The D

Robin Payne

Acknowledgements

Special thanks go to my parents for always encouraging me to read, just please don't read this!

Huge thanks to Stuart Cosgrove, without his advice and guidance at the very start (I thought I was at the end at that point, but what do I know!), I wouldn't have got this far.

Thanks also go to Ronnie, for his comma expertise, to Fudge, for enduring a very early draft, Lucy, for printing services, Matthew and Rachel, for their cover skills, to Kenny, for his wisdom and to Johnny, for some very usefull advice.

Last, but definitely not least, thanks to everyone, for the mischief and laughs over the years that inspired me. It has been a riot.

All the very best.

R

Contact: **robin.payne30@yahoo.com**

Socials:

Twitter / X - @OpPayne

Instagram - rab.payne2016

This tale is dedicated to my old pal, Mark Houston
Always on my mind
X

Prologue

Let me take you back in time for a moment, to a local store in the North West of Scotland's Capital. Three young lads stand together looking shifty in their local scheme's Co-Op. Already feeling guilt for a deed not yet performed. They were dressed in their primary school uniforms of grey shorts and black v neck jumpers, finished off with scuffed cheap trainers. Their heads crowned with the obligatory early 80s bowl cut fashioned from their loving mother's kitchen scissors. Their scrawny legs covered in mud and cuts from football in the hard surfaced school playground. Two from trying to tackle the other boy who would enjoy skipping past them on a daily basis with a worn size four mould master football. He would ghost past them and their class mates as if they didn't exist at all. His legs were also marked but by frustrated kicks and by his overzealous celebrations. A boy who at the age of nine was already infamous for going too far.

All three held bottles of Coca Cola, the real stuff, the kind their pocket money wouldn't stretch to. That was of no consequence as not one of them had any intention of purchasing them. Two of them were visibly nervous, the wilder one amongst them was whispering to them. Like an orchestra conductor he was directing them to open the bottles and place them on the floor. He then reached into the pocket of his shorts with a manic grin across his young fresh handsome face. Producing a packet of colourful sweets from the tiny pocket, he carefully handed out one each, while keeping another in his hand for himself. Clearly he had done this before. Glancing up he noticed the shop assistant had spotted them from behind the till. Hurriedly he signalled the other pair, who now looked close to bottling it that it was now or never. Simultaneously they dropped their sweets into the top of the bottles.

All three stepped back in awe as the black sweet liquid frothed from the bottles spurting high in the air and spreading all over the recently mopped linoleum floor.

'You little bastards, I know your fucking mothers, they'll hear about this. Don't you fucking move,' the hefty lady screamed, prompting two of the boys to begin their escape as they laughed hysterically. Strangely, one of the boys never ran, seemingly mesmerised by the scene in front of him. The lady moved as quickly as her large wobbly frame would allow. As she neared the only remaining boy, she slipped in the dark juice that now covered the whole aisle. Her thick ankles, encased in cheap brown nylon tights, shot into the air and she landed with a thump on her back.

Boom! Her fall triggered a reaction in the boy's consciousness. He saw a blinding light that transported him to somewhere cold and distant. He could see a tunnel, with a large man lying hurt on the ground where the lady had lain moments before. The man was unfriendly with a frightening face, but he was badly injured, the boy knew he was dying. Three strangely familiar men, he felt he knew them but just couldn't place from where, were standing looking at the man. One looked like his father, but he was sure it wasn't him. Then the men began sprinting desperately down the corridor towards a warm friendly circular bright light in the distance. All were obviously scared, running quickly as an all consuming fire engulfed the darkness behind them, hunting their every step.

The boy's vision was broken as his pal grabbed him by the arm dragging him towards the door and the safe summer sunshine. 'Run Housty, run,' his young high pitched voice urged. The boy came to his senses just in time, managing to scramble past the portly lady's outstretched arms, as she flailed around on the floor. He burst out the shops doors into the light, his friends were laughing uncontrollably, almost to the point of being unable to breathe. He didn't laugh. He shivered, standing quietly at their side. What had he seen this time?

Chapter 1

The One and Only Yorkie

'Nae bevvy, nae fucking bevvy, ya cunt,' was all the panicking, shaking, shivering Steven Malone could mumble to himself as he desperately searched his kitchen and living room, for anything containing alcohol. Well it wasn't strictly true that there was no booze. There was some, but it belonged to Steven's grandfather and was therefore not even up for consideration. His grandfather was currently upstairs, in his cave like bedroom, sleeping off the day's third hangover. He was a drunk of legendary status. He only accessed the upstairs of the house due to social services installing a chair lift. No one knew what was wrong with the old bastard, but he had had difficulty walking for years, most likely because he was constantly hammered. The chair lift was his favourite toy and the closest he got to exercise. He took great joy in sitting in it, going up and down the stairs, while slurping from a can of high strength syrupy lager. Tennent's Super was his drink of choice. It was the only lager that's high alcohol content could relieve him of which ever crushing hangover he was currently being punished by. However, if he was feeling a bit exotic, you may have found him sipping from a bottle of some supermarket own brand vodka, with his Hearts scarf tied around his neck, singing about Hibs fans in a derogatory manner.

Steven, or as he was more commonly known in the scheme, Yorkie, (a name given to him after a very public fall from grace while playing for York City Football Club) found himself in a bit of a quandary. He couldn't afford to meet his mate Housty in the boozer. He'd been free loading enough recently and he was aware that Housty, like many others, was also not employed any more. Yorkie's mouth was drier than Terry Waite's greenhouse tomatoes after being chained to a radiator for half a decade. He needed a bevvy, so in his stoned and cabbaged state, from a mixture of skunk and his dead grandmother's vast pill collection, he decided to cook up a bit of a cocktail.

This wasn't the first time he had made his own drink. It was all about using what was available. Being creative, resourceful. There was no point in going to the garden shed this time. The white spirit, that he usually relied upon as a base for his elixir, had been finished, when he had hit a previous all time low. These were becoming ever more frequent he acknowledged to himself. Beggars cannot be choosers, and if this run of luck continued, he could see himself sitting on one of Princes Street's hallowed, broken paving slabs pleading for some cash from one of Edinburgh's many unsuspecting foreign visitors. It had never got as bad as that yet, but he did appear to be on a gradual slide towards that particular unwanted situation.

A vet's bill had dropped through the door this morning. It might as well have been an atom bomb, as when his mother saw it, the fallout would be similar. Even for his beloved feline friend, Smokey, a scale and polish costing two hundred quid did seem a bit fucking excessive. Still, you couldn't dice with the health of an animal. Yorkie hoped his mother would see it this way too, although even through the thick mist that blanketed his senses, he knew she wouldn't. This meant a bevvy was even more important, something to fortify him for the trouble that surely lay ahead.

Standing in his kitchen, in a stained pair of pink Ellesse swimming shorts and faded green Lacoste polo shirt, a plan only a desperado could come up with --was forming. Unlike his clothes, Yorkie was still in decent shape for a Scottish man in his early forties. He had never been a great trainer during his years in football, but fortunately was blessed with natural fitness and a lean physique. He rummaged through the kitchen cupboards selecting the Brasso, household bleach and the remnants of his grandfather's cheap vodka. He poured it in a pan then went to the fridge to see what mixer was available. There was more food in a 1980s Russian supermarket than the Malone's family fridge. Yorkie and his grandfather were not big eaters, both generally agreeing it was a major hassle that got in the way of getting smashed. Yorkie's mother on the other hand ate very healthily but that tended to be during the hours of work or after training. For her, there was a correlation between stress and spending time in the house. Therefore, although she paid the bills, she tended to be under the roof as little as possible. The fridge contained a number of tins of his grandfather's lager which were strictly out of bounds and a couple of plastic bottles, both near empty, containing dribbles of flat lemonade and budget cola. Not one to be deterred easily, Yorkie looked further. Bingo, he thought as he spotted a frosted plastic bottle at the back that looked like it housed some fresh apple juice. He cracked open the plastic lid and took a quick sniff. Yorkie's middle aged, lined face, screwed up in revulsion and his head involuntary sprung backwards as if he had been inhaling smelling salts.

'Jesus Christ man, ya fucking cunt,' he said out loud. It smelled like methylated spirits enhanced with military grade jet fuel. His sinuses were now clearer than they had been in years. The pensioner up the stairs must have stashed this and forgot. In the pot it goes he laughed as it mixed with the Brasso, sprinkles of bleach and the vodka, creating an evil smelling vapour that swirled around the small kitchen, clinging to the extremities of the room.

As Yorkie began stirring the cocktail in the pot he lit another skunk joint. 'Turbo sooooook,' he giggled out loud as his lungs were engulfed in the pungent aroma of his home grown. For reasons even his ridiculously high brain couldn't explain he lit the gas cooker and carried on stirring probably imagining he was making magic mushroom soup.

After bringing the concoction to the boil, he turned off the hob and ladled some of the pot's contents into an almost clean glass that was sitting at the sink. Yorkie raised the glass and examined the liquid. It looked like whisky, although due to it being reduced in the pot, it had an almost thin gravy like consistency. He lowered it to nostril level. His now clear nasal passages meant he had no problem appreciating the powerful aroma emanating from the glass.

'Ho, Lee, fuck,' he announced to the kitchen, with an animated expression, lighting up his rough but still handsome, cheeky face.

Taking into account Yorkie was a thoroughbred piss artist, from excellent stock, even he was wondering if his stomach could tolerate the drink he held- before him. 'Chin chin,' he said, and knocked back about two fingers worth of the oily elixir. He staggered backwards a couple of steps bumping into the worktop. 'Ya cuuuuuuuunttttttttttt,' he rasped, while staring wide eyed at the near empty glass in his hand. He could have sworn he could feel the pale orange liquid entering his veins. His head swam and his heart was thumping noticeably faster in his chest. The initial rush calmed, settling into an amphetamine and ecstasy, psychedelic like high. What the fuck was happening? He turned and bolted for the Technics stereo system that had sat in the corner of the living room, untouched since his mother had bought the surround sound for their sixty inch TV. The TV had been kindly delivered by Yorkie's friend, Big Andy, for a mere two hundred pounds. It had arrived without the usual packaging, a very thoughtful touch from his big pal, Yorkie had assured his mother. Going on to explain it reduced the need for recycling, she was not at all convinced but had to admit the TV was a beauty. Dusting down the tape deck he rammed in one of his old Hacienda tapes and started pogoing round the living room making shapes. Even the sound of the chair lift in the hall kicking into action did not dampen his unbelievable high. He was a fucking chemist genius. What a rush. Not wanting to ruin this Mount Everest high he was on, he bolted out into the hall and pulled the plug out the stair lift, just as his grandfather came around the stair's first corner. As was customary, he was clutching an almost empty can of super strength lager.

Once the old man realised his afternoon fun had been temporarily cancelled he screamed abuse at Yorkie. 'Ya wee bastard,' he yelled and to his horror let the can in his hand fly down the stairs. It bounced off the living room door and spilled its evil contents onto the carpet. Realising he had been left high and now very dry he went berserk. 'Ya fucking wee junky waster, twat, fuck, cunt, cunt.'

As he tired of screaming obscenities, he understood through his hangover, that the racket coming from the living room had got louder as his darling grandson chose to ignore his colourful complaining and turn up the bass heavy repetitive music. The type of music a Northern Soul fanatic like himself could not abide.

And now for my next number we return to the classics, blasted out the speakers making the room shake and Yorkie's legs go ever faster. *Soap on a rope and I don't do coke*. 'Never mind coke Rhythmic State, I am going to change the world with this shit,' he sang to the empty room.

Rhythmic State were a blast back to Yorkie's youth. A group of local lads from Blercrae had formed a happy hard-core rave band. He had been a massive fan following them around the UK and Ireland whenever he could. The highlight had been attending Rezerection in 1993 at the Highland Show Ground next to Edinburgh Airport, only a few miles from Blercrae. A mental night of unrelenting, chaotic, joy.

Yorkie was experiencing a massive high. This really was like stepping back in time, he would have to give Housty a shout later and let him have a wee sip of Yorkie's own brand whisky. After about thirty minutes the chemicals in his brain returned to as normal a balance as they could inside the house of horrors that was Yorkie's skull. He decided another reefer was in order but not until he had relieved himself. He had almost lost control of his bowels as he raved. Opening the living room door he was initially shocked to see his wasted grandfather slumped in his chair on the stairs. He recalled in the initial rushes he had unplugged it. Smirking to himself he leaned over inserting the plug back in the socket and jumped back in the room closing the door in one swift motion. He then opened it again to see the old bastard being carried down the stairs as he began to come round.

'Alright auld yin, bevvy time again is it?' Yorkie cheerfully sang to the confused mess in the chair.

'Aye, son get a drink for C-o-l-i-n pal,' his learned grandfather wheezed. He never said his name, but annoyingly for everyone who had the misfortune of meeting him, he spelled it out. As time went on everyone that knew him had started doing the same. Wearing some unfashionably big, stained blue Kappa tracksuit bottoms and an old Hearts football top, with more fag burns than a blind junkie's carpet, he descended the stairs accompanied by the whirring sound of the lift's motor.

As they sat in the living room, on the threadbare matching sofas, Yorkie knew there was no point in asking for one of the prized cans of lager. If he was honest, he was feeling a bit nauseous anyway, so opted to sit for a blether with the old boy and have a spliff to try and level out. His grandfather's mood and conversation improved as the strong lager fought off the fifty year hangover that had been progressively building up throughout the decades. He was usually back to his brilliant best after two cans so as Yorkie puffed away they ended up having quite a laugh. It was great to see C-o-l-i-n's red face light up. Yorkie loved these moments and wished they were more frequent. Reminiscing about holidays in camp sites down in the Scottish Borders or the midge infested gorgeous Highlands. These were happy memories for both of them. Yorkie's grandad would spend a lot of time with him then. Afternoon walks (between bars), animal hunts (with obligatory carry out), visits to castles and even swimming in the sea and lochs. His mum and granny would sit and blether away all day while the two of them wandered around laughing and joking. Both were silent for a few moments as they contemplated how their lives had changed since those summers. His gran had passed away about fifteen years ago from a rare and horrible disease. This had hit his grandad hard and the family had watched him lose himself in even more alcohol. Yorkie always blamed the rave scene for his demise, which may have been partly true, as the entire city had been engulfed by a delicious warm wave of ecstasy in the early 90s. The summer of love, his friends and him had called it at the time. Obviously, in Yorkie's case, the rave scene was probably

8

partly to blame, but having the will power of a goldfish was undoubtedly a contributing factor.

Yorkie snapped out of it, realising it was time to feed the old goat, before he passed out again. It was similar to looking after a baby, but he had substituted milk for alcohol crammed lager.

'Fancy some special cheese on toast, old yin?'

The sudden break in silence woke his grandad from his catatonic pre bevvy coma like state. 'Aye son, that would be good, C-o-l-i-n can feel his belly rumbling.' He said this as he rubbed his not insubstantial stomach while licking his parched, chapped lips.

The two of them lived on special cheese on toast. It consisted of white bread, sliced smoked sausage, with some grated cheese on top. Real gourmet scran for the boys. Yorkie made a couple of bits each and the two of them sat watching Sportscene, another horrendous display from Craig Levein's Hearts team, was enough to send his grandad reaching for another comforting can.

'That fucking Levein is killing me, pal. That's no fucking football, son,' whinged his granddad, as Yorkie sat lapping up his discomfort. He was still revelling in the bold attacking football he had just witnessed from a newly promoted Hibs side.

'Never a truer word spoken, old yin. He is one specky boring bastard and long may he stay in Gorgie,' Yorkie laughed.

Feeling somewhat euphoric after another block busting performance from Hibs, Yorkie thought it was time to up his game and try some of his space whisky again. Pouring it carefully into an empty bottle of cheap diluting juice, he transferred the dregs into a half clean tumbler, he found on the kitchen's window sill. After stashing the diluting bottle in the old coal cellar, he went through to the living room, to find the old boy slumped on the couch in front of a dreadful recount of a Hamilton Motherwell game.

'No wonder he's fucking sleeping, watching those amateurs,' Yorkie said out loud, while smiling warmly at his grandfather.

Sitting himself down, he tanned the lethal contents of the glass, and almost immediately felt its dangerous potency, again seeping via his veins into his limbs and brain. His feet began tapping and a manic grin gradually spreading across his face. Yorkie sprang off the couch, hitting play on the old rave tape, before bounding over to his granddad, dragging him off the couch and trying, in a ridiculously naïve attempt, to get him to dance. C-o-l-i-n slumped on to his knees, platoon style, before his face accelerated towards the carpet. Yorkie's heightened senses meant that in the short space of time before the old boy's face hit floor, he managed to reach over, grab one of his mother's cushions and throw it down on the carpet quickly enough, to rescue his grandfather's barnacle nose. That nose had had enough punishment over the years, from bar brawls and drunken falls. Chortling and smirking to himself, Yorkie got behind him, put both his arms under his grandad's armpits and dragged him through to the hall. As delicately as possible he lowered him into the stair chair lift. He then stood back in wonder at the state of the old boy. He really was a marvel of human endurance. Suddenly overcome with an urge to hug him, probably due to the constant rushes he was experiencing, he grabbed his grandad's head with both hands and slapped a big wet kiss on his clammy, reptile like forehead.

'Time for beddy byes, ya old rascal,' he whispered, while simultaneously hitting the on button, so his grandfather could begin the journey to the top of the stairs. As Yorkie waved goodbye, he noticed the security light at the front switch on. That meant his mother had returned from work. Shit, he thought, I better get this place sorted out, she'll notice am out my tits. Yorkie hurried through to the living room. Taking his skinning up tray, that was covered in his smoking paraphernalia, he stashed it under the TV unit before heading through to the kitchen. As he looked at the mess that greeted him and considered the imminent arrival of his mother, he took the only option open to him. He began cuddling the fridge laughing. He was truly slaughtered.

Yorkie's mother Lynne did not approve of his extracurricular pastimes. She had taken up karate when her mother had passed away and was now a Second Dan instructing at one of Edinburgh's top clubs. The karate had been great for her, she had lost weight and was now fitter than most women half her sixty or so years. Her hobbies and Yorkie's could not have been more different. Lynne opened the door, immediately seeing her father heading up the stairs in an absolute state.

'That's C-o-l-i-n going for a wee lie down, hen,' he slurred. Trying his best and failing to appear coherent.

'You don't fucking say, old yin,' she muttered, her stress levels rising with every step she took into her home.

Taking her coat and shoes off, then putting her slippers on, she took a deep breath and mentally prepared herself for whatever she may find as she opened the living room door. First impressions were good (apart from the hammering techno music). There was a stale smell of skunk, but the place looked relatively tidy. Striding over to the stereo she switched off the awful noise and headed for the kitchen. The scene that greeted her was not quite as positive. In fact, it was a millions miles from positive. Yorkie had been attempting to dance with the fridge and while swinging on the door managed to pull the entire white good on top of himself. Much to his amusement, he lay underneath the fridge with its limited contents all over the floor, shrieking with laughter, his feet still tapping in time to the now non-existent beat. Looking to his side he saw his mother glaring at him, she was one scary woman.

Time to brazen it out he thought still feeling euphoric. 'Thank god yer back ma, this thing just fell oan me,' he struggled to say, while wrestling his body out from under the fridge freezer.

'What in the name of suffering fuck are you doing now, son?' came the retort. Sniffing the air she was now aware of an alien chemical smell. 'And what the fuck is that smell? In fact I'm not sure I want to know,' she said accusingly.

Yorkie was doing his best not to make eye contact. However, he knew if he was to find his pathway to redemption, he would have to man up. A proper bollocking was on the horizon. They worked together to get the fridge upright and then rocked it back into position. Once it was back where it belonged Yorkie braced himself for the verbal assault that was to come. To his delight he noticed she was focusing not on him but on the kitchen worktop.

'What is the old yin's urine sample doing out the fridge?' she said, picking up the frosted plastic bottle Yorkie had used to make his afternoon's entertainment.

Staring at it more closely she noticed it no longer contained a sample. 'It's fucking empty, what have you done with it? Do you know how long it takes him to pass urine? His body is dryer than the Sahara bloody desert.'

The implications of what his mother was telling him sent a wave of nausea through Yorkie as he realised he had been drinking his grandfather's fermented pee.

His mother was staring at him, understanding that his shocked facial expression meant he had definitely been up to something. Something he was now trying hard to process in his jumbled brain.

She started sniggering. 'You've no gone and drunk it, Yorkie? Ha, that will be the strongest bevvy to ever pass your lips, what on earth were you thinking?' His mother had a massive grin on her face whilst shaking her head in astonishment.

Yorkie's rushes were subsiding rapidly now but there was still enough power left in them for him to ride this out. Gathering all his strength for the piece of phenomenal acting that was to come, he went for it.

'Dinnae be daft, ma! I caught the old yin tanning everything in the fridge earlier. I had to drag it oaf him and he spilt it. Whit the fuck would I be doing drinking that?'

12

He could tell he was swaying her so pressed on. 'It's because of him the fridge fell, he did something to one of the feet while he was staggering about, I was trying to fix it when it fell oan me.' Judging by the softening expression on his mother's glowing face, he had gone some way to convincing her. One nil to Blercrae's star striker. Back of the fucking net.

'Right, let's get this place sorted out, son. I've got to get a bite to eat before training. I think I will be going back to Sensei's for extra training tonight.... again,' she added sheepishly. Now it was her who was avoiding eye contact.

Yorkie recognised this as a chance to get back on an equal footing. 'Oh aye, extra training at the Sensei's? Is that what you call it karate kid?' he teased, while attempting to giving her a nudge in the ribs. She of course had blocked it before he got close.

They both looked at each other and started laughing. It was good to see his mother happy again Yorkie thought. She had been good to him and if he was honest, had put up with an awful lot. In fact, the woman was a fucking saint, all things considered. Having cleaned up with an unusual and surprising amount of help from Yorkie, his mother had made a simple dinner of pasta with a tomato and chilli sauce. She was now getting ready for the karate club. Even before arriving at training she would go through her ritual of stretches and movements. Occasionally, if the mood took him, Yorkie would join in, amazing them both with how agile and supple his body remained. Tonight though he was slumped on the couch willing her to leave so he could have another shot of his creation. Dressed in her Adidas tracksuit she folded her freshly ironed fighting pyjamas into the holdall.

'Right son, that's me heading off. Make sure your daft gran faither is not smoking up there. He's almost burnt this place down more times than those fat greedy twats in parliament have lied.'

'Right, Ma,' Yorkie replied. 'What time ye hame or am I right in thinking you're staying all night in the dojo?' he said winking.

Her face flushed slightly. 'Shut it you, just try and make sure there's a house for me to come back to after work the morn.'

As the front door clicked closed, Yorkie leapt off the seat rescuing the liquid from the coal cellar and pouring a double helping into one of the freshly washed glasses at the sink.

'Chin chin,' he announced to no one at all, downing the urine laced mixture.

The familiar warm glow, like lava gradually spewing down a mountainside, began to creep through his veins. It began in his stomach and crept gradually to his extremities sending his brain spinning beautifully towards the cosmic clouds.

'Ya fucking beauty,' he shouted, while punching the air. With the click of a switch techno music began pumping from the speakers whilst thoughts of parties and shenanigans sprinted crazily through Yorkie's dishevelled brain. Time to get Housty up to the house he thought. He was due his friend a good night out and with this stuff to hand it was bound to be mag fucking nificient.

Chapter 2

Awakenings

Mark Houston awoke in his ex council flat deep in the Blercrae estate on Edinburgh's west side. Only close family and former work colleagues referred to him as Mark, to everyone else, including himself, he was Housty. He realised with a horrifying jolt that his day was already fucked. The haze in his eyes, brought on by Yorkie's mental whisky the previous night, would take a cunting naval vessel's industrial strength windscreen wipers to clear. He was still melted. What had his longtime friend actually given him to drink? Certainly nothing he had ever consumed before. Going on his past behaviour, this was impressive, as he was not a shy lad when it came to having a good time and experimenting.

Blercrae was a large council housing scheme, built in the 1950s to reduce the overcrowding in old tenement flats, which were being demolished across the city. It mainly consisted of the same robustly constructed three bedroom semis or four in a block, two up two downs. Although Edinburgh's schemes were all built around the same time, they all differed due to their locations and design. They all nestled nicely into the picturesque capital city, and apart from one, were far enough away from the historic city centre to be hidden from the continuous waves of tourists. Blercrae over looked the River Forth, its three bridges, the Ochil Hills and in the other direction, the Pentland Hills. Muirhouse and Pilton had the luxury of a closer, more personal relationship, with the Forth Estuary with fabulous views of the river's many islands. Niddrie and Craigmillar had their very own castle and could stare at Arthur's Seat, the extinct volcano in the centre of Edinburgh. Maybe luckiest of all were the residents of Dumbie Dykes. It hugged Holyrood Park and Salisbury Crags and was only a few minutes walk from the city's most ancient thoroughfare. To residents it would always be the High Street, for the tourists and outsiders, it was The Royal Mile.

The Blercrae estate had once been a rough, honest, hardworking place with a good community ethos, but not now, not in the same way. Not since Thatcher's buy your own council house policy had set an unstoppable tide of bankers and insurance workers from Edinburgh's once booming finance sector to dilute the bams in Blercrae. The bams still remained, but they were slowly being banished to the deepest reaches of West Lothian or Scotland's once industrious coal mining kingdom, Fife. Those that remained had realised that they could thrive in this new look community by paying the workers a visit whilst they sat at work behind a computer screen in a modern glass fronted office in the town. These types of visits were never welcome and tended to begin with the breaking of a triple glazed PVC window. Ever more frequently they ended with the victim writing a letter of complaint to their uncaring Member of Parliament. These letters would centre around the fact the glazer was there to answer their emergency call, three days before the perpetually overstretched and underfunded police, bothered to turn up.

Having managed to peel his miserable face from his pillow, Housty stumbled towards his bathroom, splashing his face with freezing water. As his face lifted from the sink to the mirror he was pleased to note he didn't look nearly as rough as he had expected. The usual bags under his forty something year old eyes were there, but not as prominent as he had anticipated. Whatever he had been drinking had potent effects and equally as powerful healing properties. Having washed and shaved he dressed quickly in football shorts, an old Napoli top displaying an outline of Maradona's distinct face and a Boss tracksuit top. He was now prepared for a gym visit that seemed improbable, in fact impossible, about ten minutes previously. A massive bowl of crunchy nut corn flakes and some fruit juice later and he was on his bike heading for Perfect Gym in Granton.

Housty used to visit a plush gym in a hotel on Edinburgh's George Street, but sadly his circumstances had changed. Since the financial collapse and the inevitable unemployment, he had been trying to stay in shape, but his dole money didn't stretch to luxury anymore. He blamed all the bottle merchant politicians, who had spent so many years arguing amongst themselves, indulging their completely unfounded sense of self importance. The finance jobs had disappeared as the upheaval of Brexit and independence took its toll on the country's fragile economy. What were these things anyway? Countries no longer existed in reality. It was multi national companies and family dynasties that ran the world, not daft wee politicians. Just as international football was replaced by the big business sponsored soulless European Champions League. A competition for the morally and financially bankrupt clubs. Financial meltdown was just round the corner for everyone, apart from the super rich. Employment prospects for your average office worker in Edinburgh were not looking good, a fact Housty knew and for his sanity did his best to ignore. The effect of long term unemployment, on his ability to pay his mortgage, was a constant worry.

Locking his bike up with all the others in the feeble shelter, designed to protect from the river Forth's unforgiving winds, but not the Pilton and Muirhouse gangs, he strolled into the gym. As always it was busy with students, fatties and oldies trying to scare off the ever approaching and unforgiving natural circle of life. He noted happily, that the usual team of women in their early twenties, sporting ridiculously tight leggings and sports bras were present. He smiled to himself as he thought every male gym member owed a pint to whoever had made these outfits trendy.

Starting with back, then shoulders and chest he finished with some stretches, a salute to his past days practicing the noble martial art of karate. It was funny to think one of his best mates' mums was now addicted to it. One of these days he would go back, if only his knee hadn't been ruined by tracing paper thin astro turf pitches, that were laid on solid concrete in the nineties. These pitches were all the rage at the time but had destroyed many an average footballer's knees and ankles.

After some small pleasantries to the bored Facebook engrossed staff, Housty typed his number into the key pad and stepped into the late morning Edinburgh drizzle. Looking out towards Fife he remembered the huge light blue gas storage tanks that were once so prominent here. He wondered where they now stored all the stuff. Probably best out the way with all the fucking head cases in the world just now intent on blowing us all up he mused. He remembered fondly, trips with his mother and siblings to Trend Centre. It was the original out of town super market, built on reclaimed land, just below where he now stood. Best time to chum your mother shopping was Easter, when all the kids had pillaged every chocolate egg, on their way round the cavernous store. Housty and his siblings would let their small hands slip into the holes in the packaging, taking a bit of the half devoured eggs for themselves. Not really classed as stealing, when every jumble sale clothed child in the surrounding estates, had done the same. Trend Centre was now gone, just its foundations remained, as a reminder to those of a certain age where most of North Edinburgh did their shopping. The surrounding area was being regenerated, now unrecognisable to the wasteland it had become. Edinburgh had moved on from the drug ridden ghettos of the eighties. All brought on by a local pharmaceutical company's factory having a slack view on security.

As he turned away from the Forth he focused on the bus stop like bike shelter about twenty metres to his left.

'Fucking raaaaaddddddggggge,' he screamed, as a hooded figure leapt on his bike and began peddling toward the supermarket that was adjacent to the gym.

Due to Housty's shout he was obviously now aware of his presence, increasing the haste of his getaway. Housty realised standing and shouting was not going to bring his bike back. He was incandescent with rage. Petty thieving really pissed him off. The miniscule amount of cash the robber would earn didn't get close to the value Housty put on his two wheeled ride. He was close to six foot in height and well built, and could still handle himself. He sprinted towards the far side of the shop hoping to cut the thief off. As he rounded the corner the hooded man was cycling towards him, concentrating on his escape and no doubt the smoke from the crack pipe he looked forward to, when he off loaded the shitty bike he had just pinched. Half full water bottle in hand, Housty flung it powerfully at the thief, missing him but following up with a right hander to the chin as he passed. Housty heard a strange cat like scream, coinciding with a loud crack, as the cyclist fell off the fast moving bike. He collapsed onto his side and then lay there moaning, clutching at his damaged face and ribs. If he hoped this display of pain, would deter Housty from dishing out more damage, he was wrong. As Housty went to stamp on his knuckles, his phone starting ringing in his pocket. He held his foot on the injured man's hand, with enough pressure to stop him fleeing and answered sharply saying he was busy. He wasn't surprised at all to find it was Yorkie and that he was babbling down the phone in his usual incoherent manner. Housty cut him off quickly, his patience with Yorkie could be thin at the best of times.

'Av no got time for this, Yorkie mate, some wanker just tried to nick my bike and a need to deal with it.'

Yorkie blethered on oblivious to Housty's business. 'I'm just making some mare oh that cocktail this morning pal, fucking dynamite eh?'

Good point Housty thought, 'What the fuck was in that, Yorkie? I was absolutely cunted.'

Yorkie went silent and muttered something about his grandad's fish.

'What the fuck are you on about, Yorkie?' an impatient Housty replied. He could see the thief was now trying to wriggle free. Fucking JKs Housty thought. If ones not nicking his bike another ones calling him and talking shite.

Yorkie said, 'Ah accidentally put some of ma Grandads pish sample in the cocktail a made, a thought it was apple juice.......that's what we drank last night, man.'

At this point two explosions took place. One wreaked havoc in Yorkie's mother's kitchen, another began at the pit of Housty's stomach as he realised what his friend had just divulged to him. Honey nut corn flakes made their way at an inhumane pace out of Housty's stomach, splattering the semi-conscious, ever more panicked ned at his feet. He cut the call without thinking. The effects of his stomach's dump, on the stricken youth, made Housty bellow with laughter. Some of the shocked on lookers turned away for fear of losing their own breakfast. It was at this point Housty became aware, that he and the cereal stained JK, had attracted quite a crowd. He thinks he can hear a faint siren in the distance. The law is so fucked up these days he'll probably be looking at ten years for spewing on the manky, North Face hooded, wee prick. He smiles looking down at the pleading thief blanketed in a soup of snot, blood and cheap Scotmid sweet nutted flakes.

He releases pressure on his hand allowing him to stagger to his feet and begin his undignified escape. As the thief rises to almost full sprint mode Housty's foot connects, as hard as his cloth trainers will allow, with the bone above his arse, almost forcing him to the ground again.

Looking round at the crowd and with the last of the water from his smashed bottle mixing with the body fluids on the pavement, Housty decides it's time to head home. Obviously, he'll need to make a detour past Yorkie's to get an explanation for his revelation and the following mayhem Housty had heard at the end of their call. Picking up his bike, refusing to look into any of the onlookers' eyes, he heads off as fast as his chuckling will allow. Wondering if his uncrushable good mood, is at all linked, to an alky grandad's urine sample. What kind of monster could pass a liquid so potent?

Chapter 3

Scrabble and Fish

Boom! Crash! A substantial noise wakes him from his slumber. The large cube shaped tank comes into view as one of his blood shot eyes blinks open. The other is glued down, by a thick gunge like the yoke of an egg that surrounds his eyelid and has formed a crust around his eye lashes. He's happy to just use one of them for the moment, as long as he can see his favourite wee pal, sucking the water in and then powering himself across the near three hundred litre fresh water tank. The yellowy green fish had been the last one he had bought, not that any money had exchanged hands. The assistant manager in Dobbies Pet Centre, on the outskirts of Edinburgh, had seen to that. As C-o-l-i-n had staggered out the large shop, with three relatively rare and expensive specimens, his attempted escape had not been difficult to spot. He had been on a watch list since his last visit to acquire fish for the prized tank. When C-o-l-i-n had been confronted, the manager had taken a degree of pity on him, due to his unkempt appearance. His grey hair was matted to his brow and he was sporting a large cut on his forehead from a recent fall down the stairs in his home in Blercrae. Strangely, that painful fall would bring him luck. The manager was a decent sort and recognised C-o-l-i-n's desperate, sorry state, and therefore, reluctantly, allowed him to head off to the bus stop with one of the fish without having to explain his behaviour to the local police force. To C-o-l-i-n's delight, the man who was in his early twenties, did not realise that the fish the haggard pensioner had chosen to keep, was the most expensive one, the Green Spotted puffer. A beautiful, wee elegant creature, although in C-o-l-i-n's case, the Red Eye puffer fish may have been more pertinent.

Shuffling off to the bus stop, for the long trip home, he had to smile to himself. Not only had he acquired the fish, but due to his recent fall, the council had agreed to come and fit a stair lift for him. That was back in 2014, almost four years ago. Seemed like decades ago now as he eventually managed to free up his other eye, giving him the pleasure of watching the tanks inhabitants with full vision. He had always loved the puffer fish, as like himself, it was a solitary creature. He hadn't always been. There were the Labour Party days, Northern Soul and the scrabble tournaments, but these were in the past. One ruined by changing social dynamics and poor leadership, the others by his behaviour and his new, more all consuming hobby, bevvy.

His last scrabble tournament had been in a church hall in Granton, down by the Forth estuary. He had, as always, won all his games with relative ease. The only danger to C-o-l-i-n's scrabble crown was the cans of lager he had stored in a bag by his feet. After each match he would nip outside and shotgun a couple of cans, before retuning inside to defeat the next victim of his word sorcery. His skill and vocabulary knowledge was legendary, as was his increasing drinking and sadly back then, aggression. He could have been a national champion and had in the past qualified to play at the finals in Torquay, only to make up an excuse at the last minute. Fear of failure was the issue then, whereas now, it was most definitely alcohol. Both went hand in hand, the booze removing the fear, but also the ability to perform. In his final official game, it was late afternoon in Granton church hall, when his opponent had used a word C-o-l-i-n had sprung in a previous game that day. The noun, Chutzpah, meant audacity and fittingly C-o-l-i-n knew full well his challenger only learned the word that day from him. With the alcohol levels now approaching maximum, he had picked up the board and chucked it at his opponent, but more questionably, had then followed it up with the heavy church stool he had been sitting on. Due to the amount of cans he had consumed during the day, his attempted escape had been a disaster. He only managed a couple of staggered steps before crashing through the table of another couple of shocked tournament participants. Unsurprisingly, this act had cast him into the scrabble wilderness and a jail cell for the night. Now his only connection with the game was his long time friend Jennifer, who although not being impressed by his behaviour, valued their friendship more. A friendship that had spanned decades, going all the way back to their early Labour party days, in the late 1960s. His only chance to play was during their monthly meetings, he valued these two hours more than any others, and always looked forward to them. It was during these games that he still hoped to be able to use the word 'indefatigability'; a salute to George Galloway's well publicised meeting with Sadam Hussain that led to him single handedly destroying the US senate in 2005. What a glorious moment that was and one he enjoys replaying on YouTube when he gets peace in the house. George's only crime, in his eyes, being he supported a Glaswegian football club having been born in Dundee. He now keeps his remaining forays into intellectual enjoyment to himself, preferring to appear the drunken fool in front of others. It was just easier this way, less chance to ruin peoples' expectations of himself.

The room he lies in is an absolute mess, but the tank standing on the plinth in the corner, could not be cleaner. As his life falls apart around him, sinking deeper into chronic alcoholism, the tank stands like a beacon. His own lighthouse of Alexandria to his past glories. He watches the fish intently, as he always does, when he wakes from the numerous naps he now takes throughout the day. Being a pisshead is an exhausting hobby after all. Are the fish the only things that drink more than him, he half smiles to himself, in a self loathing moment of clarity? Not a man to remain bitter for long, he cheers himself up in the way he always did, he lets his mind wander back to his youth, back to his first job in the pet shop. The shop was Dofos, situated on Blenheim Place, where London Road meets Leith Walk in Edinburgh's East end. He fucking loved it from the beginning. The colourful fish mesmerized him from the minute he saw them. He had got the Saturday job through a friend of his mother's and what was initially meant to be a couple of hours cleaning up rabbit shit and straw, became an almost daily obsession. Back then he had lived near Powderhall stadium so it was only a short walk and one he took whenever he could escape. The owner kept saying, I can't keep paying you son, it's only meant to be a couple of hours on a Saturday. He would have worked for nothing, as long as it meant spending time staring into those kaleidoscope like, bubbling fish tanks. This would remain his lowest paid but happiest job ever. He was devastated when his tenement flat was condemned and his excited mother told him about the new house the council was going to give them in Blercrae. A brand new house with their own garden, parks, lots of open space, but he knew he could no longer walk to Dofos every day. His mother assured him he could still go and see the daft fish at the weekend, but even that would not last long. By the time he was fifteen he had left school and was in an apprenticeship like everyone else he knew. He swore to himself, as soon as he could, he would buy his own tank and fish. Even now with so much lager under the bridge, the noise from the tank's gleaming filter and pump remained hypnotic.

His quiet contemplation is broken on that spring day in 2018 by crashing and banging sounds coming from the kitchen below. He realises that these have been going on for a while now, but he is only now fully conscious of the racket. The most prominent noise, that had initially woken him, had been accompanied by a fairly significant vibration that felt like it was shaking the whole building. What was his grandson Steven up to now? The lad was a one man wrecking ball. The government should send him into conflict zones and save the country wasting billions on weapons. Tony Blair never found weapons of mass destruction but C-o-l-i-n knew there was one in the room below him right now. Steven or Yorkie, as everyone now called him, since his failed and destructive time in the English football league at York City FC. A stage in their lives that had been a huge disappointment to C-o-l-i-n as he had seen his grandson repeating his own past mistakes. His was a path he never wanted to see his grandson walk. When his contract was cancelled, it had really brought it home to him, what his own excesses had stolen from him. C-o-l-i-n hated the name Yorkie. As well as being a constant reminder of past failure, it also made him sound like a fucking chocolate bar, but then who was he to judge? He had an annoying habit of spelling his own name out and expecting others to do the same. He liked to think it was a throwback to his other obsession, scrabble, but he couldn't for the life of him remember if this was actually the case. Like many other memories, the constant assault of alcohol to the brain had been methodically and irreversibly erasing his past.

His thoughts were broken by Yorkie bursting into his room. 'Right pal, there's been a wee accident an ah need tae get you outside pronto. No ma fault, just a wee miscalculation. Nowt tae concern yourself with.'

Before he had a chance to respond Yorkie was leading him to his chair lift and out into the sunshine at the front of the house. His grandson was refusing to even acknowledge his questions regarding the smoke and noxious vapour pouring from their kitchen.

Chapter 4

A Soldier and Fireman

The Pentland Hills provide great views of Edinburgh and Fife and were looking particularly beautiful as Matt trudged up from the car park at Bonaly, through the steep wooded section and on through the farmer's gate, onto open moor land where his mongrel dog Roxy could enjoy some space. The dog was well trained which was just as well, as only last week, he had met a monumentally pissed off farmer who had just shot another walkers dog for chasing some of his sheep into one of the many reservoirs dotted around the hills. These reservoirs had once provided the city with its water, until the massive Megget Dam had been constructed in the Scottish borders, along with gigantic pipes which took a direct route to Scotland's capital. They were buried, for about forty miles, under the hills to the city. These pipes made sure the capital had a clean long term supply of Scotland's finest natural product. The reservoirs were now used for fishing and swimming, although this was actively discouraged by Scottish Water, due to a number of teenage deaths. Not that this had deterred Matt. A few years ago, when Housty and him had been jumping into the cool water on a particularly warm summers day only to be told very firmly, by an irate Scottish Water worker, that they were fucking stupid cunts. He went on to explain that the small metal pier that they were jumping off, was above, what was effectively a huge plug hole. He pointed out that if they had been lowering the water levels they would have been sucked through the plug hole faster than an exocet missile.

As Matt's vantage point rose he could look back over the city taking in the majestic view. He felt a smile build on his large, friendly, sun tanned face. Matt was one of those guys who, despite being in their early forties, still had managed to retain almost a baby face. His head turned towards the bridges and then south to the Bass Rock and Berwick Law. All prominent and impressive features in their own right. What a fucking place he had been lucky enough to be born in, and then return to, after serving in the armed forces. As his gaze returned to his present point, they rested for a second on the hill, where he began his military training; all those night exercises and crazy times at the shooting range where the new recruits would take great delight in gunning down an unfortunate sheep that had strayed into their line of fire. That seemed like a life time ago. Slightly closer to his current position, he saw the woods that he had camped in as a boy with his best pals, Housty and Yorkie. They had experimented with magic mushrooms and giggled for hours, watching fir trees march up the grassy slopes towards them. He remembered Yorkie and him laughing hysterically at a very paranoid Housty because his long brown curly hair at the time made him look like Jesus. Great times. He would have to meet up with the boys for a drink and to reminisce about old times and some of their crazy teenage antics.

The army had initially had a good effect on Matt. While Housty had got a place at college and Yorkie had taken that ill-fated train to York, to start his brief professional football career, Matt had enlisted. His mother had been mortified when he came home at the age of seventeen and announced he had signed up for the Royal Scots. Acceptance had followed once it was clear he was not going to change his mind. On reflection the army had been good for him. There was the lingering PTSD issues, but he was sure it could be handled. It was the reason he had managed to get out early from his most recent tour. The older he got, the more he had realised that they hadn't been actually helping the world or indeed the country they occupied. It was all for rich greedy men. Arms dealers, oil companies, property deals or currency manipulation. The real masters of war. It all seemed so pointless and depressing now. Arriving in a country that was functioning, then leaving it a physical and economic wasteland. Thousands of people displaced, childrens' futures destroyed. He remembered how they would try and prepare you for this. One night, he and a group of recruits had been ordered to dig a trench system of enormous proportions. On completion of this, and as the grey dawn stretched across the Suffolk sky, their commanding officer had emerged from his warm comfortable bed in Colchester Barracks. Barely looking at their impressive work, he had barked something along the lines of, 'Get this fucking hole filled in pronto. Someone might fall in it.' Matt couldn't believe it, it had taken a huge amount of self-control not to give the boy a slap.

There had been highlights though. The off road driving course in Canada being one. The British army's Land Rovers putting the waddling heavy American Humvees in their place. The off road driving had been preparation for Northern Ireland. At any point a patrol may have had to evade a paramilitary ambush by leaving the road in daylight or darkness. Ireland hadn't been traumatic, just boring and disheartening. The high walls and fencing slicing through once happy neighbourhoods and communities. Africa had been interesting. A big beautiful wilderness sprinkled with some extreme human poverty, although unlike in Western Europe, the poor seemed relatively happy and healthy. The final straw had been Syria. The scale of devastation was impossible to comprehend. Once thriving cities had been blown back to the Stone Age. The worst bit being having to stand back and watch as Syria's own army carried out atrocities on the people it should be defending. It was during this period that Matt had realised it was time to get out. He had seen an army doctor and then a psychiatrist. Having looked up PTSD online, he knew the symptoms and was surprised to see he actually did have some of them. He certainly had rage but that seemed natural after what he had witnessed. For the first time in his adult life he had started having nightmares, his brain revisiting the same distressing situations night after night. As soon as he mentioned the rage, this was a red flag for the military. Men with guns, in combat zones, experiencing rage, is not encouraged. Matt was flown back to the UK and after more tests and interviews, he was eventually discharged.

Still, he had enjoyed the army and lasted a good deal longer than Yorkie had in the historical city of York. Matt had struggled to even communicate with Yorkie after he had ruined his brief stint as York City's most high profile player. Maybe just high would have been a better description. Yorkie had quickly gained a reputation in the quaint English town as a total head case. The club had tolerated his much publicised behaviour, due to his goal scoring exploits, until he had inevitably managed to outdo even himself. After a post-match all nighter he took a couple of girls for a wee sailing expedition. Yorkie had hotwired one of the many tourist boats that cluttered the banks of the River Ouse. He had then sailed off, fully armed with the lucky ladies, more wine than a French Chateau and a pocket stuffed with white powder. As with most rivers, the Ouse meets the sea, and that is where the good Captain Yorkie took the (very) Jolly Roger. It was around this time that the three occupants of the tourist vessel realised that its small two stroke engine was no match for the receding tide and they soon found themselves miles offshore being pulled further out into the North Sea. When they were eventually rescued, Yorkie was still in fine spirits, after consuming vast amounts of the cocaine and wine. The life boat crew could hear him shouting about invading Scandinavia just like the Vikings had done to them. The girls, on the other hand, were distraught. It proved to be one escapade too many for the York City board and management team. After short spells and very long team nights out in the even lower leagues in England and some unsuccessful stints in Scotland, it was decided within the football community that he was better left to his own devices. It never failed to amaze Matt that this disastrous part of Yorkie's life hadn't dampened his spirits one bit. On reflection though, it was probably because despite a number of years out of football, he was yet to sober up.

The wind was picking up and he could see dark clouds begin their march towards Edinburgh, slowly obscuring his view of the magnificent three bridges that spanned the River Forth. Although a bit of rain didn't bother Matt, he was always prepared, the army had taught him that at least. His Gore-Tex Berghaus jacket would protect against the rain and his sturdy waterproof boots meant he would be fine but Roxy on the other hand was a fair weather wanderer.

Putting two fingers to his lips he let out a loud whistle signalling to Roxy that it was time to return to the car park. Tramping back from their vantage point, they headed towards Matt's Land Rover, yet another reminder of his previous life. He had fallen in love with Land Rovers while doing the off road driving course in Canada with his unit. He smiled, thinking of the American soldiers' faces as the British off roader gave their version of the off road warrior a thorough spanking. Much to the delight of Matt and his super fit army pals, this had upset the Americans so much that a large fight had broken out. Matt almost started laughing out loud as he remembered the large American soldiers being shocked by the ferocity that the smaller, wiry Brits fought with. The American soldiers were like their prized, over weight and too chunky vehicles, far too slow. The top brass had not been chuffed, that a joint training operation, had ended in a full scale riot. Still, at least it showed the soldiers had a bit of fight in them. It was just a case of channelling it more positively in the future.

The one good thing, really, really good thing to come out of his military service had been his son. The first time he saw him was a light bulb moment. Something went on in his head; an overwhelming need to protect this tiny newcomer to the world. A world, he had felt at the time that he was instrumental in helping to destroy. He had met the boy's mother Emma on one of his many nights out in Colchester and they had shared time together whenever he was back at the base. After dinner in a restaurant in town on one of these nights she had broken the news that she was pregnant. Both liked each other but also knew they were never going to be life partners. For once, Matt had approached this new challenge with some thought and deliberation, trying not to jump in with both feet, fists and his forehead. Maybe he was finally growing up. He had been present at the birth having remained close friends Emma during the pregnancy. She had insisted the lad would be called Thomas after her father, laughing at Matt's Scottish suggestions, like Hamish and Angus. He wasn't too bothered as, unlike her, he knew Thomas would soon become Tam north of the border. Matt had moved back to live in Edinburgh but would be back down south to see the boy fortnightly. He had just returned from one of these trips about a month ago where Thomas had been feeling ill. He received a frantic call from Emma saying that he had been rushed to hospital. It turned out that Thomas had fallen into a diabetic coma. Matt had rushed back to be at his side and from there had begun researching the illness. Although the treatment had been good and the staff had done everything they could, Matt wanted to give Thomas the best possible chance. He had invested in an insulin pump for Thomas that was not available on the NHS, and was now paying the ongoing costs. This was crippling him financially as he already gave Emma more than he could afford. There was also the small fortune that he spent on travel to see Thomas whilst spoiling him when they were together, as absent parents do. He was acutely aware that his savings were taking a good solid kicking and would not last much longer. Matt needed to start earning money, proper money, and soon.

Retrieving the key from his jacket, Matt opened the passenger door for Roxy and then climbed into the driver's seat, instantly relaxing in the familiar surroundings. His phone's Bluetooth immediately connected with the stereo, picking up Frankie Goes to Hollywood's debut album Welcome to the Pleasure Dome. Matt loved this album. Sitting back for a second to enjoy the intro, he thought, I can't believe that a bunch of pansy boys made music like this. Mind you, he thought to himself, Queen were fucking brilliant and the Petshop boys were magic the year he had seen them at Glastonbury. Obviously, touching other men helped the creative juices flow, so to speak, he laughed to himself prompting Roxy to give his owner a curious look. He had to stop thinking like that. Being homophobic in the army was acceptable but Housty always told him to behave. Live and let live was his motto. Matt was beginning to see what he meant, the more distant the army barracks got. As they say; life is too short and he was determined to stay positive, and try and see the good in everything. This was easier said than done when you lived in a deranged, passionate, basket case of a country like Scotland.

As he reversed out of the car park, and navigated the bumpy crumbling track, he felt his phone vibrating in his Stone Island combat shorts. He wasn't really into all the designer gear nonsense, but he had purchased these at a fraction of the recommended retail price, from his big pal Andy. Blercrae's ever industrious, premier delivery driver.

The call connected to the bluetooth in the car stereo, cutting out the opening section of Two Tribes much to Matt's annoyance. Yorkie's name appeared on the digital display on his Sony car stereo. The high pitched noise that came through the cars speakers startled Matt and Roxy.

'Help ays Matty, hhhheeeeeeeeelllllllllllppppppppppppppppppp. I've blown up ma kitchen man, ma mas going to go fucking radge. I need you now, pal'

'Yorkie, calm down man, what the fuck are you ranting about?' a slightly narked Matt replied. It always annoyed him that his friend's life was a continuous war zone. What is it with bams that they can't take even a day off?

'Ah wis creating my masterpiece in the kitchen when the place just went boom! Can you get down here pronto? A know you are a trained fireman.'

'How the fuck am I a trained fireman, ya rocket?' Matt retorted. Yorkie was an absolute space cadet, making Matt consider cutting the call and getting back to Frankie and Two Tribes.

'Mind pal, you were driving about in they auld, green engines when the real firemen were striking, a mind you telling us about that.'

'Yorkie, that was those ancient Green Goddesses, we were much better soldiers than firemen. We would have been better just pishing on the fires. The hoses were crap, man. Anyway, is your house on fire and if it is where is C-o-l-i-n?' Matt used to hate spelling out C-o-l-i-n's name, but as time passed it became second nature. It would now have felt odd just calling him Colin.

'What do you think I am? I got the auld boy down the stairs, he's sitting in the front gairden doing his nut an contributing fuck all to ma dire situation.'

'Good,' an exasperated Matt replied. 'Can you confirm the house is not burning to the ground?' Matt was surprised how easily he slipped back into confident combat mode. Evaluate the situation, then shout like fuck was the modern army way.

'It better no be mate, my ma will go radio rental, get yer skates oan, mucker,' an ever increasingly manic Yorkie replied.

'Right man, I'm on my way,' Matt responded, ending the call and beginning to piss himself laughing as he accelerated towards certain carnage. Yee ha, *when two tribes go to war, moneys is all that you can score*. Matt began singing along, knowing that whatever he was about to witness, would be comedy gold.

Chapter 5

There's a fire in the Disco!

He parked up on a grass verge at the cross roads about three doors down from Yorkie's mum's house. From his vantage point Matt could already see that this was going to be hilarious. Well worth jumping the lights in Colinton village and hammering it through the bad lands of Wester Hailes. In saying that, not many people slowed down in Wester Hailes, not those with any sense or feelings of self preservation anyway. The police were missing a trick not having a speed camera on that particular section of dual carriageway, which ran passed the abomination of a building that was the WEC. The Westerhailes Education Centre. A breeding ground for bams.

Matty could see Yorkie marching up and down the pavement in front of his mum's house, puffing on what looked like a massive joint, whilst gesticulating wildly at an obviously shit faced C-o-l-i-n. It appeared C-o-l-i-n seemed to now be enjoying Yorkie's panic. Yorkie was walking like he was on an electrified pavement in bare feet, with jerky, almost robotic movements. Like Iggy Pop after disastrous double knee and hip replacement surgery. Yorkie always hates it when the lads called him Iggy. It's not that he wasn't a fan, but the man looked a state. The boys insisted that there was a certain resemblance in the manic way they both moved.

Leaving Roxy in the van to sleep off the fresh air and avoid the carnage, Matt locked the motor and stepped onto the pavement. He immediatly heard the squeal of bike brakes from behind and turned to see Housty appear, looking fresh and jovial.

'Alright, brother,' Housty said, getting off his bike and walking alongside Matt.

'No bad, son,' Matt replied, as they shook hands.

Both friends were already struggling not to laugh at Yorkie's demonic state and it was nothing to do with the clouds of skunk smoke coming their way. The thick smoke assaulting their freshly exercised, clear lungs.

'Wait til I tell you about this nutter getting me to drink Father Jack's pish last night,' Housty said to Matt. Father Jack was one of Yorkie's grandfather's many nicknames as he did have an uncanny resemblance to the celebrated drunken old priest in Channel Four's Father Ted. Matt returned a confused look towards his friend. Housty could not elaborate further as Yorkie had spotted them and was now almost upon them. Baring down on them quickly while ranting on about the state of the kitchen.

'Thank fuck you two are here, my ma is going to go off her nut,' a wired Yorkie announced.

'Right pal, show us the damage,' Matt said, whilst striding past C-o-l-i-n high fiving the hammered old lunatic. Like many locals, Matt still had a great deal of respect for the old guy.

Housty was right behind him, giving C-o-l-i-n a big smile and a wink, with Yorkie at the rear. The house smelt like a chemical factory and although not very smoky, there was a lingering, deep haze embracing Yorkie's mothers recently decorated living room. She would not be amused. Both Matt and Housty really liked Lynne. She had been good to them as kids and had had a lot to deal with. How she hadn't kicked Yorkie out was testament to her having more patience than the Dalai Lama on pure pharmaceutical heroin.

The kitchen door was wide open and the haze was much thicker here. The lads put their noses inside their t shirts simultaneously.

'What the fuck were you up to, Yorkie?' Matt said, almost to himself, as the others would struggle to hear him with his t shirt muffling the sound. Before going through to the kitchen, Matt leaned over and opened the double glazed living room windows. Matt and Housty entered the kitchen and looked at each other in a mixture of disbelief and amusement. If they were not struggling to breathe, they would have been roaring with laughter. The three by four metre room was a state. If it wasn't for their respect for Lynne they would have turned round, got in the Land Rover, and wet themselves laughing for half an hour. Unfortunately, for them, they needed to try and rescue the situation.

This time, Housty leaned over, opening the kitchen window, while Matt headed through to the adjacent dining room that led out into the back garden. Once there he opened the patio doors and front facing window. By this time Yorkie had come through and looked in serious distress at the mess his distilling skills had caused. They led him out into the back garden to allow the smoke to clear and give them time to have a good laugh at Yorkie's expense. From the back garden they could here C-o-l-i-n singing at the front, 'We are the Gorgie boys.'

'Listen to that auld wanker! Our house is just about wrecked and all he can fucking do is sing about that maroon bunch of tramps,' Yorkie whinged.

Matt caught Housty's eye and the pair of them started creasing uncontrollably. Shoulders shaking and bent double with laughter.

'No yous in all,' Yorkie wailed. 'What am I going to do, boys? My ma will be practising for her 28th Dan on my pus the night if yez dinnae help aiz.'

Catching his breath, Housty composed himself and replied. 'Tell you what, tell me what mischief you were up to and what on earth you were doing giving me C-o-l-i-n's pish to drink, an we'll sort this place out. I was banjoed last night, but for whatever reason feel no bad today, when under normal circumstances, if I was in that nick, I should

36

have been rolling about my flat licking the condensation off the windows.'

Yorkie knew it was cards on the table time. Like many people with his self destruct tendencies, he found it easy to come clean. Not much embarrassed him these days. 'I was desperate yesterday, Housty. I didnae ken it was the old boys pish sample, all ah did was try and make ma self a drink. Am skint, pal, totally brassic,' Yorkie confessed in speedy sound bites.

'Let me get this right,' Housty replied. 'You made that drink that you gave me ah thought was whisky spiked with MDMA? I felt fucking magic after drinking it.'

'Aye, it's the best of gear, man. I've not experienced anything like it in years.' Even Yorkie started smiling now that the shock was wearing off. 'We got high on C-o-l-i-n's pee supply,' he laughed, whilst taking out of his pocket his trusty bag of skunk and beginning to roll his third joint of the day.

'Ah cannae believe it Yorkie man, you're one sick puppy. What else was in it?'

Yorkie ran his tongue along the king sized rizla paper, struggling to get any moisture from his almost furry white dehydrated mouth, before answering Matt.

'Brasso, bit of bleach, some really cheap vodka and, well, you ken the rest,' he replied. A wide grin spread across his face.

Shaking his head, whilst looking back into the dining room and realising that the worst of the potent haze had now cleared, Matt said, 'Some boy, some fucking boy. You could not make it up.'

Housty was also shaking his head in disbelief. 'How are you still alive, man?' he enquired, laughing and slapping Yorkie on the back.

Passing the spliff to Housty, Yorkie just shrugged. If he was honest with himself, in his few moments of clarity, he had often thought the same. He had attempted to clean up his act in the past. Obviously, considering his current predicament, without any success.

Smoking wasn't really Housty's thing. Like Matt he had enjoyed it in his late teens and early twenties, but who wants to go about in a coma all day? Taking a couple of puffs he passed it on to Matt quickly.

'When in Rome,' he said winking at Yorkie. Matt took a few puffs, passed it back to Yorkie, who greedily sucked it to the roach.

With their understandably low tolerance levels, Matt and Housty were feeling the effects of the skunk. They were both now nicely light headed following Yorkie back through to the smoke cleared kitchen. The damage wasn't as bad as first thought, but it would take a minor miracle for Yorkie's mother not to notice. A metal pot lay in the corner of the room next to the fridge, two floor tiles were cracked where the pot had landed and there was a dent in the plaster on the ceiling, most likely due to the pot hitting it. The walls were stained by the thick smoke and steam, along with the liquid that had been boiling away. Yorkie stood in the centre of the kitchen, looking very worried, whilst Matt and Housty looked in from the dining room laughing like hyenas.

'Fuck sake boys, this is fucking serious. I should never have given you light weights a smoke. About as much use as a fuking chocolate fire guard now,' Yorkie moaned.

Realising, in his suicidal state, that he could hear his grandad shouting uncharacteristically aggressively, he went out the front to see what was going on, leaving his friends to enjoy his downfall. The old boy was apoplectic with rage. Yorkie found him slavering and gesturing towards two ten year old lads on the other side of the street, who were in a similar state of hilarity to Housty and Matt at the other side of the house. The reason for C-o-l-i-n's anger was the broken eggs on his forehead, which were sliding down his face, impairing his already dreadful vision. Yorkie could see other egg shells scattered round the old goat. The boys had taken up the chant of, 'You hearts bastard, you hearts bastard,' in their squeaky pre pubescent voices. The old drunk could only curse and swear whilst trying to clear his eyes, most probably so he could find his drink. Yorkie leapt over the small garden fence, chasing the boys down the street. Luckily for them, it was a half hearted attempt, as even in his current state he still had the burst of pace that had earned him his sabbatical in the historical walled Yorkshire town. Giving him the one fingered salute and shouting, 'fuck the hearts,' they disappeared round the corner.

Not wanting for a moment to be considered a supporter of those in maroon, Yorkie shouted to whoever was in earshot, 'Am no a fucking jambo, ya smelly, wee rodent cunts!'

Turning and heading back, he got C-o-l-i-n tidied up, refusing to clean his already soiled hearts top, he manoeuvred him into his stair lift to go and sleep off the first or second hangover of the day. It was increasingly hard to keep track.

Meanwhile, in the kitchen, the others had partially recovered from the most recent fit of the giggles and were discussing how to get the place sorted out.

'I'd forgotten how much fun you could have just by popping in to see Yorkie and C-o-l-i-n. The pair of them barely function,' Matt said.

'Aye I know, man. Comical stuff, mate,' Housty replied, his head slowly and methodically surveying the kitchen.

They laughed and joked whilst wiping the walls down with kitchen roll and mopping up the liquid that had spilled on the floor. Matt was looking at the broken tiles. 'I can fix these easy. Hopefully, there are a couple of spares.'

As he was saying this, Yorkie came in. 'Aye, there's a box in the hut my man,' he replied, feeling chirpier now that he could see the lads had finally grasped the gravity of his situation. Yorkie retrieved the hut key from the drawer and Matt followed him down the garden.

The hut was surprisingly well organised. Matt could sense Lynne's presence. It certainly wouldn't have been either of the other inhabitants of the property. As a result of this, they immediately found the tiles underneath a neat pile of the family's old camping gear.

'Perfect,' Matt said, taking two undamaged tiles from the middle of the box and choosing a couple of the tools hanging on the shed walls. After picking up some adhesive, he was ready.

Yorkie appeared to have forgotten why they were in the hut in the first place and was going through the camping gear. 'Bingo,' he said, dragging an old gas canister and camping stove into the garden. 'No stopping me now, pal,' he winked at Matt. 'Am going to cook up a storm in the hut. My ma will be none the wiser.'

'You are off your fucking nut, Yorkie.'

'Na man, you don't know ma genius yet, but ye will pal, mark ma words, you will,' he said, laughing. He headed up the garden as Matt followed him smiling at his lunatic friend's approach to life. How had he suffered with depression and anxiety, when this permanently caked bam seemed to crash through life without a care? Mental man, absolutely mental, he thought happily.

Using the tools he had taken from the shed, Matt began removing the old tiles. They both came out easily thanks to the damage from the heavy pressure cooker that Yorkie had used and which they had initially thought was a simple pot. Housty had found the buckled lid on top of the upper kitchen units. No wonder Yorkie had panicked so much, it must have felt and sounded like a small nuclear explosion.

The tiles were done. Windows, walls and doors wiped clean. Matt had managed to fill the hole left by the lid hitting the ceiling so it looked like Yorkie was in the clear. He was ecstatic.

'Fucking diamonds you pair, the best. Franck Gaston Henri fucking Sauzee of mates,' he said, grabbing them both in a hug. 'I owe you both, big time, but DO NOT FEAR.' Raising the plastic bottle above his head that contained the last of the cocktail, he continued. 'You will be rewarded, yeee ha, whos for a nip of Yorkie's rave whisky?' he enquired.

'No danger, pal,' said Matt, without any hesitation. 'I am not drinking anything that has worked its way through C-o-l-i-n's body. Anyway I need food pronto. All the fresh air and hilarity has made me hungry.'

Housty agreed, about the food that is, but he was swinging towards trying the potion again. 'Matt's right, lets go and get some scran and we can head back to mine. You never know, we just might have a wee nip of that rather exquisite, lowland malt whisky,' he said, whilst smiling and winking at Yorkie.

'That's the game,' was Yorkie's response, as he gathered up his smoking paraphernalia. Housty put his bike in the back of the Land Rover, whilst Yorkie checked on C-o-l-i-n, delivering two not so refreshing cans to his room along with a family bag of bacon flavoured Frazzles.

'Lunch is served pal. Living the dream, old yin,' Yorkie sang, as he exited his grandad's cave like room, the only source of light coming from the fish tank. Locking up the house with a wide grin and a spring in his step, he was delighted. The boys had rescued him and now armed with the remainder of the cocktail he was heading for an afternoon out with them. If Carlsberg did afternoons, he was sure this was going to be it.

Chapter 6

I love it when a plan comes together

Swinging past the local bakers, Matt and Housty opted for three steak pies each whilst Yorkie decided on a cheese salad roll. 'That'll not fill you up, mate,' Matt said.

'You dinnae ken what kind oh meat is in they pies, mate. Probably racoon from China.'

'Dinnae talk nonsense, man,' Housty replied, both him and Matt laughing.

'You've been drinking fermented wee wee and your worried about eating a pie,' Matt said, through a fit of the giggles.

Even Yorkie had to admit to himself that Matt had a valid point. Not that he chose to share this with the other two.

Armed with a couple of full cases of Stella and their late lunch, the boys drove up to Housty's flat, after dropping Roxy off at Matt's mother's house. Housty's place was in one of the few blocks of flats in Blercrae. He had one side of the top floor of the six story block. It was the perfect bachelor pad. Two good sized bedrooms, a bathroom and kitchen, and best of all, a balcony. Chaining his bike to the landing banister, Housty then opened the door and they trooped in, taking their shoes off in the hall. Housty was house proud, the place was always immaculate and this seemed to encourage the lads to treat it with respect.

'Place is looking spanking as usual,' Matt said to Housty as he admired the living room.

'Aye, palatial, tidy Heidi,' Yorkie laughed, whilst enjoying the feeling of walking into the lounge on the thick carpet and plonking himself down on the luxurious, tanned leather couch. His house would look like this if it wasn't for him and C-o-l-i-n he thought, making a mental note to try and help his mother out with the domestic duties a bit more. Having all demolished their lunch (over plates of course) and accompanied by a can of Stella, Yorkie began his post food ritual of skinning up. With the Stone Roses, Second Coming album playing in the background, *heavens gates won't hold me, I'll saw those suckers down*; the lads blethered away, enjoying each other's company. When the three of them were together, it was a challenge agreeing on what to listen too. They usually end up with the Stone Roses, or something earlier, like the Doors or Jefferson Airplane. It was very rare for them to meet up and not at some point play the classic Jefferson Airplane tune, White Rabbit. This tended to happen when they were well oiled and all three would attempt to copy Grace Slick's haunting vocals. *One pill makes you larger and one pill makes you small, and the ones that mother gives you, don't do anything at all.*

Yorkie disappeared into the hall bringing back the plastic bottle containing his concoction. 'Who fancies being a shambles for the rest of the day?' he said, shaking the bottle around. Matt was the only one who required convincing, Housty was intrigued to try it again while he was still sober.

'Let me have a look at that,' Matt said, reaching out for it. Holding the bottle up to the window, he moved it from side to side, watching the light brown liquid sticking to the sides of the bottle, before slowly creeping back down the side. 'You are one sick individual, Yorkie. This stuff looks like treacle, serious hangover time.'

Yorkie just gave him a knowing gaze before Housty piped up, 'After the state I was in last night, I honestly thought I would have felt like a reptile this morning, but not a bit of it, mate. Was at the gym early doors knocking ma pan in. Unbelievable recovery time, like being a teenager again.'

'Give us it here ya massive jessie.' Yorkie was bored of the debate. He reached out for the bottle and took a decent sized sip. Almost immediately the familiar sensation of it travelling through his veins began, his heart picked up the pace and his eyes rolled about in their sockets, like washing in a tumble drier.

'Smashing, just fucking smashing, my fine, fine friends,' Yorkie drooled.

Housty needed no more convincing after witnessing it taking effect. He hopped across the room swiping the bottle from Yorkie's shaking arms and took a slightly more measured swig. He put the bottle on the coffee table and began moonwalking back to his seat. He never made it to the seat before he was overcome by the mysterious liquid. With a huge grin on his face he stumbled back towards Yorkie. Cupping his friend's screw ball scrambled face in his hands, he gave him a big slavering kiss on his cheek, before singing along to the music. 'You should have been an angel, it would have suited you.' Turning to look at Matt, he mumbled, 'Get it down ye, GI Joe, this sort of stuff made the British army.'

'You wouldn't win a square go with a squirrel the now, look at the state of you,' Matt said, as he began laughing. Yorkie and Housty were now staggering about the living room smiling manically.

Fuck it, Matt thought; am no sitting here straight while these two rockets have all the fun. Taking the bottle, he unscrewed the lid and sniffed the contents. The potent vapour seeped into his nasal passages immediately. As the others began clapping and chanting, 'Do it, do it, do it,' he lifted the bottle and allowed a mouthful of its contents to pour down his throat, trying his best to avoid any taste buds on the way down. This was a skill he had mastered when eating army field rations. Gourmet food they were not. With the bottle safely back on the table, he sat back, aware the room was now quiet as Yorkie and

Housty surveyed his behaviour expectantly. He looked at the four beady eyes and two hanging jaws in front of him. He felt his toes, then feet, moving about and then realised he was on his feet with his arms around the pair of them.

'Ya fucking cunt ye. There's a fucking firework show going off in ma head ya couple of bams,' he slavered. 'Jesus you are one mad, mad scientist, Yorkie man.'

'Are we etched in stone or just scratched in the sand,' they all began singing together whilst hugging and dancing around the living room as The Stone Roses classic, Tightrope, belted out.. The next hour passed quickly in a euphoric haze as they danced and blethered about old times while singing along to songs from their youth. As the effects wore off, they found themselves back in their seats chatting, drinking and smoking.

'That was incredible, Yorkie. Unbelievable,' Matt said. He was astonished at how high he had been.

'Mental eh? I knew C-o-l-i-n was full of pish but I never expected to drink it,' Housty laughed.

'Aye, he may be a failed footballer but he's a fucking dangerous chemist in the making.'

'Am not a failed fitballer, man. Fitbaw failed me, there was nae support when a needed it maist,' Yorkie whinged.

'Ha ha, you got loads of support, from bars, nightclub seats and tarts beds, man,' Housty replied, making all three of them start giggling again.

As the day wore on, the lads ventured out to replenish the carry out and get some nourishment. Chicken kebabs and a few more cans were consumed while they hatched a plan to try and recreate Yorkie's masterpiece.

'It's not safe to cook this stuff up in one of our kitchens,' Matt told Yorkie after he had suggested using one of theirs. His was now a no go for obvious reasons.

'Well luckily, I've goat an alternative,' Yorkie winked. 'Mind the camping stove and that I found in my hut?' he said to Matt. 'Well how about we use that and go to my grandad's old allotment in Stenhouse? Ken the ones right next to the railway line?'

'Aye, I mind going there to pick raspberries years ago,' Housty said.

'So do I,' Matt agreed. 'C-o-l-i-n would take us after school on a Friday. Mind he taught us how to plant different vegetables? It's sad to think of him then to now.'

'The drink has taken a terrible toll on him,' Yorkie nodded sadly, oblivious to the evidence that suggested he was on a similar trajectory. Not an unfamiliar path to far too many Scots.

A plan was hatched, they would meet tomorrow and head over to the allotment.

Chapter 7

Can you see the real me, can you, CAN YOU?

Although C-o-l-i-n had always been a heavy drinker, he had only made the transformation to full blown, almost bedridden alcoholic, once his wife had passed on. In his younger years, he had been very passionate about the Northern Soul scene. He would put on nights in the local pub's large function suite to supplement his occasional trips to the famous Wigan Casino. On its legendary wooden sprung dance floor, he had even won some dancing competitions. His tall athletic frame meant he could manage dance moves that some less fit men could only dream of. The rigorous all night workout kept him in good shape and meant he was never short of admiring glances. It was during this time that he had met Yorkie's grandmother. It was hard to imagine now but he had been a well respected member of the community and had once stood to be a Labour Councillor. He received huge backing locally and would have got in if it wasn't for all the Tory voting suburban districts that surrounded his own scheme. The self interest brigade were never far from your doorstep, in what even back then, was a relatively affluent city.

A keen footballer, he had captained the local team Blercrae Star. It was widely recognised that his grandson's skills had been passed down from him. Unlike Yorkie, he had been the midfield general of the team. A solid, dependable driving force that constantly urged his team forward. As soon as the games were over, he was more often than not, inclined to urge the boys straight into the nearest boozer as well.

He was articulate with a good work ethic, this didn't go unnoticed at the pipe works in Gorgie, where he had worked since leaving school. He was promoted to foreman early on, initially meaning some of the older more experience men resented him. This didn't last as he proved himself more than capable and very fair with everyone. He had been a positive force in the union but unlike the famous Jimmy Reid, he had not promoted the no bevvying rule, especially where he was concerned. Even as a young man, he had a weakness for drink, after all being Scottish meant he was amongst like minded people.

There were many neighbouring families that could thank him for getting members of their household's jobs in the factory. There was a time when worried parents would turn up at his door and ask if he could help their wayward boy. The answer was always yes. The number six corporation bus was eventually crowded, carrying C-o-l-i-n and the local lads, to Gorgie every morning. The stale smell of alcohol, even then, was radiating from him on those bus journeys. This was when he was an evening drinker. He would enjoy a few drinks in Stratfords, just along the road from Tynecastle Stadium, when his shift was done and then he'd wash his tea down at home with a large carry out.

Like many others, eventually the morning hangovers were only dampened by another tipple. The sound of the clink of glass bottles could be heard as he climbed onto the bus in the mornings. A few bottles of pale ale and a quarter bottle of vodka would see him through the morning. Soon, lunch time drinks became the norm as did the warnings from his bosses at the factory. It was one thing turning up hungover, but another when he was staggering around shitfaced. The large gas pipes, they manufactured for Scotland's blossoming oil industry, were huge cumbersome objects. The potential for a devastating industrial accident could not be ignored. Due to the respect of the men and bosses alike and the knowledge that he was having to watch his wife suffer with illness, he had been given more time than most. In the end, the inevitable happened and he was laid off. The bosses had made sure he had got what was due, but there was only one place that money was going to end up. Like the unions, the pits and all of Scotland's heavy industry, he was in a seemingly irrepressible, steady decline.

Not long after this, his wife died and the call of the can was irresistibly stronger than ever.

Chapter 8

Cooking

Matt drove round to Housty's the following morning, amazed at how fresh he felt. Considering the state he was in yesterday, he couldn't believe that he could function, never mind the fact that he had already been out and about. He had been awake early, to his astonishment; had breakfast, video called Thomas, picked up the motor and took Roxy for an early walk out to the tidal island at Cramond. For once, he had arrived at the shore and the tide was out. He had breezed along the causeway, managing to visit all his favourite spots, even the hidden WW2 bunker in the centre of the island. Afterwards, Roxy had been dropped once again at his mothers, an arrangement that suited them both. She loved having him and it meant that he wasn't going to get in the way, or more importantly, blown up by Edinburgh's maddest narcotics scientist, Yorkie.

Upon arrival at Housty's flat, Matt was further taken aback to find Yorkie up and dressed. Housty was just finishing his second breakfast after another trip to the gym. Yorkie had chosen to stay at Housty's after receiving a few irate texts from his mother about a vet's bill, for cat's teeth cleaning. Yorkie had tried to explain to her that bad teeth ran in the family so it was important to look after Smudgies. This just made her even angrier, judging by the last text. 'It's a fucking cat, not a family member you fucking muppet. You and your grandfather will be the end of me son.'

The three of them got in the Land Rover, the morning's itinerary being a visit to the supermarket for supplies and then to head to the allotment. Before going there, they drove round to Yorkie's, all three pleased to see his mother had left for work. No one wanted to see her after the previous day's events. As well as being annoyed about the vet's bill, she had also enquired about the strange smell in the kitchen. She was a hard woman to lie to when she had you cornered, all of them had been there at some point. Obviously, Yorkie more than most.

'A hope C-o-l-i-n has another sample in the fridge for us, lads,' Yorkie said.

Strangely, Matt or Housty had not considered the fact that they would need more. 'Do we have to use that again, man?'

'Why is he leaving bottles of pish in the fridge anyway?' they enquired.

'He's having liver problems so the docs have asked for daily samples, lucky for us eh?' Yorkie laughed. 'They will be going nowhere near the docs, that's for fucking sure.'

'Aye well, if you keep stealing the samples, what is the doc going to test, ya bam?'

Yorkie's face screwed up in confusion at Housty's question. He hadn't considered this. 'Ah'll take it oot and then just refill it wi ma own golden shower,' he decided.

'Even better, let's get some pregnant lassie to do it, that would really confuse the docs,' Matt laughed.

'Or even a dug,' Yorkie started creasing.

Housty thought he had spotted a bit of a flaw in this line of thinking. 'C-o-l-i-n is not going to get any better if the doctors cannae work out what is wrong with him, messing about wi his sample is not going to help.'

Almost immediately he realised how stupid he was being as Matt and Yorkie started creasing.

'Whats wrong with him?' Yorkie snorted, incredulous that Housty could be so stupid. 'You're meant to be the clever gadge.'

'He's been a hardcore drinker for most of his life, I have never seen the old radge sober,' Matt laughed.

'Aye, fair point,' Housty conceded and then started sniggering too. 'Lets really freak the docs out, lets get Roxy, yer dog, to provide a sample.'

Arriving at the house, Yorkie ran in, retrieving the stove, damaged pressure cooker, allotment keys and one of C-o-l-i-n's samples. He emptied it into another container, marvelling at the shade of brown the old goat could achieve. Even after his three day benders in York, he had never managed to pee that colour. Taking the empty sample container up to the bathroom, he refilled it and checked in on his grandad. He looked fast asleep but as Yorkie went to shut the door he heard. 'Is that you, son? Get ays a tin, pal. C-o-l-i-n needs a wee livener.'

'Right nae bother. Grandad. Geez a minute, bud.'

Replacing the sample container in the fridge, he snatched a prized tin and bolted back up the stairs, placing the can on the bed side table.

'Cheers pal, Hertz rule ya wee radge,' he mumbled.

'Aye so they do, auld yin,' Yorkie replied, smiling as he gently closed the door before bolting down the stairs and locking up. The boys had all the gear in the back of the Land Rover and they were soon heading to the local super market for supplies. Brasso, bleach and vodka purchased as well as some food and drinks to keep them going. They headed for the allotment.

While driving Matt began to shake his head, turning to the boys, 'Still mental that here in Edinburgh we have two high schools in the same campus, one for Catholics and one classed as non denominational. What the fuck is that all about?' Neither of them disagreed with him. Scotland was a country with an extraordinary amount of bams, in all sections of society. Why it chose to create more problems in society, by educating kids separately due to something as inconsequential as religion, was a mystery to most.

The allotment was located between the main rail route out of Edinburgh and Broomhouse, another of Edinburgh's housing schemes. Just over the road from the school's in question. There was parking on an old road lying adjacent to the main road. They began unloading the gear while Yorkie unlocked the gate and led the way to the far corner of the group of around twenty allotments. The place was a bit overgrown now, but still in decent nick. It was obvious Lynne had not completely abandoned the plot to brambles and weeds. Opening the rusted padlock on the shed door the boys had a look about. There were some old cloth seats that Housty took out and started wiping the worst of the mould and dust off. Yorkie was straight in there clearing some space on the paving slabs that made up the floor. There was also what looked like a small set of bunk beds at the back of the shed. Yorkie's mother had probably installed them to escape C-o-l-i-n and her lunatic of a son. Matt for once was hanging back, looking worried while surveying the shed.

'Matt, take some of these, man,' Yorkie said, trying to hand him a collection of cracked plant pots stuffed together like Russian dolls.

'Na mate, I cannae help you there, far too many spiders' webs, bud,' he responded.

'Whit the fuck are you whinging about? You're meant to be a big hard soldier, ya massive camel's toe,' was Yorkie's response. No matter how much the other two badgered him Matt refused to help until the place had been given a good going over. He had almost knocked Yorkie out when he had pretended to throw a spider at him but it turned out to be a bit of earth. Once the place had been given the all clear, he was right in there with Yorkie getting the stove and damaged pressure cooker set up. Housty was happy to leave them to it, he was enjoying the midday sun, sitting on an old deckchair watching the trains pass. He had tried to say hello to another allotmenteer (or whatever you called them), but they had given a half-hearted wave back. This convinced

Housty that they would have to be discrete, although, how they would manage that with a space cadet like Yorkie in tow was a mystery. Luckily, the older man was on the other side of the patch of allotments so would hopefully not be able to hear their conversations, although he would have to have had his nose removed not to smell one of Yorkie's jazz fags. Thankfully, so far he was concentrating on cooking and not origami. Having got the stove alight with little difficulty they got the pressure cooker as secure as possible on it using bricks piled up at either side. Then came the potion mixing.

'Right pal, over to you,' Matt said. He got the earlier purchases out the bag and lined them up on the hut's worktop. Housty had now begun to show an interest and was loitering around the door watching.

'Am feelin a wee bit oh pressure here, ya cunts,' Yorkie laughed. 'Let's get fucking cookin boys, yee ha,' Yorkie shouted, punching the air.

Housty flinched and immediately had a quick scan to see if the old bastard had heard them. He had and was looking over shaking his head. Fuck him, thought Housty, we'll only be doing this once anyway. What would the police do if they did turn up? Lift us? Probably not, but there a good chance they would lock us up in the loony bin.

Yorkie started talking them through how to create his masterpiece. 'Right lads, gather round,' he beckoned them both into the hut around the pot and stove, which was now burning. He had gone into serious mode, reminding Housty of how he looked when playing football. No matter how smashed he had been, when the whistle sounded, he seemed to be able to find his focus. Unfortunately for him, he had never been able to focus enough off the pitch.

'First add the vodka to the pot. Never the bleach or Brasso first. Then bring it to the boil.' They chatted about the weekend's football matches, all delighted to see Hibs back in the premier and playing well. Yorkie was stirring the pot with one of his mother's wooden spoons that he had requisitioned from the house. As the third bottle of vodka began to boil. Yorkie, now in full Delia Smith, mode began pouring the bleach in. He judged about a quarter of the container should do it and then added half the tin of brasso while continuing to stir.

Yorkie noticed that Matt was not concentrating on his TV chef impression. 'Get off your phone, ya ignorant cunt, you are watching a master craftsman at work.'

'Am taking notes on how much of each you have put in the mixture, ya fuckin bam,' was Matt's response.

Almost together, the other two came back with, 'Oooo, how very British army of you.' They always did when Matt had his sensible head on which was more frequently than Housty and infinitely more than Yorkie.

Thinking this through Housty said, 'Taking the pish aside, that's a very sensible idea. Whoever invented all these synthetic drugs that you can buy up the town must have been doing the same. If we can recreate Yorkie's original formula, this stuff will sell quicker than real ale and luxury pies at a wanker's convention.'

They all nodded in agreement as Yorkie removed the lid from his grandfather's sample. As before he felt obliged to take a quick sniff. 'Oh ya cunt ye.' The other two took a sniff both recoiling involuntarily.

'Fuck me backwards, that is honking,' Matt said. 'You could clean the fucking oven with it, man.'

Yorkie emptied the entire bottle into the boiling liquid. The hut instantly filled with a potent gas, forcing all three friends out into the bright sunlight.

'Now I can see why you blew up the kitchen, Yorkie. Plenty of ventilation needed,' Housty said, whilst jamming the door open with one of the old plant pots. He noticed the old man was now looking over, giving them some unwanted attention. 'Look busy boys, that beechgrove garden twat is staring over.'

Matt and Housty did a bit of weeding whilst true to form, Yorkie skinned up some weed. The initial strong reaction from the urine in the pot seemed to have weakened so Yorkie returned to the pot and began stirring again whilst the other two sorted out the unkempt raspberry bushes, trying their best to look productive as beechgrove garden was still keeping a close eye on them. After another ten or so minutes, Yorkie turned the stove off. 'That's the cookin over, boys. Time for some dookin,' he announced. Matt and Housty just looked at each other shaking their heads and smiling, both heading back into the gloom.

'We'll need to let it cool and then bottle it,' Matt said.

'Aye and then test it, muckers,' Yorkie confirmed, obviously trying to cement his plan in the other's heads that they would be testing it ASAP. Not one to put the burden on others, unlike these big companies using animals for testing, he was more than happy to be the guinea pig.

The steaming hot liquid was lifted off the stove using a pair of gardening gloves and placed on a couple of slates on the work top. As the day's main task was now complete they took time to tidy the hut further putting the stove and left over ingredients away.

'This place is like the fucking tardis man and in pretty decent shape,' Housty said, surveying the shed.

The bunk beds had cleaned up nicely and with one of the boys sitting on them, there was room for a couple of chairs. As it had started raining, they ate their supplies, purchased earlier from the supermarket, inside. All were glad to see that the nosey beechgrove garden boy had packed up for the day.

'There must be about three full bottles worth in that pot,' Matt pointed out

'Aye, we might have gone a bit OTT,' Housty suggested.

'Light weights,' Yorkie laughed. 'I want to use a couple, to see if there is a business opportunity for my currently unemployed pals and a former professional footballer gadgy.' Yorkie then continued in a posh accent, 'I think we deserve a bit of the high life and I mean, high!'

'Who the fuck are you going to convince to buy this stuff? A drink laced with JK's pish is a hard sell,' Housty suggested.

'Am no going to tell any cunt that it's C-o-l-i-n's pish, am a ya tube? Na, am going to have a word with Big Andy. He's had a few dealings with the silver fox recently. It's worth a go. We cannae go to Ray while he's inside an there's no way am speaking to that Harvey cunt.'

At least they all agreed on that. Harvey was Ray's sidekick. Ray was a popular local, and not so local drug dealer, who was currently serving time in jail due to some serious misdemeanours.

The others didn't see this as a business opportunity, more just a laugh, although Housty had a mortgage to pay and Matt needed to start earning to keep his close relationship with Thomas. They had both agreed to come along today because they had enjoyed yesterday's mayhem. It was good having the three of them back together again. Both knew Big Andy well, Blercraes delivery man, but Ravanelli, the Silver Fox, was a step further into the underworld. A step neither of them were comfortable making. He was a Ray equivalent, but if rumour was true, they tended to deal with different customer bases. Ray knew every bam across the city and beyond, but Ravanelli knew those types with money; businessmen and politicians who were too scared to deal with Ray, preferring Ravanelli's more sophisticated discreet approach.

Once the liquid in the pots had cooled the contents were transferred back into the now empty glass vodka bottles that they had used earlier.

'Right you pair, who's for testing the goods?' Yorkie said, holding up one of the bottles.

The others just looked at each other smiling and raising their eyebrows. Their mate really was a grade one head banger.

Sensing an air of hesitation, Yorkie carried on, 'Am no fucking joking me auld muckers, a cannae take any auld pish to Ravanelli, it's got to be spot on. Tip fucking top.'

As much as Matt was tempted, he had to drive. 'Tell you what, we can head back to mine so I can drop the motor. There's no danger I'm leaving it here in Comanche country.'

Before Housty could get a word in, Yorkie had the remainder of the day planned out for all of them.

'Right, fair doos captain sensible, myself and Mr Marko Houston will enjoy a nip of this fine Lothian malt.' He had reverted back to his posh voice whilst holding up the bottle. This batch did again look like whisky due to its golden tinge.

Matt winked at Housty, 'Get in there, pal. You are in safe hands.'

Yorkie had unscrewed the bottle, taken a quick sniff, nodded at them like it really was a fine malt and he was a connoisseur of Scotland's national drink. He took a fairly big mouthful before licking his chapped lips and handing the bottle to a nervous looking Housty.

'Fuck it,' Housty said, whilst taking a swig, being careful to take less than Yorkie. Yorkie had always been greedy. If they went clubbing and had one pill, Yorkie needed five. A few beers for them and he would have some ching and nips, just to satisfy the muckle, aggressive silver backed gorilla on his back.

As Housty felt the warm glow begin to run through his veins, Yorkie began pogoing out the hut singing. 'When will I, will I be famous,' 'We're going to win the league.' He then began some atrocious rave dancing as the four pm train to Glasgow passed. Luckily, the train was going to Glasgow so its occupants were well used to seeing bams being bams.

Housty grabbed hold of Matt, trying to focus on his eyes. He slurred, 'I am fucking buzzing, this stuff is dynamite, that maniac may have actually struck gold,' as he pointed out the hut at Yorkie, who was now jogging on the spot while point up at the sky singing, 'I am the witch doctor, ooow ooow, I am the witch doctor, ooow ooow.'

'Right, I need to get you pair up the road before someone phones the bizzies, look at the state of that,' Matt nodded in Yorkie's direction. He was punching the raspberry bushes now. 'I'm bigger and bolder and rougher and tougher in other words sucker there is no other.' He skipped over to Matt, appearing to come out the trance like state, giving him a big slobbery kiss on the cheek.

'Take me back to your place, hot stuff,' he slurred, whilst slapping his arse and laughing. This set Housty off into fits of howling laughter.

'Right, for fucks sake, let's get locked up and get out of here,' Matt said, shaking his head and trying to look annoyed but thinking; I want a wee bit of that too. Yorkie may have been on to something big after all.

Chapter 9

The historical village of Davidsons Mains

Having managed to get them in the Land Rover, Matt was forced to listen to a number of shocking duets as Yorkie and Housty ruined his enjoyment of the Petshop Boys album that he had been playing. A particular low point was West End Girls, it was during this he eventually gave up and switched it off. This only succeeded in forcing the pair of them to start the usual wind ups about him liking bufties music and how he should have joined the navy instead of the army. To Matt's relief, they had both stayed in the motor whilst he picked up Roxy from his mothers in Blercrae. He then stopped for another carry out and headed down to Davidsons Mains where he lived in one of the old council four in a block. Matt had one of the downstairs flats which could be annoying when the folk above had a party. Other than that, he loved it. D Mains, as it was called by locals, was originally an old village outwith Edinburgh. Residents from the crowded city centre or Leith, would get the train there for a day out, to get away from the smog and filth in its large park. The railway had closed in the 1950s and the city had now spread, making D Mains, like Blercrae, just another suburb. It still maintained a village feel though with a few pubs scattered along its main street. There was no way Matt was taking Yorkie or Housty in his favourite haunt though, no matter how keen Yorkie was. He played darts in one of the locals and taking that pair in just now would result in an almost certain barring. Yorkie had definitely overdone it with the potion. Matt almost had to carry him in to his home and dump him on the sofa. He was pleased none of his neighbours had been around to witness this. Thankfully, Housty was now showing signs of returning to reality.

'It's not like Yorkie to go too far, eh?' he said to Matt, pointing at the former athlete slumped on the couch, smiling and drooling onto his Keep the Faith, Northern Soul T shirt. One of the few things in recent times that his grandad had given him. An old friend from the scene had been in contact and sent C-o-l-i-n a few T shirts that he had designed. Sadly, C-o-l-i-n had seemed thoroughly disinterested and was more than happy for Yorkie to take them. This was just another example of how drink had taken hold of him, blanking out most of his former interests and hobbies. When a person becomes hopelessly dependant on bevvy, sadly there's not much room left for anything or anyone else.

'I will be with you in a moment, chaps,' Yorkie said, smiling further. 'Keep the faith, my fine, fine friends,' he mumbled, whilst raising his clenched fist.

About ten minutes later, Yorkie had come around and was blethering away with the other two over a couple of cans of strong Belgian lager. Further indication that the potion's affects were receding was his insistence that Matt had a taste, which obviously gave him the green light to take another hit. Matt was open to this now as he was relaxed in the familiar surroundings of his sparsely decorated but smart home.

'Fucks sake man, this place needs a bit of colour, bud,' Yorkie pointed out. 'I feel like I have woken up in a tin of white emulsion.'

'Aye, there is more colourful cells in Saughton right enough,' Housty agreed.

'Am a bloke, you couple of pansies, minimalistic means it's easy to keep tidy and when I leave here and buy my but n ben in the hills, its ready to be sold, so stand easy soldiers,' was Matts response. He had plans. As soon as he could he was out of the city. Roxy and him would wander the hills every day, breathing fresh air and avoiding all the lunatics that now inhabited the city. Had it always been so manic? He didn't think so but maybe it was just him getting older. Wherever he went in Edinburgh, there always seemed to be someone wanting to have a go or being out of order ruining it for everyone else. Sometimes the perpetrators didn't even have to be there but the mess they have left behind was enough to really piss him off. A number of times when walking the dog he had found himself putting other folks rubbish in a bag. Matt loved Edinburgh and Scotland and hated seeing it being ruined. He had yet to decide whether to head to the highlands, islands or borders but either way he was escaping. He would have his son, Thomas stay with him as often as his schooling would allow. Finance was the only thing holding him back, jobs were scarce in these areas and good, well paid jobs, even scarcer.

'Get the damage in you, big guy,' Yorkie said, handing the bottle to him. Matt took a sniff and then gave the contents a dubious look.

'What the fuck am I doing?' Matt said, shaking his head.

'Get in about it, GI Joe,' Yorkie laughed. Matt took a very small gulp and handed the bottle to Housty who was also careful. Yorkie snatched it out of Housty's hand before he had a chance to pass it over and took a full mouthful in one fluid motion.

'Chin chin, lads,' he slurred, with a gaping droopy grin. His face beaming with chemical happiness.

Matt was already feeling the rush as was Housty. As usual Yorkie was way ahead of them in the getting smashed race that he seemed to be permanently in. He was on his feet, looking at Matt's Sonos speaker wondering where the CD went.

'What the fuck is this sorcery?' he slavered, looking at Matt. 'Get the techno on, I like to boogie on a Saturday night,' he sang, while pretending to waltz up the living room. Matt had to agree, it was time for techno, well not techno but maybe some House. *Jack had a groove and from that groove came the groove of all grooves............and House music was born*. Yorkie had picked up the bottle and was holding it above his head shouting, 'I am the creator, you see I am the creator.' They were all up dancing and singing now, 'Our house music.' It was like they had stepped back into the Calton Studios in the 90s. It was a big club on the grubby Calton Road behind Waverley Station in the centre of Edinburgh. Calton Studios had been a regular haunt for the three of them. A place famous for putting on the harder club nights. Let there be house!

An hour later the music had changed, the Inspiral Carpets were playing as the three of them sat around reminiscing, laughing and drinking.

Turning serious for a moment Yorkie spoke. 'Am going to meet up with Big Andy tomorrow in the pub, this stuff is dynamite. If he can sort out a chinwag with the silver fox, we could be in the money, boys.' The other two still looked dubious so Yorkie continued. 'This is our chance lads, life has been tough the last couple of years for all of us, come on we need to give it a go,' he pleaded. In the back of Yorkie's mind, he knew he didn't have many chances left. It had not escaped his attention that he could easily become the next C-o-l-i-n if his life didn't improve soon. He just had to convince the others, he had to.

'I don't know how you have done this bud but I cannot deny that that stuff gets you high as fuck, barry feeling with no obvious hangover. In fact, I felt brand new this morning,' Housty said, turning to Matt to gauge his reaction.

Matt had to agree with Housty. 'Aye it's mental and I can't believe I am saying this, I'm in, lets meet Ravanelli.'

'Yeeeeeessssssss,' Yorkie screamed, jumping off his seat with both hands in the air. 'Ok, I'll get in touch with him,' was the final word on it from Yorkie before they got back to talking nonsense again.

Chapter 10

Deliveries

Big Andy Forrest was well known in Blercrae. He had been a delivery driver of sorts in the area and around Edinburgh for most of his adult life. He was a formidable character physically, but not one to bully or lean on people. His demeanour and looks were enough to deter anyone taking liberties. On the surface, he was one of life's simpler people and was well liked for it. Everything was black and white to him. Treat people properly and expect to be treated the same. Old school thinking and good luck to the man that attempted to make a fool of him.

Andy would tell anyone who would listen that he had been delivering for forty years, man and boy. 'Started with the fucking Herald and Post and ma career just took oaf fae there, cunto.' His older pals would usually pipe up and point out that dumping three hundred free newspapers in the local woods hardly counted as delivering. As soon as he had his driving licence, he was out picking things up for people in an ancient Bedford van that he had bought for a couple of hundred quid. In the past he had worked for different delivery companies but it had just got in the way of his main source of income. This had forced him to become more freelance. It was rumoured that he was now delivering for the darker side of society; mainly the local gang headed by Ray. Others who were more in the know had also heard that he was working with another dealer, whose real name was not widely known, but was referred to as Ravanelli.

Big Andy had, in his younger days, been affectionately known by the nickname Biffa. This had begun at his local Boys Brigade when one of his pals had brought in a copy of the adult Geordie comic, Viz. It was quickly pointed out that he resembled the character Biffa Bacon, even from an early age. Back then, he had had short hair and a fag hanging out his mouth. Now, he had no hair but the fag remained at the side of his mouth, stuffed in between crooked teeth. It was an almost permanent ornament. Andy was one of those people that the smoking ban had hit hardest. Although the name Biffa hadn't stuck, he had to admit, even now that there was an uncanny resemblance in his appearance to the unfortunate Newcastle born comic book character.

Andy had had a busy day, far too busy for his liking. A job with far too much to it had come up and he had delivered a massive trampoline to a house in Corstorphine and been paid to erect it. He had done this with questionable competency. Andy was hoping that the customer wouldn't notice the large fag burn in the rubber. Within ten minutes of finishing the job, he had had a call from the customer, and to his great relief had nothing to do with the melted rubber. They did in fact ask him to take it down, return it and pick up an even bigger one which he was then to assemble. Fucks sake, he thought, the first one was fuckin massive. Bet that milf in the bank outfit just wants to see big Andy at work again, probably wants tae pump me oan it. He often thought this about customers, but unfortunately for him, it was a one way thing. He informed the milf bank worker that he'd smash the job the morn and headed off to the Blercrae Inn for a pint and his mysterious meeting with his long time friend, drinking and smoking buddy, Yorkie. What does that fuckin head case want wi me now? As with most of his thoughts, this one disappeared almost immediately as he remembered that he hadn't had a fag for the past three minutes. So lighting up, he headed down the road waving at every second car as the horns sounded in greeting.

Having extinguished his third cigarette consumed in his five minute walk to the pub, he pushed open the double door to a friendly cheers of, 'Here's the cunto' and 'Andy, ya cunto.' Cunto was Andy's favourite word and was used regularly to describe all situations and people. The underlying meaning could be identified by his tone.

Scanning the large public bar, he saw Yorkie playing pool with another local celebrity. As with most of these guys, he had achieved celebrity status by getting absolutely hammered every day for about fifty years.

Yorkie immediately spotted Big Andy coming over with his pint just as he was about to granny Jacks the plumber. Jacks, like C-o-l-i-n was a consistent performer in the Blercrae drinkers' top division. A man that had shown incredible consistency over the years. Winking at Big Andy, Yorkie slammed the black into the middle left pocket.

'Fucking skelped you there, pal,' Yorkie said to Jacks, putting his arm around him.

'Guaranteed pal, guaranteed,' came the standard response from his permanently pickled friend. 'I better get down the road, paaaaal,' he slurred. He shook Andy's hand as he registered his presence, before picking up his work bag which actually contained lots of warm cans of lager and practically nothing that would help with his chosen line of work, plumbing.

'See ya later, cunto,' Andy replied warmly.

'Guaranteed, pal. Guaranteed,' came the jovial and predictable reply.

Jacks left the pub to head home in order to make inroads into the day's third large carry out. Andy and Yorkie retired to one of the booths at the far end of the bar, away from the other afternoon drinkers. Their initial conversation followed their usual roughly monthly piss ups together. Andy would always enquire about C-o-l-i-n's health. Even now after being house bound for so long, people still asked after him, usually with a sad expression, as his current predicament was widely known. There was always the token football discussion. Big Andy was a Hibs fan too and in his younger days had been involved in the casual scene. When the focus of the police had been turned on football hooligans, Andy recognised any connection to trouble could bring implications to his business ventures, so he had taken a step back. When he no longer attended games, he realised it was not the actual football he enjoyed but the circus that surrounded it; the away day train journey, obligatory piss up and guaranteed fight with whoever was game enough. Now he only had a passing interest, he would check on results and occasionally attend the derby games.

They had a good blether about what chaos was being caused locally. In a housing scheme the size of Blercrae, there was always local dramas. Big Andy had told him about his (not so) close encounter with the trampoline milf, obviously embellishing the story, saying that he was onto a sure thing when he was round there tomorrow.

Returning to the table with the fourth round, Yorkie thought it was time to broach the subject of a meet with the fabled Ravanelli which he hoped his friend would facilitate.

'Right cunto, time to discuss business,' he said, taking a gulp from his fresh pint. He enjoyed drinking with Big Andy, as they both drank at full pelt, not slowing down until the sixth pint at least. Although his grandad was a master piss artist, he was as much use as a sewn up arsehole after three strong tins. The curse of the professional JK. They love getting hammered, but just can't keep up once they hit oblivion, which they are only ever a few drinks away from. The secret was to allow yourself to sober up enough to enjoy the next session. Real drunks never sobered up, the extent of the hangover could actually kill them.

'Business, cunto?' Big Andy questioned. He was under the impression they were here for the sole purpose of getting smashed.

'Aye, I have got something tae sell and I was hoping you could introduce me to the silver fox, you still see him?' Yorkie asked, while attempting to appear relaxed about the question. In truth, he was far from relaxed, his entire plan relied upon him convincing Big Andy to help facilitate the meeting.

Big Andy stiffened up. 'You mean Ravanelli? Which cunto told you I see him?'

'You did ya bam, you tell me almost every time we meet up. You said he had moved to Aberdour, just over the bridge. In fact, you had been there that day, the last time we had a bevvy, buddy.' Unlike most others, Yorkie rarely suffered from memory loss no matter how drunk he managed to get. This could be an asset, but also had the ability to haunt him for days, depending on how he had behaved.

Looking worried and quickly sobering up, Big Andy was desperately trying to think who else had been drinking with them that day. Ravanelli was obviously not his real name, in fact Big Andy was one of the very few who knew his real name was Bill. He was originally from Middlesbrough and had been in the RAF. He looked like an RAF cunto; well groomed and always smart. His silver hair and beard looking like it was clipped by a professional, daily. Mind you, if he was from Middlesbrough, he can't have been a posh cunto, probably just filled the jets with fuel and let Sir Shagalot actually fly the things.

'I wisnae talking about him in front of anyone else was I?' Big Andy said hopefully, his face now portraying how anxious he was.

'Na man, it was just you an me, bud,' Yorkie confirmed, not really giving it any thought. Most of the other afternoon drinkers in here had gherkins for brains, so even if he was, they wouldn't recall.

Relaxing a bit, Big Andy made a note to not discuss his booming wholesale delivery business again. 'There is no danger I am introducing you to that cunto. He's a good cunto but am no wanting to tickle that particular tiger the wrong way.'

'Fuck off, man. You deal wi Ray, he cannae be worse than that.'

'Ray's one of us though, bud. Ravanelli is different. All well spoken but a cold cunto,' Big Andy warned.

'Look man, I dinnae want tae pump the boy, just present him a business opportunity that could make us all some good pennies. You dinnae want to be delivering all your life do you?'

Taking a minute Big Andy thought, aye I do, I love delivering. It's about all am good at. The thought of a pay day no matter how unlikely made him reconsider. 'Right, tell you what, ah'll be seeing him in the next couple of days. I will ask him right, whit kind of opportunity? Al need a bit more tae go oan.'

Yorkie's face broke into a big smile. 'Ma man, ma fucking man,' he said, grabbing Big Andy's chunky shoulder. 'I have a new designer drug that I want tae start punting. It's no fair keeping it to me an ma boys. Not only that, it's dynamite cunto, we will make a killing.'

'Which boys? You better no be getting me in bother.' As much as Yorkie was Andy's pal, he was also a nutter and like most nutters, had many unreliable acquaintances. The last thing Andy wanted was to get mixed up with anyone he didn't know and couldn't rely on.

'Easy brother, it's Matt an Housty. Sound as a Scottish pound,' Yorkie's face beamed back at him.

The thought of them being involved settled Big Andy down. They were good lads not complete radges like Yorkie. Hopefully, their presence would be a calming influence on their troubled friend.

'Mon outside, we'll have a celebratory smoke,' Yorkie said, standing up. He sensed Big Andy was coming round to the idea. Delighted he skipped towards the side door that led to the beer garden. He had been worried Big Andy wouldn't go for it, he had had to tell a wee lie to his mate there. Big Andy had only mentioned Ravanelli once or twice and only when really hammered and badgered by Yorkie. He had heard elsewhere, from Harvey in fact, that he had moved to Aberdour. As usual Harvey had taken this as a victory, banishing a rival to the wastelands of Fife. Little did he know that the village of Aberdour was full of money and actually signified that Ravanelli was doing very well and that possibly Ray's power was failing. If it was failing, this would be down to Harvey himself as Ray's hands were currently somewhat tied due to being in a cell for twenty three hours a day.

Big Andy did not need convincing to go for a smoke, he realised at least thirty minutes had passed since his last cigarette. Not that Yorkie had any intention of smoking plain old tobacco. What would be the point in that?

Chapter 11

Ravanelli, The Silver Fox

Yorkie hit redial again on his phone, wishing his big pal would answer. He had not heard anything from Andy since their session in the pub. A good few more pints had been consumed and they had been joined by a few others. He was hoping that Big Andy had not forgotten. He shouldn't have let him smoke all those spliffs with him. Andy attacked a joint in the same way he attacked a fag, blitzkrieg style. He wasn't used to smoking skunk in Yorkie's quantities and was a bit worse for wear when the two of them stumbled up the road. Cursing himself as the phone went onto answer machine again, he headed upstairs to see if C-o-l-i-n needed another can. It felt like his plans were becoming increasingly tenuous. Housty had not been in touch and he knew Matt was down south in Colchester to see his son and no doubt hooking up with some army pals for a carry on. In the days that had since passed, Yorkie had tanned the rest of the bottle and was gutted that he had left the other two at Matt's place, along with the keys to the allotment shed.

Arriving at the upstairs hall, he saw Smokey sneaking out of C-o-l-i-n's room. Why did that cat sleep with Scotland's number one JK and not him? Fucking cute little traitor. Leaning down stroking him he said, 'If it was up tae that auld goat ye widnae have teeth that good wid ye?' In true cat form, Smokey started purring and rubbing himself along Yorkie's legs. 'Ye are a wee cutie right enough, pal.'

A familiar croaky voice interrupted their bonding session. 'Is that you, son? Get C-o-l-i-n a nice tin, pal. Av got a hangover bigger than your beautiful auld granny's arse.'

His phone began to vibrate in his pocket and his heart skipped a beat when he saw Big Andy's name on caller ID. 'Alright cunto, hows you?' Yorkie enquired, trying his hardest not to sound desperate for news. Always best to try and retain the veil of coolness.

'Cunto, av got to nash but av goat you a meeting wi the silver fox oan Friday. Al pick you up at nine am sharp, we've to be in Aberdour by half nine. Do not fuck this up. You owe your pal Andy one massive session. Nine am sharp,' he repeated, hanging up.

'Ya fucking beauty,' Yorkie shouted as he bounded down the stairs. Cold can now in hand he sprinted up to see C-o-l-i-n, handing the sweaty mess the tin and giving him a big slobbery kiss on the forehead.

'Get fucking af me, ya Leith batty boy,' he said, trying to shove Yorkie away from him.

Laughing Yorkie left the room feeling right up for it. 'Pump up the jake, pump him up, coz his heed is thumping and his heart is jumping,' he started singing. In the hallway he shouted through to C-o-l-i-n in his posh accent. 'Bye for now old friend, I have business to attend to, business of the highest importance.' Time to phone the boys he thought. That muckle lump of old soldier better get himself back up the road pronto. He opted to phone Matt first. It was Wednesday which didn't give him much time if he was still playing sticky biscuit with his soldier boy comrades. In fact, worse than that, he remembered the initiation race that Matt had told him about where the new lads had to run round the parade ground with a biscuit jammed in the crack of their arse. The loser then had to eat the other recruit's biscuits. Animals, fucking animals, he thought, smiling and hitting dial when Matts name popped up on his phone screen.

To his delight the call was answered within two rings. A muffled, distorted voice, 'Yorkie bud, hows you?'

'Matt is that you? I cannae hear ye, pal.' Matt's voice was disguised by the static disrupting the call.

'You're on bluetooth mate, I've just crossed back into bonny Scotland. Passing Eyemouth, should be back in the Burgh in an hour. Depending on the traffic mind, it was fucking murder passing through Geordie land. Queues of traffic longer than Ray's charge sheet, man.'

Yorkie was pleased that Matt sounded in good spirits, his son must have been on good form. 'Stroll on my man. Big Andy has sorted out a wee chat wi the silver fox on Friday morning, you need to be there, pal,' Yorkie pleaded. Yorkie didn't expect any issues but if things took a turn for the worse, Matt was a good person to have by your side. He sensed hesitation from Matt. 'C'mon man, this could be the big one, ah mean WE, need this, brother.' He emphasised the we and he meant it. The three of them catching up had been great and Matt had appeared happier than Yorkie had seen him in a long long time.

When it came to Yorkie, Matt was protective, so with a sigh to himself, he agreed to be there. 'Right man, I will be there. Just keep the blethering to a minimum, man. Sometimes better to say nothing than too much. Oh and lay off the drugs before it.'

'It's at nine thirty am man, even I should be straight at that time of day,' he said, as he decided to get up extra early that day to have a spliff in order to calm any pre match nerves. 'Be at mine for nine am sharp. Big Andy is picking me up then. You can follow in the lanny.'

Completely unconvinced by Yorkie's response, Matt signed off the call. 'Right man, see you at nine am, do not fuck this up.' He hung up using the stereo and went back to the Charlatans; Between 10th and 11th. *Theres no soldier in me, I want my guts where they are.*

Why does everyone tell me not to fuck things up? Yorkie thought, annoyed for a very short instant. He soon forgot about Matt's words of warning though. He was delighted to have him on board, getting Housty along would be so much simpler now. God knows why either of them needed convincing, they had both tried the cocktail. It was fucking mental gear. If Ravanelli could get it into some sort of sellable state, every head case in Scotland would be on it. 'Guaranteed,' he said out loud laughing, imitating his crazy pal, Jacks the plumber.

Housty felt his phone vibrating in his suit jacket. He had been at another job interview, for a job that he didn't want, but really needed. It had gone okay although it was hard to tell with these HR slime balls. All nicey nicey to your face, giving you a bit of hope and then nothing. The knock back letter always said that if you wanted feedback, please just call. Aye right, you would get the usual text book waffle that they had been taught on some dull training course. Pulling his phone from his pocket in the hope it was good news on the job front (and in a way it was), he couldn't help but be disappointed when he saw it was his childhood pal. 'Alright, man,' he said, with no enthusiasm whatsoever.

Immediately sensing Housty's mood, Yorkie thought it best to fire in straight away with the good news. 'We are on my man, we're meeting Ravanelli on Friday morning buddy. Fucking magic, eh?'

Christ, Housty thought, here's me trying to get a job to sort out the mortgage arrears and he's getting excited about meeting a bam with some crazy cocktail made with his grandad's pish.

Yorkie continued, 'Mon man, whats up? Matt is in. Nine am at mine Friday morning. Do not be late,' he barked

'Sorry man, just had another job interview which a will no doubt get fuck all from.'

'Job interview? Dinnae talk pish, mate. Once we get this little enterprise up and running you'll be wiping your arse wi fifty squeeb notes and getting hookers tae make ye yer tea.'

'Aye sure,' Housty retorted. 'I've got a mortgage to pay and am no sure getting off my tits in an allotment shed is going to do that.'

Give me strength, Yorkie thought, slapping his forehead with his freehand. Firstly, why anyone would want a job was beyond him and secondly, what could possibly go wrong? He knew they were on to a winner. Housty could be so dull at times, talking about mortgages and jobs.

'Positive mental attitude, my fine, fine friend,' Yorkie said, trying to pacify this dour version of his best pal Housty.

'Matt has agreed to this then?' came the monotone response.

'On Smokey's cute wee feline heart, he has me old mucker. Nine am at mine Friday. You will be there aye?'

'Aye, right see you then, man. Fuck all else to do have I?' Housty hung up and headed along Princess Street to get the twenty six bus home. What on earth had he just agreed to?

Simultaneously Yorkie looked around his living room in disbelief. 'Ungrateful cunt,' he said out loud. Here he was trying to make their lives better and more industrious and Housty had the cheek to complain. He was doing him a bloody favour.

That Friday morning, Matt had picked Housty up at quarter to nine and the two of them arrived outside Yorkie's house ten minutes later. They stood in silence, Housty ringing the bell. They had been discussing what they were doing agreeing to this meeting. It was a sign of how far their lives had fallen or in the very least changed. When Yorkie was so enthusiastic, he was a hard man to turn down. Both felt protective of him as well so, if their presence increased his chances of making it back to Edinburgh alive, that had to be a worthwhile reason. Both looked at each other when there had still not been a response after the third long ring.

'He's still in his fucking scratcher,' Housty said, looking at Matt incredulously. 'After him telling us not to be late in all.' Both friends were just shaking their heads when they saw Big Andy's van pull up.

Yorkie had heard the ringing in his sleep, wishing it would go away. He opened his eyes, realising he was slumped on the couch, trousers round his ankles, with the adult channel still playing in pristine HD quality. Sitting up straight, he saw that he was clothed from the night before, with a couple of cheap bottles of wine and a wrap of ching in front of him on the coffee table. All were empty. Feeling a crushing sense of doom, he remembered being so excited about Friday's watershed moment in his life that he had ended up getting banjoed. Just as he so often did in his football career before big important matches. Small ones as well, and training sessions in fact when he came to think about it. He leapt off the couch, pulling up his trousers and trying to fix his hair whilst slapping his face in an attempt to wake himself up. He would have to brass neck this one out. Game face on, he bounded for the door, opening it as Big Andy came down his garden path cheerily greeting Housty and Matt with his usual, 'Alright cuntos.' All three turned to see the door open and a horrifically rough looking Yorkie greet them.

'Morning lads, great day eh? Just give me a second an I'll be right with you,' he said as cheerily as he could muster. All three just stared at him and then looked round at each other in horror, none in the least bit convinced by his bravado.

'Fuck sake, man,' Matt said.

'Look at the fucking nick of you, Yorkie,' Housty carried on for his friend.

'Aaww fuck, cunto,' Andy added, shaking his head angrily.

Not one to give up easily, Yorkie tried once more to convince them that he was fine. 'Boys av just slept in, that daft cat kept me up. Wee rascal.' Even whilst smiling and winking at them in a way that made it look like he had mild Tourette's, Yorkie could tell he was losing the battle.

'Yorkie, you have a fag end stuck to your cheek, you smell like a French vineyard and its fucking obvious you have had less sleep than Billy Idol on one of his many meth binges,' Housty pointed out.

'Right cunto, you have two minutes to sort yourself out. All be in the fucking van,' Big Andy said, pointing at his pal. Cursing repeatedly, he lit a fag and headed for the familiar comforting surroundings of his motor.

Yorkie had already sprinted upstairs, chucked cold water on his face, rubbed some tooth paste about his red stained mouth and thrown on a semi clean Paul and Shark t shirt that he found lying on his bedroom floor. He could hear C-o-l-i-n stirring in his room but there was no time to fetch him a can. Bolting down the stairs, he ran out to Big Andy's van. Opening the front door, he realised that there were no seats spare. Housty and Matt were already in the two front passenger seats and Big Andy was obviously sitting in the driver's.

'Back of the van for the late cunto,' Big Andy barked, not even smiling now. He was pissed off and made no effort to hide it.

Yorkie could tell that there was no time for arguments. Swearing, he trooped round to the back, got in and sat on an upturned crate just behind the driver's seat. For him, the journey over the bridge was a quiet one. It became obvious that Big Andy was not amused with the state he was in. He had initially asked why they didn't just take Matt's car as well. Big Andy's response had been a very curt one. 'Just because, the less cars arriving at his house the better.' No friendly cunto reference was used, alerting Yorkie that he was in the dog house or more accurately the back of the van. The others blethered away casually, Big Andy and the other two having a good catch up. All three admired the bridges as they crossed the River Forth and caught a few glimpses of the aircraft carrier being built at the Rosyth naval dock. Big Andy summed it up accurately in his own special way. 'Fucking massive cunto oaf a ship.'

Aberdour is about a twenty minute drive from the outskirts of Edinburgh. It lies on the beautiful Fife coast, looking across the Forth to Inchcolm with its Abbey and further east to the fair port of Leith.

The boys drove in to the town past the old Woodside Hotel and sand stone church before turning right down towards the town's beach and harbour.

Aberdour could not have been more different to Blercrae. It was a quaint town that once entertained the kings and queens of Scotland in its beautifully laid out, now ruined, castle with elegant gardens. Blercrae's spacious modern layout was replaced by a village main street, old stone buildings and some impressive mansions that sucked in the majestic view of Edinburgh from the Forth's Northern shore.

'Some nice pads down here,' Housty commented.

'Not short of cash,' Matt agreed.

'Rich cuntos,' was Big Andy's predictable smoke encompassed response.

Big Andy turned left at the bottom of the hill, directly in front of an inviting sandy beach and continued on to a large villa that overlooked the quiet harbour. He parked outside, next to a large fancy looking Range Rover and an old Black MK1 TT.

'Lucrative business,' Housty said quietly. The mood in the van had changed. It was time for Big Andy to be serious. Ravanelli was an important part of his livelihood and he didn't want the relationship soured by any idiotic behaviour. He had had some hard times when Ray had initially gone down and he liked working for Ravanelli. He always got paid and it meant that he didn't have to deal with Harvey. Like everyone else, Big Andy hated Ray's sidekick.

'Cuntos, do not fuck this up. He's a good cunto but takes nae pish,' Big Andy said, his eyes firmly focused on a rather sorry looking Yorkie in the back.

'Loud an clear my man,' replied a nonchalant Yorkie, doing nothing to convince Big Andy or the others that he had taken any notice.

'Right, game on cuntos,' Big Andy said, stubbing out his fag and walking round to let Yorkie out the van. Matt and Housty were standing looking at the vast villa which was a cross between a Spanish mansion and a Welcome Break Hotel. The beauty of the setting could not be argued though. It faced out across the harbour which was littered with colourful sailing boats. Arthur's Seat could be seen in the distance looming across the Capital city.

'Nae smoking, cunto,' Big Andy warned Yorkie. 'An his name's Bill, nae fucking mention of silver foxes or Ravanelli. He's no fucking daft.'

He led the boys to the entrance and rang the bell. Almost immediately, the door was answered. Ravanelli stood there looking every inch the upper class drug dealer. He was tanned, with silver styled hair and neatly trimmed silver beard, wearing a pair of smart black trousers and expensive looking black v neck jumper. To finish off the look, he had suede loafers and a watch with a bigger face than a fat lying politician.

'Andrew, great to see you,' he said, shaking Big Andy's hand. It was clear Ravanelli liked Andy as he looked genuinely pleased to see him.

Making a sweeping gesture towards the other three, 'I take it these are the gentlemen you told me about? Hello, I am Bill.' His eyes scanned the three of them resting on Yorkie longer than the other two. He had clearly noticed Yorkie looked absolutely fucked. Matt and Housty both offered their hand and he shook them in turn smiling. As Yorkie stepped forward there was a small pause before he accepted his hand. Ravanelli was trying hard not to show his obvious disgust at the state of the man in front of him.

Not trying very hard to hide his revulsion, he invited them all in and directed them through to a huge open plan living area that overlooked the beach and island. 'Make yourselves comfortable please, I'll get some drinks for us all.'

As Yorkie had let himself fall onto the couch, he then jumped off it and bolted over to the window where a large, very hairy black cat was sitting. 'Hiya pal,' he said, stroking the cat. Turning to Ravanelli he began slavering, 'Av goat a cat in aw, barry things. Mines called Smokey, he's a wee smasher. What's this furball's name?'

'Fez,' came the curt response from Ravanelli who had his eyes firmly fixed on Big Andy's, with a look on his face saying, why have you brought this muppet to my house. Big Andy returned an apologetic shrug. He wasn't a babysitter after all and if people couldn't behave what was he meant to do?

Matt had laid the rucksack that contained the remaining two bottles of party whisky down in front of him. He had kept a close hold of them since picking up Yorkie. When Yorkie was in this state, he could not be trusted one bit.

'A love cats man, barry pets,' Yorkie confirmed, to no one in particular as he gave Fez one last tickle before slumping back on the expensive leather couch.

A woman entered the room with coffees for everyone. Only Yorkie looking disappointed that it wasn't something stronger. His head was hurting big time, a monumental hangover was just around the corner. Once she had left, Ravanelli was keen to get down to business and no doubt get them out of his house sharpish.

'Right gentlemen, our mutual friend Andrew tells me you have a business proposal for me,' Ravanelli's eyes, focusing on Matt and Housty, deliberately cutting Yorkie out of the conversation.

Housty sensed Yorkie was about to speak so cut him off quickly. 'Yes, we have two tester bottles of a, erm.......a kind of cocktail we have developed that has some pretty impressive results when taken in a small quantity.' Matt had taken the two bottles out of his bag and laid them on the table.

'It's a mental dunt ye get oaf it, pal,' Yorkie chipped in, with some less than impressive sales skills.

Ravanelli ignored him completely. Picking up one of the bottles, he looked at the liquid that it contained before unscrewing the top and nervously sniffing its contents. He didn't allow his nose to hover over the bottle for any more time than necessary.

Looking up at the four expectant faces staring back, eagerly waiting for his response, he said, 'Certainly smells potent. I have an acquaintance of mine here, who if it's all right with you, I would like to try it so I can understand its qualities better. All happy with that?'

'Aye, no bother,' Housty replied, as the others nodded.

Ravanelli rose to his feet and walked to a side door where they could hear him whispering to someone. He came back into the room, followed by a character that looked in a worse mess than Yorkie. He was introduced as Scotty and looked like the long lost brother of Gollum from Lord of the Rings. Even Yorkie looked a bit concerned about the state of him. Scotty hadn't even looked at any of them, just sat himself down on the sofa next to Ravanelli and stared straight ahead. It was obvious the boy was absolutely hanging. A good meal would have been more beneficial rather than the drink he was about to test.

'Please go ahead and pour a sensible measure into the glass on the table and Scotty will do the honours.' Matt leaned forward and did just that placing the glass in front of Scotty. All eyes in the room were now on him, a position of focus he was clearly not comfortable in.

'Down the hatch Scotty boy,' said Ravanelli, with the first hint of real amusement on his face as the shaking hand of Scotty raised the glass and slammed the cocktail home in one professional movement. Within seconds, his eyes were more alert and then he was on his feet with the room's full attention.

'That is some fucking hit, Bill. Some hit,' he said. His head was shaking from side to side as an enormous smile appeared on his gaunt face. This exposed a set of teeth that looked like an ancient neglected dry stone dyke. He was doing a strange dance at the window and looked to be waving at the boats in the harbour. Leaving him to enjoy himself Ravanelli returned his focus to the lads.

'Andrew tells me one of you is a military man, I presume it is one of you two?' he said, nodding towards Matt and Housty

'Aye, I served in the Royal Scots for twelve years,' Matt confirmed.

'Excellent, I spent time in the RAF. Teaches a man discipline,' was the response as Bill evaluated him.

Yorkie was next to speak. 'A was a pro footballer for York City, star striker man, that's why a get called Yorkie now. It's a wee blast to ma football past.'

'Mmmmmm,' was Ravanelli's only response to Yorkie's unwanted announcement.

Trying to find common ground, Yorkie pressed on, oblivious to the others in the room wishing he would shut up. 'Aye a played at Ayresome Park in the FA Cup for City, scored a couple so a did. Aye Big Andy, erm a mean Andrew telt us you were a Middlesbrough boy.'

'He did, did he?' Ravanelli said, turning round and giving Big Andy a funny hard to read look. Scotty was getting more into the massive high he was experiencing. Trying to moonwalk, badly, and doing some terrible robotic dancing, much to the irritation of Ravanelli and the amusement of the others.

'Andrew, I know how much you like a smoke, be a sport and please take Scotty out on the balcony and give him a cigarette would you?'

'Aye, no bother,' replied Big Andy, getting to his feet and ushering the spangled wretch out onto the balcony. Andy was more than happy to vacate the room for a smoke.

'Oh and please make sure he is quiet and doesn't bloody jump,' Ravanelli called as the sliding doors shut.

'Gents, judging by the state of my friend, I am a little surprised to say I am very interested in dealing with you. Can I make a proposition?' he said, knowing fine well that these amateurs in front of him would agree to anything. He was met with a chorus of Ayes. He continued, hardly waiting for them to respond or caring what the response would be. He wanted in on the action.

'Firstly, am I right in thinking that the recipe is a secret and will remain so?'

'Aye, it's ma own wee creation, man. A bam never reveals his secrets,' Yorkie confirmed, tapping the side of his nose and winking.

'In that case, I would like to take these two bottles and ask a friend of mine, a chemist, to devise a way of splitting them up to make distribution easier. Are you all okay with that?' Again, he hardly waited for a response. 'Good, as a show of good faith I'll pay you one hundred pounds for each bottle.' Misreading the looks of surprise on the boys' faces as annoyance at what he himself thought was a paltry offer, he said, 'Okay one hundred and fifty per bottle. We can come to a proper deal once I see a clearer way forward. For now, can I suggest that you begin upping production? Going on Scotty's reaction, I can see huge market potential. There may be some very profitable times ahead,' he concluded, smiling with his hands clasped together.

To everyone's dismay, an ecstatic Yorkie reached over the table and took a celebratory mouthful from the already open bottle.

'Oh for fucks sake, Yorkie,' Housty said angrily.

'Ma heed is burst, man,' was all Yorkie could say as waves of euphoria engulfed his brain. He was quickly on his feet again and with the new found energy he went back over to Fez to stroke him and slaver in the poor beast's ear.

Ravanelli, obviously now keen to get these lunatics out his house, handed Matt the three hundred pounds which he counted out from a much larger wad of notes he had in his side board. He then rescued Big Andy from a seriously caked Scotty who was ushered out the room via the door he came. He passed a now equally spangled Yorkie who laughed at the state of him mumbling something about being a light weight whilst slavering in the distressed cat's ear.

Ravanelli had got them all back to the front door when Yorkie took his chance. 'Any ching on the go, big man?' he slurred into his ear. His rancid all nighter breath polluting the air around Ravanelli.

An obviously now pissed off Ravanelli looked at him coldly and said, 'I think you've had quite enough,' before dismissing him with a sweep of his hand in the direction of the van.

Housty thanked Ravanelli and dragged Yorkie towards the van before he made an even bigger cunt of himself. He was off his face.......again.

Leaning in towards Big Andy and Matt he hissed, nodding his head towards Yorkie, 'That boy is a fucking liability. Do not bring him here again. From now on, I deal with you Matt. I can be contacted through Andrew. Now if you will excuse us, I need a quick chat with Andrew alone.' He signalled to Big Andy to join him back inside. His accent briefly showed his working class roots in his native Middlesbrough.

Matt strode over to the van getting in the front alongside Housty, pleased to see Yorkie had been put safely in the back again. Yorkie however, was not sitting but was standing gesticulating wildly. 'What a cunt, an arrogant drug dealing cunt. Its ma fucking invention and ingenuity that got us here and he treats me like a fucking loser.'

Punching his chest for dramatic effect as his head bumped off the van's roof.

'He spoke to you like that cause you were off your tits,' Housty pointed out.

'Fucking embarrassing, man,' Matt agreed.

'Did you get the doe of the grey heeded cunt?'

'Aye,' Matt snapped, not even turning round. For the first time in a long time he was tempted to flatten Yorkie. Judging by the look on Housty's face and the way his fist kept clenching, he was experiencing the same dilemma.

'Tidy, I need to pay Mr T for last night's powder. Goin give me ma share, an dinnae bother taking the hump about that skinny silver heeded bake off boy looky likey.'

'Aye right, that money is going on ingredients. We are going to spend the next few days in the allotment shed making as much of this stuff as possible. A ton fifty a bottle, easy fucking money. '

This made Yorkie stop and think for a moment. 'Aye, a suppose I could delay Mr T. As the business boys on the telly say, let's make the money work for us. Luckily, I have been storing C-o-l-i-n's samples. We're going tae need them!'

'Am more concerned about him watching the bake off, you must be tempted to eat the telly when you've got the munchies,' Housty said as he began to cool down and see the funny side. After being subjected to Yorkie's antics for years, it was hard for Housty to remain angry with him for long.

'Shut it, Housty. It's no me that watches it, its C-o-l-i-n. I reckon he's got the hots for the wrinkly one that looks like a stretched Yoda. She's the only person still breathing with more wrinkles than him.'

As Yorkie was speaking, he could feel his phone vibrating. It was his mother, no way was he answering that. He had left the house in a right state and she would not be amused. Almost immediately a text came through. It was again from her. 'I've just had the doc on the phone. Have you been giving your grandad a smoke? There were traces of weed in his urine!!!! We need to talk.'

Yorkie was completely oblivious to the other's anger. In this mood, he was more socially ignorant than an Eton educated Tory. He didn't hesitate to interrupt the others who were mumbling quietly to each other.

'You pair are going to have to start giving me your pish to replace C-o-l-i-n's sample. The hozzy have detected weed in his…..well mine really,' he said smirking.

With perfect timing, Big Andy got in the van to hear them discussing urine samples. He just turned looking at them all, 'I dinnae even want to know, cuntos,' he said, smiling despite the fag he had expertly placed in the corner of his mouth. He had in his possession a well wrapped package which he stashed safely under his seat before starting the van and heading back to Edinburgh. He had been intending on giving Yorkie a rocket for his conduct but unbeknown to the others, Ravanelli had slipped him a sweetener as thanks for bringing them to him. He had reiterated his point that he wanted no more dealings with Yorkie though, a request that Big Andy was more than happy to cooperate with. Although he had work to do, he kept the van well within the speed limit. Not only did he have a melted Yorkie in the back, he now had a special delivery to make, courtesy of Ravanelli.

Chapter 12

In Business

Matt could hear the Stone Roses, Tell Me, in his dreams. *You can't tell me, you can't tell me anything, I love only me, I love only me. I've got the answers to everything.* His eyes opened with him realising that he was not in King Tut's tent but lying in his bed in Davidson's Mains. The reason for the early rise, six am to be precise, was because they had a lot of bottles to fill with what they had decided to call, The Damage. It was Yorkie's idea. He pointed out that it was the damage and did a lot of damage, so it was a fitting name. The other two went along with it. In truth, neither cared what they called it as long as Ravanelli paid them. Early mornings had never been a problem for Matt until recently, it was a discipline thing. In the army they got up at all hours of the night and morning for training exercises and in some cases, the real thing. Since leaving, he had made a point of not getting up until at least half seven but even that had begun to drift.

Staggering out of bed, he stepped into the hallway to be greeted by a very excited Roxy. He knew his morning walk was close. Matt shuffled into the bathroom and just as he began to empty his bladder, he remembered. 'Fuck sake,' he said to himself. He held the pish in as he waddled through to the kitchen to get the sample bottle. Filling it up nicely, he felt much better. He then flushed the toilet out of habit and placed the bottle on the window sill. He would have to remember to take it with him to replace C-o-l-i-n's sample when he picked Yorkie up. Since it became clear that the hospital did actually check the samples, the three of them had decided that Housty and Matt would take turns. There was a good chance the drugs squad would be at the door if Yorkie continued to be the donor. A quick cup of tea followed by a banana and him and Roxy were in the park. They were back in the house by just after seven. Matt had some porridge, brushed his teeth then hurried out, dropping the dog at his mums before going to get Housty.

'Fucking early, man,' was all Housty said as he climbed into the lanny yawning. 'Usually go to the gym in the morning to waken myself up. Hanging about wi Yorkie is bad for your health in more ways than one, dude.'

'Aye, you better believe it,' Matt replied. 'What's the chances he's out his scratcher?'

'Zero to no fucking chance, I reckon. If it's early for us then that plum will be struggling big time.' Housty had a point. The three of them had delivered supplies to the allotment shed after getting back from Ravanelli's. The allotment was busy; there were four others there along with beechgrove garden and all of them were at the same level on the nosey scale as him. They had been polite and tried to be as inconspicuous as possible but it was hard to hide a case of cheap vodka. They had even had to tend to the allotment, just to make their green fingered friends less suspicious. The lads had decided then that it would be better to arrive early and get the job done before anyone else turned up.

The lanny was bumping over the endless rows of speed bumps in Blercrae with Matt's pish sample bouncing about at Housty's feet.

'I hope you put the lid on that properly,' Housty said, pointing at the frothy yellow liquid swilling about below him.

'Aye, me in all, mate,' Matt said, laughing as they both glanced nervously down at the container and it's precious cargo.

Arriving outside his house, they both almost passed out in surprise as an alert looking Yorkie came out smiling. Bounding up the path, he opened the passenger door. 'Good morning my fine, fine colleagues and how are you on this rather brisk summer's morning?' Yorkie enquired. Catching sight of the sample, he snatched it up. The others had yet to manage a reply before he had turned on his heels and ran back into the house.

They looked at each other with concerned looks that both said, is he off his tits again?

Within less than a minute, he had emerged with a carrier bag presumably containing C-o-l-i-n's stolen samples. Jumping in the back seat, 'Right chaps, tally ho,' he said in his best Fettes accent as Matt put the motor in gear and pulled away.

'Right Yorkie, please explain,' Housty said, turning round to face him. He had never looked this fresh in years.

'Explain what ya fucking radge?' Sounding like a foul mouthed commonly born Fettes student now.

'Well you are full of the joys, at what must be an early start for a professional stoner like yourself and you look like you may even have ironed your t shirt and I would go as far to say had a good wash,' Housty replied, trying to imitate Yorkie's posh voice.

'Easy to explain my man. I feel as head of this enterprise I need to show my subordinates how to behave and part of that is to be properly turned out. You could both take note,' he said, pretending to turn his nose up at the pair of them.

'God help us,' Matt said, laughing.

'God has fuck all to do with this, mate,' Yorkie pointed out. 'This is purely about the wheels of industry. The laws of commerce. Simple economics, supply and fucking demand.'

'Did you attend open university in the past twelve hours since I last saw you?' Housty enquired. He was enjoying the Yorkie show.

'Did a fuck, nae university needs to teach me that if Ravanelli pays us, we'll make it and the more cunts want it, we'll make fucking more. We'll then get paid more and have a barry time. Piece of pish,' Yorkie confirmed.

'Simple economics indeed, ya head case,' Matt replied, still laughing. 'Am just glad you've washed, I thought you had shat yourself yesterday, man. Van was honking on the way home.'

'Funny you should say that, I did a wee shart at one point. The Damage goes straight through me mate and wi all that ching an wine, a had a wee follow through,' Yorkie admitted, without a hint of embarrassment.

Matt hit play on his phone and The Doors burst through the car speakers. He didn't want to hear any more about Yorkie's bowel issues. *Dead cat, dead rat, did you know what they were at, oh yeah.*

Handbrake on and engine off, they had arrived at the allotments.

'Thank fuck for that, that bloody droning song does my nut in.' The End by the Doors had been going on for the past ten minutes.

'Not a fan then, Yorkie?' said Matt. Although even he, a huge fan of The Doors like he was, had to admit it went on a bit.

'I wouldn't say that, some great tunes but that one is even more boring than a Craig Levein coached team'

None of them were going to argue, Craig Levein was not only a Jambo, but he had been the most boring Scotland manager in living memory, which in itself was impressive with the likes of Brown and Roxburgh to consider. To be completely fair to both of them, they had got Scotland to major championships though. Something a whole generation of Scots had sadly, yet to witness.

Matt retrieved a large holdall from the boot, before locking up.

'What you got in there, man?' Yorkie enquired. 'We put all the ingredients in the shed yesterday'

'You'll see,' Matt said, winking at him and wandering after Housty who was unlocking the padlock on the large gates.

'Am in charge here, dinnae uz forget it,' Yorkie shouted, pointing a finger purposefully into his chest.

'Aye, sure you are Field Marshal Bampot, get in here before I lock you out, ya slaver,' Housty said, beginning to close the heavy steel gates.

'No a bad security feature, eh?' Yorkie nodded towards the gates as they shut. 'We can cook up drugs to our hearts content now.' The three of them started laughing as they walked over to the far side of the allotments. Life felt pretty good for the first time in a while.

'It's a good point though, man. At least we will get fair warning before plod can huckle us,' Housty agreed. 'I have some wire cutters in the house, I'll bring them next time and leave them in the shed. If the busies appear, which lets face it is highly likely with all these green fingered do gooders that hang about here, we can cut the fence and do a runner over the railway line.'

'Aye, nice one,' Matt nodded in approval.

'This is fucking magic, boys. I've not been this excited since I took those two tarts on a wee cruise in York. I almost want to get busted so we can make our escape.' Yorkie opened the shed grinning manically from ear to ear.

'Aye, that ended well Seaman Stanes,' Housty said, laughing. Matt and him couldn't help creasing as they followed him into the hut. Not that Yorkie cared. That one incident had made him more famous than the rest of his entire football career. It was the only time that he had got a significant mention in the national papers.

It was not even eight am when all three were in the shed, their start up business headquarters. Housty sat on the bottom bunk while Matt began emptying the bag. Yorkie standing in the middle of everything obviously thought it was such an historic moment that he should make a speech. 'Welcome to our place of business gentlemen,' he announced, with his arms outstretched. 'This is a massive moment for us all and believe me when I say I do not intend on letting either of you scoundrels arse this up with your petty squabbling and childish behaviour.' Seemingly, not put off by the other two ignoring his antics, he went on. 'And let me remind you both, AM IN FUCKING CHARGE HERE.'

'Yorkie, will you shut the fuck up, man. Its fucking early and we're trying to be discreet.' There was only so much Housty could listen to. It's not that he didn't appreciate his pal's antics, he just couldn't be arsed with that volume of idiocy this early in the day.

'Worry not my fine employee, for Yorkie is the height of discretion.' If it wasn't for the fact he had seen Matt emptying another stove and pressure cooker from his bag as well as a note pad, pen, white sheet, screws and wire, he may well have continued but it was Housty that was first to comment.

'Check out this cunt, he thinks he's in the fucking A Team.'

Yorkie started giggling. 'Well, he was a crap commando right enough.'

As the others laughed, Matt was getting annoyed. 'Right you couple of lazy bastards, geez a fucking hand, you wouldn't last two fucking minutes in the army.'

'What would you do like? Batter us about the ring or is that the navy?' Matt was easy to wind up and Yorkie was an expert in the field.

'Am fucking warning you, Yorkie. Shut the fuck up and help.' Matts face was getting redder as he looked up at Yorkie while on his knees sorting everything out.

Housty sensed the danger in Matt's rising temper and moved to defuse the situation. 'What's all the gear for, mate? I mean, I get the other pot and stove but the sheet and other stuff.'

'The more we can cook quickly, the less time I have to spend listening to you bams blethering pish, hence the second stove. The sheet and wiring is to make covers for the windows. We dinnae need any nosey cunts getting a look at our set up.'

'Aye, good point.' Housty was nodding his head in agreement with Matt's thinking.

'A sheet and wiring to make covers for windaes? What the fuck are you on GI Joe?' Yorkie was not convinced.

'You thread the wire through a cut piece of the sheet then wrap the wire round a couple of screws either end of the window. That way, when we're not up to something, we can open the curtains and when we're up to something, close them. That way any nosey bastard having a look wilnae get too suspicious.'

'What the fuck did they teach you in the army? How tae kill a man wi your bare hands and how tae make a lovely set ae curtains?' Yorkie was now using his gay voice whilst mincing provocatively about in front of Matt.

'Right, come on GI sew, we'll sort the windows out while the mad scientist sets up the gear.' Housty was keen to get on. He wanted out of here before people started to turn up to tend their allotments.

'Aye, good plan. You two bufties get the curtains out and leave the mad scientist to get on wi his experiments.'

It was a bit tight for space but they managed to work round each other. Matt and Housty set about blocking the two windows on either side of the shed. They cut up the old sheet and fed through some metal wire screwing it into the wood above the glass. The finished result was some dodgy looking curtains, but at least they could pull them open and closed. Yorkie had been setting up the stove and sorting out the ingredients that they had bought. They had agreed that they would fill the empty bottles of vodka they use back up with The Damage, once it was ready. They had blank labels to put on the bottles, Yorkie had insisted that they wrote Damage on these in two stages, DAM then AGE. He had spent a lot of time waffling on about how, at their point in life, they were damming age and it was the damage. The other two agreed just to keep him quiet. He was also keen to date every bottle which the others agreed was a good idea as none of them were sure how long the old codger's pish would keep.

With both stoves set up and the allotments still quiet, the boys started the cooking process. All three were now concentrating, the only outside noise supplied by rush hour traffic. Commuter trains and Edinburgh's swanky new trams gliding along their expensive rails, only meters from the shed. Housty was sitting on the bunk with a pen and notepad whilst the other two double checked the set up.

'Why the fuck have you got paper an a pen, Housty?' Yorkie asked. Matt and Housty had decided that they would both take a keen interest in the distilling process of The Damage. It would be handy if all three knew how to make it. Housty had volunteered to keep notes, whilst Matt measured the ingredients. They both thought that it was a wise idea as Yorkie had always had the reliability of an old French car.

'I'm going to write down the recipe. We're going to weigh everything so we don't make a cunt of this. I can just imagine the silver fox's reaction if we sell him twenty bottles of simple pish.'

'Fuck sake, man. Am mair oaf a freestyler. I've never followed a recipe in ma puff,' Yorkie moaned

'Stop talking shite, ya clown. All you ever make is cheese toasties. Sunday dinner to you is cheese toastie wi chopped up smoke sausage,' Matt pointed out.

'Nowt wrong wi that,' Yorkie winked back. 'Right, enough of the chit chat you work shy dogs, let's get fucking cooking.' He clapped his hands together and started opening vodka bottles. Looking up at Housty with a seldom seen serious expression, the cooking process began. 'Go with five bottles in each pot and bring them to the boil.' As Housty scribbled this down, muttering calculations to himself, Matt and Yorkie turned both stoves to full. They had bought ten bottles of bleach the previous day. These were stashed under the work bench with the extra bottles of vodka and the brasso. 'I think for every five bottles, we should use half a bottle of the bleach.'

'Right, that's half a litre of bleach for around two litres of crap vodka,' Housty noted whilst Yorkie and Matt judged the bleach as best they could, adding it to the boiling pots. They handed the wooden spoon they had used previously, back and forward until Yorkie was happy that it was mixed sufficiently. Taking a screw driver from the work bench, he opened the Brasso. 'Let's go with half a tin of brasso per five bottles.' Again Matt and him added the liquid and stirred.

'Jesus, that already smells like serious shit, man,' Housty said. He could feel the vapour stinging his eyes and working its way into his nasal passage.

Matt got up and checked no one was about. Happy they were still alone in the allotments, he used a heavy plant pot to hold the shed door open. Meanwhile, Yorkie took the urine samples that he had collected from C-o-l-i-n. He had ten bottles.

'Worrying times boys. Ten bottles is not going tae last long. We need tae think of an alternative plan.'

'Going roughly on what we did last time, one sample per three bottles means we will be able to make three bottles of damage every day,' Housty suggested.

'Aye, spot on, ah reckon,' Yorkie agreed. 'So about one and a half samples per five bottles oh voddy.' Housty wrote this down whilst the others added the agreed amount, stirred and then fastened the lids on the pressure cookers. All of them were a bit wary of what may happen next. They all left the hut fairly happy with how things had gone. As Yorkie skinned up a celebratory reefer, the others scraped off the labels from the empty vodka bottles so Yorkie could name and date them.

'How long do we leave them do you reckon?' Housty asked, looking back into the hut nervously. Both pots were rocking back and forward already.

'No fucking long, mate. I've already blown up my ma ma's kitchen,' Yorkie laughed half heartedly.

As they were speaking the pressure cookers were looking increasingly unstable, one in particular was rocking violently.

'Fffffffffuuuuuuuuuuuucccccckkkkkkkkkk,' Matt shouted. He dived into the shed and turned both stoves off as quickly as he could, before turning on his heels and bolting straight back out to find his two pals had moved a good ten meters away.

'Cheers for the help there, boys,' Matt said sarcastically.

'Don't mention it, my pal. You're used to dangerous situations. Am the brains behind this venture and Housty is the money man,' Yorkie pointed out. 'Housty, please make an entry in your notes that GI Joe is principle stove turner-offer.'

The three of them bickered away, pleased to see both pots had very quickly settled down once the stoves had been switched off. After about ten minutes, enough time for Yorkie to smoke and the others to scrape the bottles, they undid the lids to reveal their morning's hard work.

'Fuck me, man. This stuff is potent.' A thick oily steam rose in the hut forcing them back out. 'We are going to have to be careful as fuck, it's like high octane space fuel. That's another reason to call it The Damage, Yorkie. When it ignites it's capable of causing serious damage,' Housty continued.

'Good reminder,' Yorkie said as he marched back into the hut to retrieve the labels and marker pen they had brought to feature on their very unique bottles. Writing Dam Age in jagged, wavy writing like that from a calligraphy pen, Yorkie wrote out labels for the ten bottles. Yorkie hadn't been a stand out at school but had had the neatest handwriting in his class. C-o-l-i-n had had some expensive fountain pens and Yorkie would often practice writing his signature. He had loved the way that the ink bled from the pens nib. Small dates were added in the bottom right of each label. Using the measuring jug, Housty and Matt began filling the newly labelled bottles. All ten were filled, the amber liquid looking dangerous and inviting, glistening in the glass bottles. To Yorkie's delight, there was enough left for him to fill Matt's water bottle.

Smiling, whilst admiring their work, he lifted up the plastic bottle and took a big slug. 'To the spoils of war, boys,' he announced, lifting the bottle triumphantly in the air and trying to pass it to Matt.

'No fucking way, mate, its quarter past nine in the morning ya radge.' Housty also just shook his head. Of course, this didn't bother Yorkie at all, he could feel the now familiar feeling of The Damage running through his veins.

'Only get high on your own supply,' he shouted. He was now buzzing, prancing about trying to cuddle the others and annoy them at the same time. He achieved his second goal as Matt and Housty tidied up, putting the bottles in the bag and the stoves under the old shelves that ran up one side of the hut. Yorkie just waffled rubbish about buying a speedboat and going raving in Ibiza every weekend. They ushered him into the Land Rover, glad to get away just as beechgrove garden turned up, eyeing the three of them with obvious suspicion.

Yorkie waved and shouted, 'Morning, lovely day for it old boy, tally ho, off for a spot of breakfast. Kiss kiss, bang bang.'

Housty shoved him in the back, slamming the door and nodding embarrassingly in Beechgrove's direction. 'Christ Yorkie, we're trying to keep a low profile, I thought you were taking this seriously ya fuckin head case,' Housty protested unconvincingly. He knew fine well his friend would be oblivious to his protests and even if he was aware, would take no notice.

'It's just the stress of being at the very height of business for so long. Wheels of industry, commerce,' Yorkie slurred, laughing to himself. Some drool falling from his slack mouth onto his t-shirt.

Matt drove them to the butchers at Stenhouse for Edinburgh's most famous and best mince and gravy pies. Housty and him were starving. Surprisingly, Yorkie wasn't interested in the slightest. They were glad when he was dropped at his house, although Matt had to physically stop him from taking the bag full of the bottles. There was no way that he was being trusted with anything going forward. Yorkie had seemed happy enough when Housty shoved the plastic bottle, still relatively full, into his hand and escorted him into the house. Now it was just a matter of waiting until Big Andy got in touch.

Chapter 13

Planning

Much to Yorkie's annoyance, Big Andy had called Matt instead of him. It seemed Ravanelli was as good as his word and refused to deal with Yorkie again. Although the others were obviously fond of him, they all understood and were honest enough to say between themselves that it made things easier and without doubt more relaxed. The worries about how he would behave were therefore not an issue, which meant any discussions should be more amicable than would have been the case. The meeting took place in the same house in Aberdour with Big Andy again driving. They were greeted by a very friendly Ravanelli, the reason for this soon became apparent. He ushered them into the large living room that they had previously met in. He didn't bother offering drinks this time as he was very keen to get started.

'Gentlemen, I am pleased to announce that I want us to come to an arrangement regarding the supply of whatever that stuff is,' he said, pointing over at the ten bottles the boys had brought with them.

'Nice ONE,' Matt said enthusiastically, with Housty nodding along in agreement. Of course, Ravanelli knew he was the only show in town for them currently but he also knew that Ray's release date had been brought forward. He didn't want his big rival snatching this opportunity away from him. Hence, he never mentioned it but continued, hoping to strike a deal that suited him first and foremost.

'My chemist was particularly keen to find out the ingredients. He did detect traces of cleaning products and vodka but was annoyingly unable to identify everything. Well, when I say annoyingly, more for him because he thinks he's one smart bastard. I enjoyed the look on his face, more than I should have, when he had to admit to me that he just couldn't work it out. Priceless!' he said gleefully.

'Well it was Yorkie's creation and he takes a fair bit of understanding,' Housty pointed out. 'He's a simple, yet complicated individual.'

'Indeed he does and is,' Ravanelli said, smiling slyly. 'Now, all that remains for us to do is to come to a mutually beneficial financial arrangement. Oh and I suppose I should show you the finished product.' He lifted a bag of capsules from under the coffee table, taking two capsules out that looked like big cod liver oil pills. He handed one to each of the lads. 'The chemist has judged that is the correct dosage for people to enjoy themselves without getting in the state Scotty was when you last visited. Total disgrace, do you know he shit himself in front of me after you left, wasn't even the slightest bit embarrassed. Unbelievable!'

Remembering that Yorkie had had an accident of his own, Matt and Housty looked at each other, quickly turning away before they got the giggles. Big Andy was shaking his head, chuckling deeply as he announced, 'Am away out for a smoke.'

Once safely on the balcony and out of ear shot, Ravanelli made his offer. 'I will commit to buy ten bottles per week for the next month at two hundred pounds per bottle. Can you manage to meet that?'

When the lads confirmed they could, he continued, 'All going well, if this stuff starts selling I will up the order, agreed?' He then stood up and held out his hand.

The boys couldn't believe their luck. They had made those ten bottles in roughly an hour and a half, so two grand sounded like a sound proposal. They all shook on it as Big Andy came in from the balcony. Once the money had been handed over, they were soon heading back across the bridge having agreed to handover ten bottles to

Big Andy every week for the coming month. Ravanelli had even handed a small bag of the capsules over so Yorkie could see the finished article and test them. Maybe his negative opinion of him had thawed ever so slightly.

Yorkie had made them agree to go straight to his house after the meeting with Ravanelli. They opted to get off on the main road so they had a chance to talk things over before giving Yorkie the good news. Both were concerned that C-o-l-i-n was not going to be able to provide enough of The Damage's secret ingredient.

Housty spoke first. 'Right man, two grand less say the cost of ingredients, vodka etc say two hundred squeebs for a nice round number leaves us with eighteen hundred, split three ways is six hundred cash in our hands every week. Not bad for starters, in fact it's fucking staggering. This stuff takes off we could be on to a winner.'

'Winner, winner, steak fucking dinner, mate. Unbelievable.'

'Our big issue though is how we can get C-o-l-i-n to pish more. He already drinks more than anyone I know.' Well almost anyone.

As they rounded the corner of Yorkie's street, they heard the familiar tones of another premier league Blercrae JK. It was Jacks the plumber. He was stumbling along the road with his work bag, no doubt stuffed with warm cans of his favourite lager.

'Boys,' he shouted. 'How's you ma pals?' a very excited Jacks enquired. His full head of silver hair gleaming in the sunlight.

'Jacks man, good to see you,' Housty said, shaking the skinny but surprisingly powerful hand.

Matt also shook his hand. Both were fond of Jacks. There was not a bad bone in his lager drenched body. As always, Jacks was in his brown leather bomber jacket, Scotland top, jeans and Air Max. To finish the look, he was sporting the usual bright white pair of sports socks. The boys had discussed in the past how he looked so clean and presentable when his enormous lager intake was considered. Of course, the obvious answer was his long suffering wife. Strangely, given who the boys had just been with his silvery grey well trimmed hair and stubble, meant he could have been mistaken for a half starved Ravanelli's father.

'He's going to gee me a can oh lager for every bottle oh pish I gee him, whats that aboot eh?' Jacks babbled on. 'Guaranteed lager for pish, guaranteed. Count me in ah said, pal.' Jacks was so excited at his change in fortune, he was jumping from foot to foot.

It dawned on them that Yorkie had talked Jacks into donating a sample. A stroke of genius on Yorkie's part. They needn't have been concerned. As Jacks headed down the street, they both looked at each other and burst out laughing. Jacks was an absolute legend of the game, if anyone could replace C-o-l-i-n, it was him. Within minutes they were in Yorkie's living room showing him the capsules and hearing his good news about their new found supply of special grade one alcoholic's pish.

'While you two have been shmoosing with the client, I've been dealing wi supply issues and I am pleased to say I've cracked it, boys. I have come to an agreement with the much renowned, Jacks the plumber, to supply his potentially potent pish daily in return for his choice of cheap lager. The government should get me involved in trade deals, ya cunt. Took me a fucking age tae explain things tae him, harder to deal wi than that funny looking North Korean Kim Flung Dung. Mind, to be fair to him, it's a strange request! But a goat the deal done.'

A familiar voice interrupted them. 'Get C-o-l-i-n a tin, pal. I'm feeling a bit wonky.'

'Al be up in a jiffy, auld yin.'

'What was that pal? C-o-l-i-n ears are sare, a cannae hear fuck all.'

'Right,' snapped Yorkie. 'He is doing my nut in, getting fucking worse. Need tae keep him sweet but, eh?' Snatching a can from the fridge, he bolted up the stairs. Having resupplied C-o-l-i-n, Yorkie and the boys had a seat down the stairs and discussed the way forward. Yorkie became a bit emotional when he saw the finished product. 'These things look the fucking bollox, boys. Cannae believe it. Mind the Scots have always been great inventors. The TV, the telephone and now this.' The boys just looked at each other smiling, it was hard to tell if Yorkie was joking or actually believed he was on a par with John Logie Baird and Alexander Graham Bell. 'I'll be the toast of Ibiza when these things hit the island. Who's for trying one now?'

'Na man, lets sort out finances and how we are going to meet the order every week.'

Yorkie reluctantly agreed. 'Aye fair doos, but surely a wee party once everything is ironed out?'

The others just sighed resigned to the fact that they were bound to end the day baked. Yorkie's insatiable appetite for escaping reality would be the end of them all. Once they had filled Yorkie in on the deal with Ravanelli, he was ecstatic. In his words, he was now fucking loaded, six hundred pounds a week plus his carers allowance for C-o-l-i-n meant in his eyes, he had made it. He had tried to convince them to get cocaine and hookers round to one of their flats and was genuinely put out when both of them declined. Housty and Matt had mortgages to pay, so although cash coming in was a positive and would see them through the short term, neither saw this escapade as anything but a stop gap. As it was a surprisingly nice summer's day in Edinburgh the lads decided to visit an old haunt of their youth, with a carry out (obviously) and barbeque.

The tide times were favourable; as they made it over the causeway to Cramond Island just as the tide was cutting it off again. This meant they had the place to themselves for the next six to seven hours. Cramond Island lies in the river Forth at the mouth of the river Almond. It is a tidal island, covered in old concrete World War Two gun emplacements. These were designed to deter and ultimately stop the Germans from bombing the world famous and strategic Forth Rail Bridge. As the bridge was still there, it could be easily argued that they had served their purpose. They headed for the beach at the far side of the island that faced back up the river Forth towards Queensferry and the bridges. The sun was shining, they had enough lager and barbeque food to last a few days, as well as Yorkie's usual pocket stuffed with skunk and the capsules Ravanelli had given them that morning. The makings for a very good day stretched out in front of them.

Matt and Housty were happy just lazing about while the food cooked, but Yorkie finding it hard to contain his excitement was getting stuck into the cans while smoking non-stop joints. Pulling the capsules out of his pocket, he was determined to get wired in. 'Right, who's going to give these wee fellas a go?' Matt and Housty just looked at each other, the boy's appetite for self harm was insatiable.

'No till I've had something to eat, man. Calm your fucking jets,' Housty warned. Yorkie pretended not to hear him and swallowed two rapidly. Matt and Housty glanced at each other in dismay.

'Dinnae worry, bud. More food for us,' Matt pointed out.

'Aye, good point, bud.'

As they chomped their way through the sausages on well fired rolls, Yorkie hopped from foot to foot in front of them babbling absolute nonsense.

'Oh man, these are fucking magic. Am a genius. Ho lee fuck. Am buzzin. We are going tae change the fucking world, boys. No more war, jist loads ae high folk, lovin life. Al get a Nobel peace fucking prize.'

He went on and on. It was clear that Ravanelli's chemist had got the dosage right. If Yorkie was as high as this on two, one would suffice for any normal human being. Once they had finished eating, Matt and Housty tested this theory by taking one each. Not wanting to miss out, Yorkie joined them pointing out that it was better he wasn't coming down while they were still flying high.

Almost immediately, Housty felt a buzz as The Damage entered his blood stream. 'Fucking hell, man. Ah can feel that already.'

'So can I, man.'

Matt and Housty were both on their feet now too, all three friends hopping about, shaking hands, hugging and congratulating each other. It felt like they had struck it big. These pills were the business. In that moment all three, not just Yorkie, thought this could be massive. The instant head slam of the drug lasted for about half an hour, slightly less for Yorkie due to his gargantuan tolerance levels. Once the initial incredible buzz had subsided, they were left feeling elated and energised. Taking some cans with them, they staggered round the island exploring the deserted buildings. The boys blethered about old times and the times they hoped were still to come. Making plans, for what in their current state, seemed like a certain profitable future.

As usual, Yorkie had wanted to continue the party once the tide had gone out again but Matt and Housty were sober enough now to know they needed their beds. They had work to do in the morning and planned to start early again to avoid the other allotment users.

Chapter 14

The Wheels of Industry…………come tumbling off

Housty stood in front of the three bedroom semi-detached house in Blercrae, dreading ringing the bell. He had got the short straw. While the other two were away buying vodka and the other essentials for making The Damage, he had lost the game of rock, paper, scissors so here he stood with six cans of lager about to ring Jacks the plumber's front door. It was half eight and again none of the boys felt any hangover whatsoever from yesterday's Cramond Island adventure. The Damage would revolutionise Scottish society. Finally, a drug had been found which would allow the masses to get royally smashed at night and the next day go about their business like good church going citizens. Yorkie had suggested earlier that morning that one day he would be recognised up there with scientists like Alexander Fleming or in his words, 'the cunt that discovered penicillin.'

Taking a deep breath, Housty rang the door bell. Jacks opened the door with a home rolled fag hanging out his mouth and the ever present warm can of lager in his hand.

'Morning, pal. Guaranteed.' Jacks's face lit up when he saw Housty. An enormous beaming smile that was just crying out to be reciprocated which it was immediately.

'Alright Jacks, how's you, man?'

'Living happy, pal, Guaranteed,' Jacks replied, as Housty followed him into the living room. The place was spotless and tastefully decorated, going completely against the style of the man that occupied it. Even in the summer heat, Jacks had on his jeans, Scotland top and white sports socks. The brown, ever present bomber jacket draped across the couch.

'You no working the day, Jacks?'

'Aye, pal, aye. Am workin at the old folk's home along the road, guaranteed. Been waiting on you for a couple oh hours, pal. Guaranteed.'

Yorkie had warned Housty that Jacks had been phoning him since six am wondering when they would be round. Yorkie had tried to explain how early it was but had given up after the third call and just left it to Housty to face an obviously shit faced Jacks.

'Right well, a better no hold you up any longer, Jacks. Geez the sample and I'll be on my way.' If it was later in the day, Housty would have been more than happy to stay for a catch up but he couldn't bring himself to start drinking this early.

'Guaranteed, pal.' Jacks reached down the side of the sofa and pulled out a plastic supermarket diluting juice bottle, filled to the rim with a horrific cloudy liquid. He then reached down twice, more pulling out a further two bottles.

'Jesus, Jacks. That is some amount oh pish, mate. You got a race horse hiding behind there, pal?'

'Guaranteed, pal. Ah dinnae ken where it aw comes fae,' he said, whilst downing the can of lager in his hand.

'Aye, I just cannae imagine, Jacks. It's a mystery,' Housty replied, laughing as he put the bottles in the carrier bag he had brought the lager in. The transaction was complete and he was keen to get on.

'Right bud, I better be off, Yorkie will be in touch. We cool?'

'Guaranteed, pal. Happy as Larry. I'll keep my pish for ye, pal. Guaranteed.'

Walking up the road to meet the boys, Housty couldn't help wondering what had happened to his life. Not long ago, he had a good job in the town and now here he was walking through the scheme with three bottles of urine belonging to one of the biggest bevvy merchants he had ever met. As the lanny came down the road towards him, he stopped and started laughing hysterically to himself much to the confusion of Yorkie and Matt when they pulled up alongside him.

'What the fuck have you been taking, ya radge?' Matt said as he unwound the window, his chunky bare arm resting on the Land Rover's window frame.

'Cunt's been taking mushrooms,' Yorkie said, eyeing Housty suspiciously. He hated missing out on a party of any sort.

Controlling himself, Housty climbed in the back. 'Just thinking about how fucked up this whole thing is, man. I used to be on the phone to cunts in the US and Europe talking about investments and here I am wandering up the road with three bottles full of Jacks's pish. Couldn't fucking make it up,' Housty explained, feeling amused and bewildered at the same time.

Laughing, Matt agreed. 'Aye, I see your point, mucker.'

'Those cunts in Tesco wouldnae sell us the voddy man, these new licensing laws.'

'Aye, we got everything else so we can head over to the allotment now but without the voddy we'll have to wait till tomorrow morning. I'll get it once I've taken Roxy out, then we start early doors the morn.

'Fuck's sake, man. Ah need my fucking beauty sleep,' Yorkie whinged.

'Shut it, ya lazy malingerer. Tell Big Andy to meet us Thursday so we can hand The Damage over.'

'Am meeting him for a bevvy this afternoon, al let him ken the score, comrade.'

The boys went to the allotment dropping off the supplies that they had bought, along with the urine they had collected from Jacks. Matt headed home to get Roxy whilst Housty hit the gym, leaving Yorkie to listen to C-o-l-i-n's shite patter for the rest of the day. The following morning the real work began, if it could really be described as that.

The three of them were in good spirits, the sun was shining and Matt had ABBA playing on the drive to the allotment. All three joined in the singing. *'I called her last night from Glasgow,'* Housty singing Glasgow in a rubbish weedgie accent as Yorkie sang super paratrooper to Matt.

'This is one fucker oh a summer my fine, fine friends.' Yorkie was in high spirits as he unlocked the allotment gates.

'How beautifully put, Yorkie. Ever thought of taking up poetry?' Housty asked.

'Shut it you, ya Bondi Beach cunt, I mean what the fuck are you wearing?'

Housty was sporting a lairy Adidas vest with swim shorts and flip flops while the others were kitted out in the usual cargo shorts, polo shirts of some overpriced designer make and colourful trainers.

'Aye, that is some outfit right enough, been spending too much time in that trendy gym.'

'Matt, how can a gym in Granton be fucking trendy? It's the fucking opposite of trendy. They might have knocked those varicose vein, heroin ridden flats down but it's the same bams. They're simply housed in the new places which incidentally look cheaply built so will look just as brutal as the ones they replaced in a few years.'

'A bet it's full of chicoritas though, just the place for a retired footballer like me to regain his former fitness now am back in employment.'

'Firstly, you didn't retire, you were effectively thrown into the football wilderness for being a total jake ball and secondly, this isn't even close to employment. This is a fucking carry on,' came Housty's retort.

The three of them bickered away as they began the cooking process. Everything went according to plan, the only issue being the pots looked like they might explode again. The elixir was so powerful that it became unstable very quickly. By the time they left the allotments, just before nine am, they had that week's order completed. The following day, Big Andy had met Matt in a small lane near his house in Davidson's Mains and they had transferred the two cardboard boxes containing the bottles of The Damage. Big Andy had handed over the cash and after some small talk sprinkled with Big Andy's catch phrase, Cunto, that week's business was concluded. The next few weeks went by smoothly, the only change was that Yorkie's nose was constantly streaming and he had a habit of sleeping in one of the deck chairs whilst the others cooked The Damage. His distilling career looked to be taking a similar path to his once promising football career. He had not been investing his money wisely and his excesses were beginning to take their toll. On a more positive note, according to doctors C-o-l-i-n was on the road to recovery. All his recent samples were showing no sign of any illness and very little alcohol. It was only a matter of time before Yorkie's mother Lynne sussed something was up. This had been debated and they had decided it would be prudent to let some of C-o-l-i-n's real samples through for testing. For two reasons; one being they all liked the old boy and wanted him to get treated properly and two because Jacks had taken up the task of collecting pish with great gusto. He had been peeing like a race horse. The incentive of free lager, had unsurprisingly done the trick.

After discussions with Ravanelli from which as previously agreed, Yorkie had been excluded from, the weekly order had been tripled. Ravanelli was delighted with how popular The Damage had become. There had been rumours around Blercrae referencing a new drug. Yorkie had to be warned regularly to keep their involvement a secret. Fortunately, even in his now permanently buckled state, he could see through the fog and realise that in this case, too much talk would spell the end of the party. A slurred response to Matt and Housty's warning had indicated he understood.

'Loose lips sink ships, muckers, mark my words. Ma lips are sealed tighter than an otter's arse.'

With the increase in production, it not only meant another couple of early mornings at the allotment, but also an increase in Yorkie's spending power. This had very clear and obvious consequences. There was also a knock on effect for their now main pish supplier Jacks. Luckily, not only was he a reliable source of The Damage's secret ingredient but he was also a resourceful man. He enlisted his pal Jigsaw to help meet demand on a similar deal as before. He was called Jigsaw due to the number of scars on his face. There were so many that they had begun to join up and at first glance resembled a tattoo of a jigsaw. Miraculously, neither of them questioned why the boys needed their urine. They were content with what they saw as free bevvy.

Burning the candle at both ends is a well known saying and it summed up Yorkie nicely as he slumped into the front seat of the Land Rover that morning.

'Fuck man, look at the state of you, Yorkie. This is getting beyond a joke, pal.' Housty was driving this morning as Matt was down south for a meeting with the diabetes team who were treating Thomas. He was flying back that morning and was planning on seeing them at the allotments.

'Av not been to ma bed, totally banjoed last night. These early mornings are killing me, brother.' Yorkie couldn't even meet Housty's eyes. Such was the monstrous size of his impending hangover and sense of anxiety and dread that he would have struggled to look a pigeon in the eye. He was only too well aware that he was now letting the other two down. They were about a month into increased production and he had missed mornings and spent the other ones catatonic in a deck chair outside the hut. They had pointed out that he would soon have to find somewhere else as summer was coming to an end which meant it would soon be raining constantly (even more constantly than an Edinburgh summer) and be baltic. When the enterprise had started, he had been full of enthusiasm while looking healthier and smarter than he had in years. Now, sitting next to Housty, was the shell of Yorkie. He had lost weight, was wearing an ancient, once white, Paul & Shark t shirt covered in stains. He was unshaven and his hair looked like it had been washed in a chip pan. Housty had to open the window to combat the smell. Something had to be done. Little did Housty realise that today's events would spark a big change in their working arrangements and stimulate a Yorkie recovery of sorts.

Arriving at the allotment, Housty had begun setting everything up with very little help from his friend. Yorkie had perked up when he had found a half empty, wrap of coke in his jeans pocket. Not even bothering to chop out a line or offer Housty any, he had emptied it out on one of the manky hut shelves and snorted the entire half gram in one huge, snottery, dusty, grimy second. This signalled a temporary transformation of epic proportions.

Housty felt a push from the side as a revitalised Yorkie inserted himself slap bang in the middle of the hut. 'Right, let the ringmaster in to work his magic.'

'Fuck man,' Housty had to dust himself down. 'You got ma new shirt dirty on the floor, man,' he whinged.

'Luckily, it's a cheap one then. Seriously old chum, that is some get up. Paris fashion week has missed a trick not inviting you over.'

Housty had the flip flops on again with an expensive pair of designer cargo shorts and an equally expensive and now filthy denim shirt. He had been investing his money in a different way to Yorkie.

'Am sure it's all nice gear bud but it disnae quite gel the gither. Flip flops wi a denim shirt. In fact, no just flip flops, you are sporting toe nails that look like Special K flakes. Looking at your feet should come wi a health warning. A feel the boke coming.'

'The only reason you feel the boke is coz you've no slept in about a week. How much have you been spunking on coke?' Housty enquired slyly.

'It's just a number mate and one that's nane of your spunking business,' Yorkie snapped.

'Temper, temper now,' Housty laughed. Yorkie was on the verge of exhaustion, the result of which meant he could snap at any moment. Unlike Alex Ferguson, Housty was not into man management so continued to needle his horribly wired friend. They seemed to spend their entire time together slagging and winding each other up and the next hour was no different.

Once the prep work had been done and the stoves were on, Housty realised he was starving. 'I fancy a Bains pie, Yorkie. You hungry yet?'

'Not sure al ever be hungry again, bud. Ma stomach feels about the size of a dried out old baked bean.'

'Surely, you could manage one of Stenhouse's greatest and only export, well apart from Souness that is. No fancy a hot fresh mince pie and gravy?'

'Aye fuck it, get aes one, no on second thoughts, make it two. Am bound to be hank marvin by the time you get back.'

Housty intended to be back very quickly. Matt and him had both agreed leaving Yorkie cooking on his own was risky but a couple of minutes wasn't going to matter. The butchers was less than five minutes' drive. He could be back in ten minutes if he shifted. Even a snottery, sniffing mess like Yorkie could keep things together for ten small minutes.

'Right bud. Al no be long. Do not fuck this up, stay alert.'

'Message received loud an clear, sir. Keep the faith,' came the response as Yorkie began the skinning up process.

Housty made a run for the lanny, wheel spinning the usually lethargic vehicle as it headed in the direction of pie heaven. Arriving at the roundabout he was delighted to see a space right outside the butchers. Dancer, he thought, but to his annoyance a shitty wee motor coming from the next opening beat him to it, forcing him to park in one of the side streets. He bolted round to the butcher already with a bad feeling in his stomach. Pleased to see no queue, his heart sank when he heard the butcher tell the old dear in front of him that pies would be five minutes. Fuck he thought, if anything happened Matt would blame him. The smell of those beautiful pies roasting in the oven overrode any desire to get back to the allotment and his liability of a friend. It seemed like an age by the time he was snatching his change out the butcher's hand and sprinting from the shop. As he neared the Land Rover, he heard a distant dull thump of a noise. It was an explosion, he was sure of it and even more worrying was the direction it came from. He swerved out onto the road barely looking when he turned left at the roundabout and flooring it. His fears were justified. He could see smoke coming from an area that could only be the allotment. Was that already the sound of distant sirens? As he rounded the corner, the scene in front of him was confirmation of his worst fears. The shed, their business headquarters, was no longer visible. It had disappeared. He pulled up in the usual spot and attempted to digest the sight that greeted him. Where the hut had once stood was a scattered, scorched, pile of wood. He could see bits of their cooking apparatus but even more worryingly, no sign of Yorkie.

Jumping out the lanny, he was delighted to see no other allotment owners had arrived in his absence. It was still before nine am but this did mean that the surrounding roads were busy with rush hour traffic. Glancing around, he noticed cars beginning to slow down to look at where the smoke was coming from. Sirens were getting closer. There was a fire station on the Calder Road only a short distance away.

He turned and started walking as calmly as he could back to the lanny. Yorkie wasn't there. He must have made a break for it, he thought. As Housty got in and started the engine, he felt his phone vibrating in his shirt pocket. Please be you, please be you, was all he could think as he got it out.

It was him. 'Yorkie man, are you ok? Where the fuck are you?'

'Housty, am round at those houses behind the railway line at Forresters school. Fucking hurry up, there's a crowd gathering, man. A just about died, man.' Yorkie was flustered and close to full scale panic, that much was obvious.

'Am on ma way meet me on the main road, pal,' Housty responded as calmly as possible.

Housty hung up, slammed the lanny in gear and sped out the car park. The sirens were close now, in fact he could see the blue lights coming down from the Calder Road direction. The emergency services went past him as he turned off the main road and saw an even more dishevelled Yorkie waiting for him at the entrance to the high school. Housty had to control himself as he began to physically shake with the giggles as his friend jumped up into the front seat.

'Fucking dinnae man, just dinnae.' Yorkie slumped in the seat like a man already beaten by the day's events.

Sniggering, Housty goes, 'Get the radio on, man. I think we've caused a bit of an incident When I say we, I obviously mean you, ya radge.'

As Yorkie fumbled with the stereo, his hands shaking like an old MFI kitchen unit, he began to explain what had happened.

'The pots went mental, fucking mental, man. I was outside an a tried tae turn the stoves oaf but I was too late. I started sprinting for the hole we made in the fence. Ah made it through just as the hut went up. Fucking shat ma self, bud. Bits oh the hut and that were bouncing oaf the fence.'

'Fuck,' was all Housty could say, although Yorkie was in no mood to listen. He had just suffered a near death experience and wanted to talk, big time!

'Folk in they flats saw ehs climbing the other railway fence, there was folk coming out the stairs panicking. One eh them tried to grab me but luckily I can still turn a defender,' he said, with no humour at all. Yorkie gave up with the radio, he was shaking too much. More emergency vehicles were bombing past them. An ambulance and two fire engines passed coming from a different direction from the first ones. The emergency services were mobilising big time and impressively quickly. They had obviously caused quite a stir, more than they realised. Housty parked the lanny close to his house and the two of them slunk up the stairs, both very relieved to get inside the safety of his flat.

Housty immediately put the TV on, going straight to the news channel. Both lads sat on the sofa, not talking, just watching the news nervously.

'Nothing so far, man,' Housty said, almost whispering to himself. Praying this would remain the case.

'This is the fucking national news channel, man. No danger are we going to be on this'

Yorkie had spoken too soon. The female presenter had been alerted to a new breaking story. She began speaking, her face set in serious story mode, staring directly into the camera she read her teleprompter.

'We are getting reports of an explosion in Edinburgh, adjacent to the main railway line between the Capital and Glasgow. Police are treating this as a terrorist attack. We will bring you more when we get it.'

They looked at each other. Both had gone as white as most of Yorkie's recent investments.

Chapter 15

Away

Yorkie and Housty had not moved from the couch all morning. They had been super glued to the news channels. It was now being widely reported. There were reporters at the scene, held back by armed police, firefighters exploring the wreckage and latterly, the army had arrived. Matt had got Housty's message that he was to head straight to his flat and had hurried, managing to arrive straight from the airport half way through the morning. Even then, there was not much talking getting done. It had been obvious from the headlines and the singed Yorkie that the pots had been left to boil too long and an incident similar to Lynne's kitchen had taken place. On a bigger, much more public scale. There was going to be serious repercussions. It wasn't just civilised drug dealers that they were going to have to pacify, but the law were now involved. Drug dealers and the law made for a bad combination at the best of times. Being stuck in the middle of them both was not ideal.

There were local politicians commenting and the UK Government were being kept informed. Talk of raising the terrorist threat to critical, its highest level, had even been mentioned. As the day passed, a photofit was released, that looked disturbingly like a burned, sooty Yorkie. When he had gone to the toilet, he had left a mark on Housty's leather sofa. Housty hadn't even moaned about it which just highlighted the gravity of the situation. The only saving grace was that anyone who had witnessed Yorkie's escape, would have been hard pushed to come up with a decent description of his normal appearance as he was in such a state. It was just a matter of time before the beechgrove garden cunt came forward to help with enquires. Luckily for them, the allotment was in the name of a long dead family member so it would take some time for the police to find a link to Lynne or C-o-l-i-n. Lynne was another problem. If she got wind of this, the three of them would be made into chop suey in no time.

Slight relief came when they were tucking into a Chinese takeaway for their tea. The army had quickly arrived at the conclusion that this had not been a small bomb making factory, but just some scoundrels cooking up a yet to be identified substance. As soon as this information was released, the national news teams that had gathered had a good laugh about it and buggered of to a posh boozer in town or headed straight for the airport.

As coverage died down, the boys began to discuss their next move.

'We need to get in touch with Big Andy so we can let Ravanelli know. We might have to knock this on the head. The heat is on BIG TIME,' Housty pointed out.

'Dinnae even consider that, ya sap,' was Yorkies retort. Shaking his head, he continued. 'This is the best money and easiest readies any of us have made. We cannae just shit our pants at the first sign of trouble. Where's yer spirit of adventure, man?'

'First sign of trouble, ya bam? We wouldnae be in trouble if you wernae in such a fucking mess. An I warned you about leaving him on his own. Fucking accident waiting to happen. If you had carried on much longer, we could have started distilling wi your pish. I could do without this, I've got enough on ma plate with the wee man's diabetes. It's costing me a fucking fortune, an I could do with the cash we've been making.' Matt was pointing at Yorkie and he could feel himself beginning to lose it. He was also speaking the truth. Him and Housty had discussed how much of a liability he was and Yorkie had undeniably been going the full George Best of late.

'Aye, I ken we fucked up, Matt. How's the wee man doing anyway?' Yorkie had turned the full glare of his space cadet, please feel sorry for me, pet rabbit eyes on him. 'How about you go and smooth things over with the silver fox an see where we stand, pal? He's a businessman and we were making sweet, sweet business. It's just a setback boys. The future is still bright my fine, fine friends.' Yorkie recognised this as a good time to turn on his charm.

'Right, al see him the morn. The wee man's fine thanks, man. Now shut it and lets eat this scran,' Matt said, whilst grabbing a juicy spare rib and biting into it. 'Aye, an when we've had this you can tell me in great detail what happened coz it sounds absolutely fucking comical.'

That's exactly what they did. When they had eaten, Yorkie skinned up and they went through the morning's events with him being kind enough to act certain bits out. He had them in stitches describing his escape through the fence and then over the railway line. A particular favourite was when a local resident tried to perform a citizen's arrest only to be side stepped by a frazzled Yorkie.

Getting a meeting with Ravanelli had been easy. Big Andy was already heading over to Aberdour the following morning, so as with other occasions, Matt hitched a lift. They thought it better Housty kept a low profile and Yorkie's ban from all things silver fox was even more poignant after yesterday's catastrophic events.

Big Andy picked Matt up in Davidson Mains. 'Alright, big guy?'

'No bad, cunto,' Big Andy replied with his usual fag hanging out the side of his mouth.

'I'm guessing you three cuntos are in a bit of bother. What's that cunto Yorkie been up tae this time? Nae fucking good I bet?' Andy knew without any doubt which of the three would have been behind the issues.

'Funny you should say that.' Matt went on to describe the previous day's events to Big Andy as they headed over the Firth of

Forth, both gazing at the bridges and views as they creased with laughter.

Big Andy suddenly got serious, as if he hadn't initially grasped what Matt's tale meant. 'I really hope our mutual pal finds your story as funny, pal. Cannae see him being chuffed, likes.'

'Aye, I ken.' They drove into the village in a slightly less humorous mood. As they climbed out the van they heard a cheery voice behind them.

'Gentlemen, great to see you both.' Ravanelli was walking up the drive towards them, smiling and clutching what looked like two or three newspapers. 'Andrew, Matt. I trust you are both well?' He shook both their hands.

'Alright, Bill,' came the reply in unison.

Fishing a set of keys from his pocket, he headed for the front door with the two of them following. 'No injuries or burns?' he said, winking at Matt as he held the door open for them.

Shit he knows, he fucking knows. How the fuck does he know? I'm going to slap Yorkie. Liability, absolute fucking pest of a boy. These were just some of the thoughts flashing up inside Matt's head. The three of them sat down in the living room. Without saying a word Ravanelli began placing the papers on the large coffee table in front of them. He turned the papers towards Matt, leaving them all on the front page.

Matt felt his heart rate increase as his eyes scanned the headlines and pictures of an Edinburgh allotment he knew very well.

Breaking Bad comes to the Capital

The Enemy from Within

Drugs Factory on our doorstep

Edinburgh's Meth Lab

With a funny, sly smile on his face Ravanelli began speaking. 'The only major disappointment is no one was hurt. When I say no one, I mean one individual in particular, whom I suspect you are going to tell me was to blame for this mess. This very....... very public mess.'

Time to front it out Matt thought. 'Aye well, Yorkie wasn't exactly blameless, Bill. Look cards on the table. Housty left him for a matter of minutes..........' Matt realised there was a question he should have but hadn't asked yet. 'How do you ken that was us, Bill?'

'Well, I like to keep tabs on people I work with. Let's just say I was interested in how you managed your business premises,' he explained calmly, whilst meeting Matt's eyes, ensuring that he knew they had been watched.

'I see.' Matt was now visibly pissed off. He hated the idea of Ravanelli keeping tabs on them. What else did he know? How much had Big Andy told him about them? He was enjoying the extra cash. It meant he could now see Thomas more, but it appeared to be coming at a cost that he hadn't anticipated.

Ravanelli sensed Matt's displeasure and moved to smooth the situation over. 'Look, I was handing over a lot of cash and wanted to make sure it wasn't going to come back and bite me. As it happens, I think we have probably got away with this one but it cannot happen again. Especially when I want you to up production. We have a good thing going here, but it is obvious your operation lacks a certain amount of professionalism.'

Matt relaxed a bit. He couldn't believe what he was hearing. He had not expected to be asked to produce more.

'The people I deal with tend to have stressful jobs, careers, pastimes, whatever the fuck we want to call it. So they need a way to relax. These pills, The Damage as they are so crudely named, give them exactly what they want and unlike the other synthetic and natural products on the market, they don't leave you feeling like a dead zombie for days afterwards. Everyone is raving about them. I'm told it is the cleanest high they have ever had. Only one has mentioned the side effect of loose bowels to me, but I couldn't care if these high powered self-indulgent cretins soil themselves once in a while. In fact, I would love to see them do it in public. Bunch of first class cunts. Apologies for the language, gents,' he said smiling. 'Oh and I should mention that they are willing to pay a high price for your friend's creation. He may act and look like an undesirable but he really did strike gold with this. So I have a proposal for you. One which I encourage you to accept. Especially for the safety of Yorkie as that photo fit was horribly accurate in a spitting image type way.'

'Was not expecting that Ra….. Bill but I'm all ears, go for it.'

Ravanelli did not appear to notice Matt almost called him by his nick name, although Big Andy did. He gave Matt a sharp look. Matt wondered how much Big Andy was really involved and if he was quite as straightforward as his very public persona made him look. Was he the one that had spied on them? Chances are he was, Matt concluded.

'Ok, I have here a set of keys for a caravan in a small town down the east coast, about an hour from Edinburgh. I am willing to let you use it, free of charge, as long as you can double our current arrangement regarding quantities delivered. Also, as part of the deal, I can up the amount required at any time.' Seeing Matt was about to speak, he quickly continued. 'Within reason Matt, I understand. I have been fair with you up until now have I not?'

It was hard for Matt to argue with that. 'Does it belong to you?' Matt was worried that any damage would have to be paid for. Yorkie was bound to hot rock the place and make a general mess.

'Let's just say I procured it and the original owner is not around anymore.' Matt noticed him glance involuntarily in Big Andy's direction. Although Andy's large heavy set face remained impassive, it was obvious something remained unsaid. 'My understanding is that site fees have been paid, in full, up until Christmas, which gives you a good few months to see if the new working environment is acceptable.'

What could Matt do but agree to give it a go?

It turned out the caravan was in a village called Coldingham, which lay between the commuter town of Dunbar and the fishing mecca of Eyemouth. Firmly entrenched in Scotland's beautiful south east coast. The caravan site was called Lawcross, which sounded appropriate given that they were all getting used to crossing the country's law boundaries regularly. Armed with the keys, directions and a new bigger order of The Damage, Matt felt optimistic as Big Andy and him crossed the mighty Forth and gunned it back into Edinburgh to its finest suburb, Blercrae. Matt had tried to establish just how involved Big Andy was in the silver fox's business, but was met with clouds of smoke and non-committal mumblings, that included the words cunto and deliveries.

As they waited at the lights at Barnton, on the city limits, Big Andy turned to Matt and said with deadly seriousness. 'Dinnae underestimate the cunto, he is a fucking bam. Radge as fuck. More fucking radge than Ray, an he is a total rocket. Watch yourselves.' He then accelerated away, leaving a massive cloud of smoke hanging in the air where his door window had been.

The remaining ten minutes of the journey were driven in silence, giving Matt time to digest Big Andy's words of warning. It was hard to imagine Ravanelli doing anyone any damage personally, he was relatively slight and so well spoken. The complete opposite of Blercrae's very own naughty businessman Ray. In saying that, he must be a loony if he had achieved his current position in the supply of narcotics and had worried Big Andy enough for him to warn Matt like that. His thoughts drifted back to the former caravan owner's disappearance. Yes, Big Andy was right, he would be careful.

Yorkie was already at Housty's flat when Matt arrived. C-o-l-i-n was being a real pain in the arse and Lynne hadn't failed to notice that the photofit in the newspaper looked very like her darling son. She had been less vocal in her criticism of him recently since he had left her two hundred pounds on the kitchen worktop for Smudgie's dental bill. Although a kind gesture, it raised other alarming issues in her head.

Primarily, where had he got the cash, on top of the money he was obviously spending getting out his nut. She was well aware that he had been hitting it hard, as on the few occasions she was not round practising with Sensei, the decline in his personal appearance and the cleanliness of the house was dramatic. It all clearly meant that he was up to no good. Then that night, there was a bastardised picture of him staring back at her on the front of the Edinburgh Evening News. He was being linked to some sort of drugs factory. The icing on the unpalatable cake was that it appeared he had been using the now destroyed allotment shed. She had been calling and texting so he had done the honourable thing and bolted round to Housty's. Being the decent sort he was, he had made sure C-o-l-i-n was well stocked with his favourite tins before making his escape.

The two of them were about twenty minutes into an argument that started with Yorkie calling Housty Sport Billy because he had been at the gym again.

'How can ye still be built like a beach ball when yer training all the time? When I was at ma peak for City, I was ripped tae fuck, man.' To emphasise this Yorkie slapped his slightly flabby torso.

'Cheeky cunt, am not fat ya radge, just cuddly.' Housty grabbed a hold of him and started squeezing. 'Give us a big cuddle, ya smelly jake ball.' As much as Yorkie tried to escape his friend's grasp, he just didn't have the strength. Obviously those gym visits were more productive than he was making out.

Yorkie was saved by the door bell going and the familiar knock that signified Matt's arrival. Both stopped wrestling immediately and to their surprise were nervous to hear the outcome of the meeting. It came as a revelation to Housty especially to realise that he had begun to enjoy their escapades and the tax free cash he had been earning. It certainly beat working. Let's face it, who didn't enjoy ripping off the tax man?

Matt had decided as a bit of payback to wind them up to begin with. Therefore, when Housty opened the door, he was met with a facial expression that suggested they were in deep shit.

Matt didn't sit down, trying to build on the drama. 'Well you pair have got us in some serious fucking shit. Right up to our fucking necks in it.'

'Eh? Come on, man. You serious?'

'What did the silvery slimey slug say?' Ravanelli's dislike for Yorkie was rivalled by his equal hatred.

'We've to leave Edinburgh pronto. No choice.'

'Fuck off,' was the reply from both of them.

'Aye, we huv,' Matt said smiling and pulling the caravan keys from his pocket. 'Anyone fancy a wee holiday?'

Yorkie and Housty just glanced at each other.

'Do tell, you smug twat.' Housty had known Matt long enough to know that his pal was pulling their legs but also had some interesting news for them.

'Aye, mon spit it out secret smarmy Simon.'

'It's escape to the country, gangsta style, boys. We have the use of a large family, two bedroom, en suite, luxury caravan and we have an increased order. He wasn't bothered at all. I think he found it quite funny. Especially the photofit,' Matt said, winking at Yorkie. 'Anyway, his posh well to do junky customers love our work. Game fucking on, boys.'

The three of them starting cheering and celebrating, hugging each other.

'This is better than pumping the blue noses at Hampden, yyyyaaaasss,' Housty shouted. Things were looking up. He might just catch up with his mortgage payments after all.

'Beats Arthur vs Gomez at Meadowbank, mmmmuuttthaaa ffaaakaaas,' Yorkie screamed in response. That had truly been a magnificent night in Edinburgh's sporting history. The atmosphere in the ageing sports facility was truly electric. Not only due to both fighters' epic battle in the ring but also to do with those in attendance. A huge section of the lunatic fringe in Edinburgh society, including a large element from the Hibs hooligan firm the CCS, had been there and were more than happy to fight Gomez's fans. Thankfully, the feeling was mutual, ensuring the fight in the ring was overshadowed by the full scale riot that ensued following Gomez's fifth round stoppage of Arthur. The stadium should have been demolished that night instead of being left to rot slowly for a further twenty years. It truly would have been a fitting end for the concrete monument that was Meadowbank Stadium.

When things had settled down, Matt filled them in on all the details and it was decided they should head down the next day. They were all keen to get away as soon as was possible but there were certain ingredients they would have to gather before heading down. The good news was they wouldn't need to use the small gas stoves as the van had proper gas hobs, but they would need to replace the pots that had blown up. The rest of the day was taken up getting the necessary supplies and kit. As usual Jacks had his very own supply that he was delighted to swap for cans of lager.

Chapter 16

Coldingham

Matt and Housty arrived at Yorkie's not long after ten am the next day. The sun was shining and they were both excited with what lay ahead. It felt like they were going on a lad's holiday. The only concern was that there was no sign of Yorkie. The door was open, C-o-l-i-n was passed out on the couch clothed in a truly awful purple and black Le Coq Sportif shell suit. They were both worried. The chances were high that with yesterday's good news Yorkie had decided to go on yet another bender. As they stepped back out the house into the street, to their delight a very sober Yorkie, was just leaving the house next door.

'Morning, muckers,' he waved.

'Bloody hell, that boy has amazing powers of recovery.'

'Aye, he certainly does.' A delighted and relieved Housty agreed.

A very fresh looking Yorkie shook their hands as he marched down the path past them into the house. They turned and followed him back in.

'I was just next door giving the old skag hag the low down of what is required from her while I'm away. She is C-o-l-i-n's new honorary carer.'

'Brilliant man, skag hag. I've not thought about her for years. How's she doing, man?'

'Still bonkers, the house is scary as fuck, man. There's still loads oh dodgy photos oan the waws, an she's still got the red light bulb. I think she thoat I wis roond fir business.' During Edinburgh's infamous heroin epidemic, Ruth Hinds, like many others, had had an expensive habit to satisfy. Unlike other desperate city residents, she was too much of a good soul to go round stealing and conning people, so she reverted to the world's oldest trade and turned her three bedroom semi into a good old fashioned brothel. Although she had kicked the habit many years ago, knocking her knocking shop on the head had been more difficult. Now in her twilight years and carrying a good few extra pounds, no one came to the door for business. This hadn't stopped her carrying on the tradition of turning her red light on in the evenings when she was looking for work.

'Good of her to look after dafty though, man.'

'Aye, she is sound, all its going to cost me is a bottle of gin. Sweet as a fucking sugar dipped nut. Right, pick up the bags dudes an let's get this party started. See ya later, jakey boy.' Yorkie nudged C-o-l-i-n's shoulder and got a grunt as a response.

With the lanny loaded they jumped in and headed for the city's continually busy bypass. For once, Yorkie didn't moan about getting in the back as Matt had brought Roxy along. He could stroke, tickle and generally annoy him the whole way down the coast. Not that the dog minded much, he loved the attention. The journey was slow until they got onto the A1, then the traffic opened up and they began to make good progress. All three were in good spirits and as much as they pretended that it was a work trip, it was hard not to see this as a holiday. One of Yorkie's seriously strong reefers helped add to the party mood.

'Right, what's the plan, boys? Dump the stuff and have a look round the town. A couple of afternoon refreshments wouldn't go amiss.'

128

'Fuck me, Matt. It's Yorkie's job to encourage us to get spangled not yours,' Housty said smiling.

'Count me in, Mattias.'

'Way I see it is, we need to get the stuff to Ravanelli in four days. I reckon we can do it in a day if we go for it. It's not like before where we had to work early in the morning. We can cook all day in the van and no one will be any the wiser.'

'I fucking love you, big boy.' Yorkie tried to give him a kiss. 'This is going to be a barry laugh, man.'

'I'm certainly coming round to your way of thinking, boys,' Housty said, also now laughing.

Matt hit play on his phone, delighted to hear one of his favourite songs being picked at random by the Sonos app.

'What the fuck is that you are subjecting us to now, man?' Yorkie asked and Housty echoed. A strange hypnotic beat along with some speech samples were blasting out the Land Rover's thunderous speakers.

'Dinnae get wide you, that is the fabulous Alabama 3, Mao Tse Tung Said,' Matt lectured.

'It's fucking magic, man. I cannae believe I have never heard this before,' Housty conceded.

'Aye, I ken. I feel like I should hate it but I cannae. It's like techno mixed wi country and western. Absolutely love the sampling. Fuck knows how but it works.' Yorkie was loving this new sound. He was a big music fan and just tended to wind Matt up about his taste for fun. 'It wid be safe to say you have an eclectic taste in music, man.'

'An you my pal have an eclectic taste in drugs.' It was hard to argue Matt's point.

'Aye, fair doos. Mind you would drag me up the town to watch all those punk bands at the Cass Rock Café? Mental nights. That band Sad Society were no bad. Singer was Deek fae Blercrae.'

'Magic band and the funniest album name ever. I've still got a copy in the house; it's called The Best Thing Since Hand Relief,' Matt replied, smiling happily at the memory.

The punk music was forgotten. '*Change must come through the barrel of a gun,*' they all sang as the lanny gunned it down Scotland's magnificent East coast.

Not long after Dunbar on the A1, they passed an enormous cement works and then the dominating Torness nuclear power station loomed large. A few miles further on, the turning for Coldingham came into view and was met by cheers and Yorkie drumming on the seats in anticipation. The road began to climb onto a moor where they were met with the view of a sprawling wind farm. The turbines looked to be at least a hundred feet tall and were turning at different speeds depending on what direction they pointed. It was an eerie place and all three were hypnotised by the spectacle.

'Wow man, space age.'

'How fucking smart are they? They dinnae make a sound, man.'

Passing the wind farm, the road began to descend towards the coast. After a few tight turns, a long straight took them into the village and before they knew it, the caravan site appeared on their right.

'Home sweet home, boys,' Matt announced, signalling and turning into the site's well maintained entrance.

'Ha ha, check this place out man, it's like a posh Trailer Park Boys.' Yorkie was delighted with the neat lines of caravans he saw.

'Aye, and you're Bubbles, mate,' Housty replied, referring to the hit Canadian TV series.

'Shut it Housty, ya prick. Do not start your nonsense with me,' Yorkie retorted, smiling. No amount of bickering was going to ruin today.

Not wanting to arouse suspicions or have to answer any awkward questions, they opted to take their time finding the van. There was an office with a bar attached but they avoided it. After a number of wrong turns, they found the van hidden at the end of an oval stretch of grass with the obligatory 'No Ball Games' sign. Around twenty vans circled the grass, all of them looking very much loved and cared for. Their van was right at the end, adjacent to a well established wood.

'Perfect boys, we are right out the way here.' Matt got out the car and stretched, opening the back door so Roxy could jump out and do the same. Apart from the van looking like it could do with a good clean due to pollen stains from the surrounding trees, it appeared in cracking shape.

'Excuse me, dogs must be kept on a lead at all times,' a voice announced from behind them.

All three of them turned to see an elderly bald man with his equally elderly and very hefty wife. 'You should get one for your fat……….'

Housty quickly cut Yorkie off. 'Aye, he'll be on a lead, but as you can see, we have just arrived.'

'Staying long are we?' It was obvious he saw trouble which in fairness was an accurate assessment.

'Might do pal, we'll see. Have yourself a wonderful day now,' Yorkie said sarcastically as they turned and wandered off. The boys were grateful to see their van was one on the far side of the grass.

'Nosey, fucking, cunt.'

'You better believe it. This place will be full of them along with their hideous garden ornaments.'

Housty unlocked the van, stepping into what was an absolute belter of a caravan. It had an open plan kitchen, dining and living space all of which looked almost brand new. A door to the right opened up into a corridor that led to a twin bedroom, a shower room and then an ensuite double room. Roxy bolted past Housty jumping on the double bed.

'Looks like this is my room, lads,' Matt said, laughing. 'Good lad,' he continued, giving Roxy a congratulatory stroke.

'Aye right, if I pull some local tart al be up to my boz in her in here, make no mistake.'

'No danger of that, Yorkie. You cannae even pull yourself off after a bevvy these days.'

'Aye a kin, ya radge. Solid as a rock.' So as to highlight the point, Yorkie grabbed his cock and balls in a show of strength.

'Stop talkin pish you pair and give me a hand with the gear,' Housty shouted from outside.

'I'm desperate to drop the kids ooaf at the pool' Yorkie said shutting himself in the toilet.

'Lazy cunt.'

'A heard that Matt, that's no very nice, pally wally, bing bong.'

'You were meant tae hear it, ya bam.'

Housty and Matt emptied all the gear and supplies out the lanny and into the van, stashing most of it on the floor in the double room at the back of the van. Away from the wandering eyes of the park's nosey bastards.

'Oh jesus, that is reeking Yorkie, shut the fucking door.' A horrifying smell was escaping from the toilet.

'Smells like a rhino has been in there, man.'

'Ah cannae flush the fucker, theres nae water. What kind of bog has nae water?'

'Take it easy, there will be a tap outside tae turn it on.' Housty headed out to find it. Knocking on the side of the van, 'Try it now.'

With the powerful flush now working, Yorkie responded. 'That's it oan its merry way to the beach. Tattie bye,' he said whilst waving it off.

After a further few minutes acquainting themselves with the van, it was unanimously decided to go out for some scran and a scout about.

'Let's get a bar lunch an a couple of jars, boys.' Matt was standing at the door rubbing his hands together with a psychotic look that suggested he might eat them. 'I am fucking ravenous.'

'I'll bring the ball for a kick about on the beach.'

'Kick about tends to mean you taking the mickey out of us.'

'Aye, sure does. The day will be no different even if am three sheets,' Yorkie said, with a huge grin. He had been a fabulous footballer. His only weakness being the fact he was born on the North end, of a small island in Northern Europe, in a country called Scotland. A race doomed to football failure and the permanent curse of alcoholism hunting you down.

The sun was beating down as they headed over the grass and up towards the main road, Yorkie showing off doing keepy uppies. Roxy jogged along beside them contentedly.

'No ball games. PLEASE!' The same old boy announced, in an old school teacher's voice, from the decking of his caravan. 'And I have already mentioned animals must be kept on a lead at all times.'

'You can suck ma co……...'

Once again Housty cut Yorkie off. 'Just ignore the cunt,' he hissed.

Matt just couldn't resist. 'The dog is on a lead, it's just very thin and clear so you cannae see it from there.' He pretended to hold up the imaginary lead. 'No need to apologise though, eh?'

'Aye, fucking gestapo is alive and well, sure enough.' The old boy could be heard moaning as they disappeared onto the main road.

'He will be trouble. Hope he croaks it while we're out. Old bald cunt.' No one argued with Matt.

Walking down towards the village, they passed a primary school and some houses, then found a boozer which was unimaginatively, due to its seaside location, called The Anchor.

'This place is idyllic, boys.' They were sitting on a picnic table at the front of the pub, watching village life pass them by.

Coldingham had a similar feel to Aberdour but represented the typical small Scottish village better. Unlike Aberdour, it was far enough away from Edinburgh that it hadn't been polluted with the rich, former city dwellers that so often ruined rural towns. It had managed to maintain the wee village theme, remaining sleepy and true to its history. The only change being tourism and not the agricultural and fishing industries, was now the major contributor to the economy. Where Aberdour had a castle, Coldingham had the ruins of what was once a major priory. It would have dominated the village and those that surrounded it. It seemed fitting that the boys were here to distil The Damage in its shadow. Emulating the Benedictine monks who would have made ale and mead within the Abbey's ancient carved sandstone walls.

Three pints in, they were all getting hungrier.

'We better eat soon boys or I'll be hammered and not in a fit state to eat,' Housty urged.

'Aye, good point.' Matt was also beginning to feel the effects of sunshine, lager and a very empty stomach.

'Fucking lightweights. In saying that I myself could do with some local produce. Fish an chips perhaps.' Yorkie was back in posh voice mode. A sure sign he was relaxed and enjoying himself.

The Anchor was a proper pub so they opted to head over to the other hostelry, situated further down the road. It looked more like a place you would get a decent scran rather than a game of darts and a brawl. The Old Inn also had a beer garden at the rear and they sat there tucking into huge portions of fish and chips. The owner was great bringing a bowl for Roxy and some treats.

'Quality place this, boys. I reckon we eat here and get smashed over the road.'

'Aye, The Anchor place has a pool table and dartboard through the back. I noticed it when I had a pish. Perfect.'

'Some of the boys drinking in there looked like they could give C-o-l-i-n and Jacks the plumber a run for their money. Proper steam boats at lunch time.'

After a couple more pints, the boys wandered through the rest of the village taking a path for about a quarter mile to the beach. Along the way, they enjoyed one of Yorkie's jazz fags meaning that Matt and Housty were caked and completely helpless to stop Yorkie dancing around them with the football. Wandering back up the hill, they settled in for another few pints in a hotel that directly overlooked the bay with its clean golden sand and colourful beach huts.

'This is paradise, boys.'

'Aye, thankfully Ravanelli never came down here or he'd have thought twice about handing the keys over.'

The day continued in a similar vein. They ended up staggering back into The Anchor for a few games of pool armed with sausages, bacon and rolls they bought in the local butchers. Yorkie had thought the food was for breakfast but Matt and Housty pointed out normal people survive on more than one meal a day.

The following day, Housty woke up to Yorkie's snoring and wheezing dope stained lungs whistling in his sleep. The room was honking. Looking to his side he saw a half smoked spliff and a can of beer. The fucking animal must have got up during the night for a smoke and a drink. Leaning over, he opened the window and leaving Yorkie sleeping, like an aging sloth, he went to the toilet. Going through to the living area, he saw that there was a bag of shopping sitting there and looking further, he could see Matt sitting on the caravan's white pristine decking.

'Morning, man.'

'Alright, Matt. You must have been up sharp.'

'Aye, I woke up to the smell of the wee fucker's farts. Room was worse than a Nazi gas chamber.'

'I feel your pain.' Housty went on to tell him about Yorkie getting up for a lager and a smoke during the night.

'I've had my morning video call with the wee man and been down to the shop for tea bags and breakfast stuff, bud. Make me another cup of tea me old son.' Matt handed him his empty mug.

The two of them sat on the decking enjoying another beautiful clear sunny morning whilst having a couple of hot rolls. By ten am, there was still no sign of Yorkie so they headed off to find a supermarket to get the final ingredients. The plan was to cook all day the following day and then deliver the bottles to Big Andy the day after. Speaking to people in the pubs yesterday, it had become clear that the caravan site was busy over the weekends but quiet during the week. They therefore planned to be away first thing Friday morning and not return until the Monday night. Doing this would mean that they would hopefully manage to avoid as many caravaners as possible. Having only met one, who was a total prick, they all agreed this was a sound idea.

They were both in high spirits when they drove through the fishing town of Eyemouth and back onto the A1 heading south. Matt knew from his many drives to Colchester, to see Thomas and old friends, that there was a big supermarket on the outskirts of Berwick Upon Tweed. The town lay just over the English border. They got some funny looks buying numerous cheap bottles of vodka but neither cared. Their Scottish accents were probably enough to justify it. Minimum pricing and no discounted alcohol had not reached England yet so the shop was no doubt used to Scots crossing over and buying massive carry outs. These ridiculous types of pricing policies would hurt only an already financially stretched section of society, the much maligned super alky.

They had an easy stroll round the impressive town walls with Roxy and then headed back North. As they crossed the border, Housty pointed out, 'It's funny we always got told Hadrian's Wall was built to keep us bammy Scots out, but the wall was built miles from what is now the border.'

'Aye, good point, man. Those slimy Romans obviously weren't too keen on our Northumberland brothers either.'

Laughing, Housty replied, 'Aye, it's no real surprise having had a few nights out in the big market in Geordie land. That lot know how to enjoy themselves.' Both had had many a good day in the city of Newcastle in their teens, sneaking on the train from Waverley Station in Edinburgh to enjoy an adventure in another town. Great times, although a large proportion of the journey was spent in the toilet avoiding the ticket inspector.

Leaving the A1 for Eyemouth, Housty decided he was hungry again. 'Mon man, lets go into Eyemouth. Bound to be some fine fish an chips on offer.' They headed into the town, parking close to the harbour and opted to call Yorkie.

A gritty dry voice eventually answered, 'Hallo.'

'Good morning Theo, its breakfast time,' Housty sang into the phone.

'Fuck man, where are youz?'

'We're in Eyemouth just along the road, fancy some fish and chips.'

'You pair are fucking eating machines but aye a do. I'll have a scampi supper, ta.'

'Right see ya in a mo, my good man.' Housty hung up and they walked into the chip shop to place their order, immediately being hit by the welcome smell of hot greasy cooking oil. They spent the ten minute waiting time drooling over the glass cabinet that contained an outstanding array of ice creams and sorbets.

Back at the van, the three ate in the sunshine, discussing what to do with the rest of the day. Yorkie was all for another day in the pub which, given the weather and setting, the others found hard to argue with. They had emptied all the vodka into the van, placing it in the back bedroom out of sight, before heading back down to The Anchor for an afternoon session. This time they chose the large beer garden at the back of the pub so they could enjoy one of Yorkie's special fags in peace. The afternoon passed in a predictable haze.

'Yorkie, have you noticed that you've had no class As in two days? Must be a record for you.'

'A fucking slanderous comment Housty but funny you should say that. It's no even crossed ma mind. In fact av no thought about hame at all. Hope the old skag hag is getting on alright and minding to feed Smokey.'

'Am goin for a slash,' Matt stumbled as he got up.

'Once a lightweight, always a lightweight, eh Matt?' Yorkie was delighted, he loved to see his mates struggle to keep up with his formula one pace.

Matt didn't even reply. He was feeling fucked. He just wasn't used to all this bevvying and smoke. Stumbling through to the toilets, he took the only free place at the trough like urinal. There was space for three and the boys to either side of him looked in a worse state than him. One was leaning with his forehead against the tiles, he appeared to be asleep. He had certainly finished peeing.

138

The other old boy turned to Matt, 'Alright ma pal, Bert's fucking sleeping again. His Mrs will be in shortly. Hang about for the fireworks. Mark my words, pal.'

Almost automatically, Matt replied, 'Guaranteed.' Jacks the plumber style.

'Aye guaranteed, son,' the man repeated, nodding like a wise old wizard.

The old boy left but Matt finished up and began washing his hands. In a moment of clarity he glanced along at the plumbing on the urinal. It looked like it was from the Jurassic era and in that moment he came up with a genius idea. These boys were total piss heads, of that there was no doubt. Instead of picking up C-o-l-i-n's or Jacks the plumber's pish in the burgh, they could just use these old boys. Bert's would be dynamite judging by his current state. Leaving Bert sleeping, he bolted out the bog returning to his seat feeling suddenly energised.

'Listen to this lads, I've got a fucking barry idea.'

The other two eyed him suspiciously. 'How come you've sobered up so quick?'

'You had a wee tactical spew, big boy?'

'Have a fuck.' Matt looked disgusted with the idea of emptying his stomach. 'No, just shut the fuck up and listen. We dinnae want tae have tae bring the pish down here every week, so how about if we could get a source here?'

'We dinnae ken any of these piss heads well enough to ask. It's not an easy subject to broach with a stranger, after all.' Housty did not fancy having the conversation with any of them, no matter how drunk they were.

'Right, firstly these boys are indeed premier league piss artists. One of them, a dear old soul Bert, is currently asleep standing up at the pisser.'

Before Matt could continue, Yorkie butted in. 'If you think am hangin aboot they bogs waiting oan Bert havin a kip while pishing wi a plastic bottle in ma hands, you can forget it. No fucking danger.'

'Shut it, man. Will you just fucking listen for once, dafty. It's one of those ancient trough urinals. All we would have to do is come down here late in the day and plumb in a container to the drain. An hour later, hey mutha fucking presto, we would have a tonne of prime JK's pish.'

They took it in turns to check the plan out, taking care not to wake Bert who was still enjoying his beauty sleep. Whilst ordering more drinks Housty glanced round the bar. There really was an exceptional standard of alcky. Tomato coloured, moon cratered faces that would be the envy of the former Scotland striker and now radio presenter Alan Brazil. Some even had the tell tale signs of hairs growing out their barnacled noses. More pints later and several games of pool, which Yorkie won simply because he was the only one that could see straight, they made their way back to the van. Roxy the only one that was not stumbling about singing. All were agreed that Matt's plan was a possibility. There was no way any of the pub's patrons would notice if they made a few plumbing adjustments on their next visit early the following week.

That night Housty had chosen to sleep on the huge L shaped couch that dominated the living area to avoid Yorkie's smoking, wheezing and snoring. To his huge annoyance, he was woken about three in the morning by Yorkie screaming when he dropped a can a lager onto his foot when quietly trying to rescue it from the fridge. This did ensure that Yorkie was up, not very bright but early, to start cooking. Much to his displeasure, Housty and Matt were in the small twin room not long after eight am to get him up. To his credit, once he was up and awake, he switched on pretty quickly. All of them had enjoyed their time in Coldingham, but were also looking forward to getting back to civilisation. Matt had another flight booked to see Thomas, his new found wealth meaning he could fly more often, therefore avoiding the dreaded overnight drive. By nine am the newly bought pots were on the hobs, the curtains closed and the ingredients laid out. The caravan windows facing away from the other vans were opened, meaning they had to keep their chat to a minimum, in case any dog walkers or nosey neighbours were passing.

The cooking process went smoothly, apart from the usual drama when the pots became unstable. To meet the new order, they had to go through the process three times. By the time this was done, the van was like a sauna and all three were exhausted.

They stood looking at the twenty bottles of The Damage in front of them, all feeling knackered and sweaty, but all delighted with their days work.

'Twenty bottles, that's four fucking grand sitting there, lads.'

'Aye, no bad for about half a day's work,' Housty agreed.

'Am sweating like Lawrence of Arabia in a bubble jacket. Let me out for a smoke.' Yorkie almost fell out the door with the others not far behind him.

'That's twelve hundred each, with the other four hundred covering costs.'

'Aye, sounds about right, accountant boy.'

'If this keeps up al no be looking for another boring, shite office job. This has been a fucking barry laugh.'

None of them disagreed with Housty on that. The caravan was tidied up and the lanny loaded. They had to meet Big Andy at ten in the morning which meant they could have another night in The Anchor before heading home first thing.

'You shree are becoming regulars,' the bar man slavered whilst pouring the drinks. He hadn't even asked what they wanted this time.

'Aye, been doing a bit of fishing, mate. Probably be back at some point next week.' They had decided that fishing would be their cover story.

'Fisherman and divers, that's what we get down here.' He was stumbling about with their drinks almost dropping one before Yorkie saved it at the last minute. Thankfully, the other customers were just as thirsty as the boys so his attention was elsewhere as soon as he had their cash. They nipped back out into the beer garden to enjoy the fresh air. All of them feeling a bit light headed after spending so much time in the caravan breathing in the toxic vapour.

'Ken what's funny, Yorkie?'

'No ah dinnae, so goin tell ais whats fucking funny now, GI Joe.'

'It's like what Housty was saying yesterday. Like you are a changed man down here. You have just stood in front of all those bottles of The Damage and not taken a hit. You are cured, my man. Halleluiah praise the lord.' Matt and Housty both crossed themselves while giggling.

'F f fuuukkk. I must be turning into a sappy cunt like yooz. Am going to tan some when we get up the road.'

'No danger mate, that motor is staying locked.' Matt warned, pulling the keys out his pocket to remind Yorkie where they had stored all of The Damage. Realising that there was a good chance that Yorkie would attempt and probably succeed in picking his pocket, he put it in the zip one further down the leg of his cargo shorts.

'Joking aside though boys, av no even thought about it. We're down here apparently working but it's been fucking magic. Cannae wait tae see Smokey an ma ma an I suppose C-o-l-i-n. An ken what, I cannae wait tae get back here next Monday. Cheers lads. Here's tae life at the seaside.'

Their three glasses clinked together not for the last time that day.

Chapter 17

Working Nine to Five

After three weeks in Coldingham producing the twenty bottle order Ravanelli had asked, in a demanding, you have no choice sort of way, if they could double the order. Forty bottles meant eight grand a week, the realisation of which had caused a fair bit of back slapping and celebration. They were now looking at the type of earnings that meant getting a real job was no longer an option. They just wouldn't get this amount of money working. Obviously there wasn't the long term prospects of normal employment but Yorkie summed it up very well with his own version of a famous proverb.

'Let's make hay while the kids get cunted.'

Unfortunately, a huge increase in the order also brought very particular issues. The easiest one to overcome was that they would now be forced to work for a good part of two days. The work wasn't particularly demanding, mentally or physically, although, it was very uncomfortable in the caravan while they were cooking due to heat and lack of ventilation. The next issue which they had already began to address was their supply of alcohol soaked urine. One evening in The Anchor, they had hooked up a large water storage bottle to test Matt's theory. It had gone according to plan for the short time it was plumbed in but leaving it longer would increase risks. Yorkie, who had begun his training as a plumber after his short football career, had initially been given the task of doing the plumbing while the others kept watch. He had moaned so much, which was understandable given the filthy appearance of the, pipes that Matt had taken over just to get it done. With a bit of luck, they had proved Matt's theory. The biggest issue was that The Damage had been getting some press coverage and sooner or later, the new designer drug that had begun to appear on the market, might be traced back to the allotment debacle and from there to Yorkie's photo fit. Ravanelli may well have been selling it to his posh, well to do customers, but a significant amount had been finding its way into normal circulation. All three had heard whispers about it when they were back in Edinburgh. A few of Matt's soldier mates who were based at Penicuik barracks had been encouraging him to go on a night out and try these capsules they had got their paws on. Describing them as, 'fucking dynamite, Milan missiles man.'

The forty bottle order was met for the next month with all things going surprisingly smoothly. All three were delighted to see regular money coming in. Housty's mortgage was now up to date, Matt had never felt so close to Thomas and Yorkie no longer had to beg and plunder to survive. They collected The Anchor clientele's pish on the first evening they arrived down there, usually the Monday. The lads in the pub were none the wiser and were a fine, friendly bunch. As it tended to be a Monday night that they arrived at the van, the locals had taken time out of their busy week days getting sloshed to go hell for leather over the weekend, making their urine even more potent. Ravanelli was delighted with the new strain saying his customers were raving about it even more. He had said to Big Andy that the sea air must be stimulating their creative sides. When Big Andy passed this onto Matt, they both started laughing.

'Aye, he doesnae ken you cuntos like a do. Av no worked out what you're up to an ah think it's best I dinnae ken. Let's just say there's no danger I am ever having some of that stuff.'

'You are a wise man, Andy. You wouldnae believe it if a told you.'

'You're joking, cunto. I wouldnae put anything past Yorkie. He is one crazy cunto.'

The fifth week with the bigger order started with them heading down earlier than usual on the Sunday morning. The previous week they had intentionally completed the order a day earlier so that they could get back down on the Sunday. All three had been loving the seafood on offer since they began frequenting the area. Although this never stretched past fish and chips or cray fish from a harbour van in Eyemouth, they had seen a food festival advertised in Berwick-Upon-Tweed. The festival was taking place in the now abandoned town's army barracks. Once home to the Kings Own Scottish Borderers Regiment the barracks were now used for local gatherings and events. They did still house a regiment museum which Matt had threatened to drag the others round but all of them wanted to give the seafood and local bevvy a good go. Parking up the lanny at the caravan, they headed down to The Anchor for a swift pint and to order a taxi for the short drive along the coast into Berwick.

'Am no eating anything that's no cooked, man.'

'Aye, and by cooked you mean deep fried.'

'I certainly do Housty, my good man.'

'Well, lads,' Matt interrupted, 'I am going to eat fucking everything. Am wantin oysters, squid, crab, the fecking lot.'

'I bet you would love some cockles, would remind you of those sausage parties you used to have in the trenches.'

'Shut it, you wee sea urchin, the only thing you'll be eating is some local apples that have been pressed tae fuck to make cider.' A statement Yorkie knew there was no point debating.

The bickering continued as they entered the bar, the pints being poured as soon as they were spotted by a visibly caked barman. The usual suspects were already staggering around, the Sunday club in full swing. The lads blethered to the locals, some of whom they were now on first name terms with. The local taxi driver, Tam, turned up when they were half way through their second pint but was happy to wait and have a smoke with Yorkie while they finished up. A now very stoned, heavily overweight taxi driver, squeezed into the front seat of his ancient, maroon Vauxhall Cavalier. The others joined him in the

146

car, all getting their seat belts on as they knew from a recent night in Eyemouth that he was a horrific driver. Due to his size he didn't bother getting a seat belt on, obviously relying on the fact that he was jammed in against the steering wheel. The old GTI 2 litre engine burst into life, leaving a plume of black smoke and dust for the unfortunate drinker trying to enjoy a fag outside the pub.

'This auld jambo coloured motor cannae half shift, Tam.'

'Aye pal, the motors been souped up and the suspension lowered,' Tam wheezed.

'Was that deliberate or does it just happen whenever you get in?' Yorkie said, winking at Matt and Housty who were sat in the back looking rather worried about their long term, life expectancy prospects.

'Whit you slavering about? Am a fine figure of a man,' Tam said, smiling at Yorkie. It was clear Tam was well aware of his weight issues and that he was used to people making jokes about it.

Despite Yorkie continually taking the piss out of Tam, they had a great laugh on the way down the coast to Berwick. Turned out Tam had no further booking so they talked him into joining them at the food festival. The catch being that he had to drive them back afterwards. Walking towards the barracks, Yorkie was still making jokes at a now wheezing red faced Tam who was struggling to keep up.

'Hold your belly in Tam, you'll get Scotland Yard as soon as they see the size of you. You are a food festival's worst nightmare, bud.' Tam didn't react at all, he was more concerned about avoiding a cardiac arrest on the short walk.

'Dinnae listen to him, Tam. He'll soon be off his nut on local ale,' Housty tried to reassure the big guy.

'Am no bothered a fuck, mate. Just looking forward to the scran. No eaten since aboot eleven this mornin,' the big man replied.

Glancing at his watch, Housty noticed it was just after twelve. This boy was going to go to town in this place. It was obvious on gaining entry that all four had different priorities. Matt had mumbled something about the museum to which Yorkie just scoffed and headed straight to one of at least six bars, all serving a variety of local produce. Housty had directed Matt over to the seafood van as he was starving and didn't want to get started on anymore bevvy until he had eaten. Big Tam did a good impression of a hunting hound and loped towards the nearest van selling meat products.

Forgetting about their pisshead friend and big Tam, Matt and Housty set about the food stalls. Deep fried whole crab, squid, monk fish in batter and some tasty big prawns later, they were ready for a peev. Looking around realising over an hour had past and they hadn't spotted either of their comrades, they headed off to the back of the barracks, a place they hadn't yet been to. Sure enough, the pungent aroma of skunk was instantly detected. Yorkie and Tam were huddled behind of one of the long stone sleeping blocks that circled the parade ground.

'Jesus, the last thing Tam needs is the munchies,' Housty said, as the friends wandered over to join them.

'We could smell you pair from over there.'

'Alright, boys,' a red eyed, spangled Tam slurred. He was already in a state. There was obvious signs of food down his front but also a very distinct reek of booze on his breath.

'Fuck man, what have you two been drinking? You're meant to be driving, Tam,' Matt pointed out.

'Leave him alone, lads. He's a right good cunt. We've been on the monk's juice. Some scary shit called Mead. It's fucking horrible but gives you a good dunt. Dinnae stress about his driving, his mucker just dropped af a couple of geez oh ching so he'll soon be sober as......a monk.' Yorkie started creasing at his crap joke and slapping Tam's arms trying to get him to join in. In Tam's state, it took him a bit of time to cotton on but when he did he returned the slap, sending the considerably smaller frame of Yorkie flying into the barracks wall.

'Some boy, you are some boy.' Matt headed for the nearest bar to get a fortifying drink. He was followed closely by Housty as the other pair headed for the bogs.

Ordering two drinks of mead, Housty turned to Matt, 'Good luck to Yorkie sharing a cubicle wi big Tam.' They started laughing as their drinks arrived. The laughter was short lived, both taking a drink of the golden mead and gagging.

'Fuck me man, that is rotten.'

'Spot on, let's go and get proper bevvy. No wonder that pair are looking so rough if they've been getting stuck into that.'

They headed back round to the main part of the festival in the parade ground. Standing now with a couple of pints of lager and watching some locals put on a truly terrible music and dance show, they both relaxed. Housty had pointed out another fish van, this one selling local oysters. Agreeing that they would be getting a fair wedge of their cash later, both chilled out enjoying the sight of Yorkie and Tam trying to chat to some local girls who were easily pension age. Neither appeared even slightly embarrassed when old Jean and Betty sent them packing. They then joined the others at the bar.

'Who's wantin some dust?' Yorkie whispered, not very quietly to the group.

'Aye, why no?' Housty announced, looking to Matt who just shook his head.

'No way, man. Am going to organise a military assault on that oyster van in a minute. Some crappy, local powder, will just hold me back.'

'Right, see ya in the khazi, spazzy,' Yorkie said, winking at Housty and heading off in the direction of the toilets. Housty shrugged and headed after him. When it came to drugs, Housty had always been in Yorkie's slipstream

Matt turned around expecting to find big Tam there but the not so light footed, large human, was in a queue for belly busting, spicy hotdogs. Jesus, thought Matt, even a couple of lines hadn't made a dent in the huge man's appetite. Good news was that more food would at least sober him up for the journey home.

Housty had followed Yorkie through a doorway they thought led to the toilets but was in fact the military museum. Not spotting Yorkie on the groundfloor, he headed up the stairs to find his pal in the first room, chopping out a couple of enormous, train track lines, on a display case.

'Wait till we tell Matt we had a line oan toap oh some of his poofy comrade's medals,' Yorkie slavered. He was taking his time, not even slightly bothered that someone could walk into the room at any moment.

'Hurry the fuck up, ya fucking bam, ah can hear folk downstairs.' Housty grabbed a note out his pocket and nudged Yorkie aside, slamming the generous line back. His nose felt the hit immediately and almost simultaneously his brain.

'Christ that's strong, his mate gets some good gear.'

'Aye, I might have been tellin a few porkies. A hid it in ma poacket all along, man. Goat it oaf Harvey yesterday. Hate that cunt but the charlie is barry. Rays oot soon, man.' Yorkie hoovered his line and handed the note back to Housty. Both exited the room just as a couple of tourists entered. They bolted down the stairs, not caring if they had been noticed and joined Matt at the bar again.

'Yorkie just told me Ray is out soon, Matt,' Housty blurted out. He was struggling to speak properly as he could no longer feel his tongue or throat.

'If he kens we are in cahoots wi the silver fox, he'll no be chuffed. Am glad he's getting out coz he's a good lad, but we all know the reason he is inside in the first place is because folk tried to get in the way of his lucrative business dealings. A dinnae fancy getting dangled of a fucking cliff up Blercrae Hill by ma ankles.' Even Yorkie

150

was quiet at Matt's words. They were all well aware that the Ray's release date would come but had had their heads buried firmly in the sand where that was concerned.

Housty broke the silence. 'Aye, food for thought,' he said, dismissing any concerning thoughts that were trying to push their way into his brain. He was totally buzzing so no amount of worrying news was going to ruin that. 'Still, lets get hammered.' He got another round in, trying to engage anyone that would catch his eye in conversation. The knock on effect of this being, that anyone with any social awareness, could see this and just looked the other way or pretended to make a call.

Despite it now being fully autumn, it was nice enough to sit out in the day's sunshine. More pints were drunk and lots of laughs. Tam had returned and demolished the hot dog like it was a cocktail sausage. The others just looked on in amazement. Matt then headed over to the oyster van, getting a dozen of the Lindesfarne bad boys. A few drops of tabasco and they all disappeared down the hatch. Licking his lips, he had another six before joining the others again. Although he felt sober, it was now increasingly apparent that Tam was going to have serious problems navigating the taxi back to Coldingham. He was off his tits. Drunk, stoned and flying. A lethal combination for a taxi driver. He sat next to the others but was taking very little part in the ever crazier conversations that they were having. Not long after his oyster binge, Matt began feeling cold and tired, suggesting it was time to leave. In his head, he had already decided that he would drive, so the sooner they were gone, the better. Yorkie and Housty were keen to continue but their hand was forced when one of the event organisers noticed that the cigarette Yorkie was blatantly rolling was not your average woodbine. The four of them staggered out of the barracks under the watchful eye of a couple of local churchgoers. Matt being the only one capable of being embarrassed at that moment, had tried to apologise, but his attempts were met with stony faces. Up ahead, Yorkie and Housty were marching towards the parked taxi, puffing away, whilst Tam followed zombie like behind. Matt was feeling a bit dodgy so was pleased that Tam put up no resistance to him driving. He handed over the keys instantly, without a word. Matt wondered if this was not an isolated incidence. Opening the car, Yorkie and Housty slid in the back whilst Tam crashed into the passenger seat, putting the cars springs under serious pressure. Matt got in the front seat as a huge shiver shot through his body, making him feel nauseous. He took a deep breath and forced the bile back down his throat, he then started the engine, gunning the car out of Berwick as quickly as possible.

Matt knew he was in a race against time. His stomach was groaning, he kept dry gagging and was now shivering so much that his teeth were chattering together. The other three were oblivious to this for different reasons. Tam was asleep, his chin resting on his enormous chest. Yorkie and Housty had taken another line and were blethering absolute rubbish about football losing its soul. This was a common theme amongst them, all agreeing that the huge amounts of money being showered, on the English leagues especially, had meant clubs were no longer about the fans and local community. Ticket prices were so disproportionate to the average wage. Perversely, because the clubs were paying their players such massive salaries. These were sentiments Matt agreed with and would usually have joined in, but he was struggling big time.

Yorkie then tapped Matt on the shoulder. 'Did Housty tell ye we had a massive line in the museum of wan oh they display cases? It wiz full oh loadsa crappy auld medals. Just auld junk, man'

Matt's hands clenched the steering wheel. He was summoning his anger to have a rant about having respect for the military when his stomach clenched, forcing its contents up through his throat and out his mouth, all over the windscreen. Housty and Yorkie were frozen, absolutely speechless. The car had swerved, changing lanes on the busy A1. Panicking, Matt had pulled it back under control and turned to the sleeping Tam to apologise for the mess. As he turned, his stomach lurched again and another catastrophic amount of vomit exploded from his mouth and nostrils, splattering Tam in a thick blanket of bile. He was struggling to keep control of the car as water blurred his vision.

Thankfully, the turn off from the main road was just ahead. To all their astonishment, Tam was still sleeping, completely oblivious to his predicament.

Laughter erupted from the back seats. Matt expected no sympathy and the boys duly obliged.

'Check the state of them,' Yorkie shrieked. 'The spew crew, the fucking spew crew. Matt, my man, my fucking man.'

Housty had tried to speak but was convulsing in hysterics and gasping for air. 'Spew crew,' he whispered.

They hugged each other, crying with laughter, neither able to communicate properly. Matt took the Eyemouth turning and pulled in. He was first out the car and was immediately sick again. Taking off his soiled Lacoste jumper, he wiped his face clean on the back of it and chucked it into the ditch. Turning around, he saw Yorkie and Housty had not calmed down at all. Both were peering in the window, creasing, looking at the puke stained form of big Tam. Tam had not moved and remained, fortunately, completely oblivious to his predicament.

Still struggling to control the gag reflexes that he was experiencing, Matt mustered the energy to speak. 'Boys, we need to get back to the van, pronto. Am bound to be over the limit, if the police pass, we are getting huckled.'

Housty's breathing had almost returned to normal. 'What in the name of fuck are we going to do with Tam? I mean, just look at him!' This set the pair off again.

Feeling dreadful and seriously peeved, Matt got back in the front seat. He winced as he sat in the puddle of vomit that had gathered on his seat. His clothes were going in the bin as soon as they were back. First though they had to ditch Tam and his motor somewhere safe, preferably his house.

Yorkie was now back in the car. 'This car is reeking man, I'd phone a cab but …well…..I've already got one! I'd say his taxi earnings are going to take a bit of a hit.'

'Do either of you ken where his gaff is?' Matt was again feeling sick. It must have been the oysters.

'Aye, he telt me he lived in one of the houses next to the park, the one behind the boozer.'

Housty had now fully got his senses back. 'We'll drive there and leave him in the motor. With any luck, he'll think it was him that barfed everywhere when he finally comes round.'

Matt didn't even speak, he was already starting the engine and pulling out. He needed to get to the personal comfort of the caravan toilet very, very soon. An explosion at the other end was imminent. He would never live that down. Passing the pub in Coldingham, he turned right into the park following the road round to a group of nondescript, terraced houses. It was easy to spot Tam's place. All the others had kids' toys in their well kept gardens. Tam's garden was a jungle. At the end of the drive was a recycling bin, packed with takeaway boxes of all descriptions.

'This has to be the one,' Housty said, pointing. Matt didn't need telling twice. He turned sharply into the drive and jumped out, vomiting into the long grass and weeds that dominated the front of the house. The others were out almost as quickly, the smell in the car was appalling. Matt headed straight round to Tam's side of the car and carefully put the car keys and fifty pounds in his pocket before closing the door quietly and walking back to the caravan. Matt felt awful, and so was glad when Yorkie and Housty headed down to The Anchor, leaving him to clean himself up in peace. He would have run back but was afraid he'd follow through such was his desperate state.

The boy's evenings could not have been more different. Whilst Yorkie and Housty enjoyed the pub's hospitality until closing time, both fleeing by the time they staggered the short distance back to the van, Matt had continued to be sick as well as having the pleasure of explosive diarrhoea. He spent the whole night going back and forward to the toilet. Thankfully, the big room he had crashed in had the ensuite, so he didn't have far to go. He didn't sleep at all. Toilet trips and violent shivering saw to that.

The caravan was quiet for most of the morning. Matt had got up for water, well aware that serious dehydration was now in the post. Lying in the living area were the fully clothed forms of his friends. Each lying on the large couch, snoring loudly, the remnants of last nights after party scattered around them. It was clear that they had kicked the arse out of the rest of the day while he suffered. Almost managing a smile, he wondered how big Tam's morning was going. That would be a rude awakening for the big man. Taking the glass of water back to his bed, Matt got under the covers, hoping sleep would take him. As he drifted off his thoughts turned to Roxy. He missed the wee guy, but was glad he had left him with his mother, no danger could he have taken him for his morning walk. The dug would have had to pick up his own crap for a change!

As Matt shook like a Swedish flat pack wardrobe, the full extent of yesterday's overindulgence was coming crashing into Housty's and Yorkie's consciousness.

'Fffffuuuuuuuuccccckkkk,' Housty yelled, as he rolled onto his side. 'A feel fucking brutal man. Ma mouth feels like the bottom of a bird cage.'

'Me an all, mucker. This is how that jake ball C-o-l-i-n must wake up every day. My tongue is stuck to the toap oh ma mouth. Ma fucking mouth feels furry.'

'My throat's like the Gobi desert, man, I think a badger sneaked in an shat in ma gob.'

Both were now sitting up, surveying the mess they had left.

'We better go and check on Matt.' Housty struggled to his feet taking off his jumper that he had slept in mumbling to himself, 'Roasting man.' He headed through the caravan, opening the bedroom door to see Matt curled up in his sleeping bag, snoring away. Going by the smell that hit Housty's nostrils as he opened the door, it had been a long night for his pal.

Christ, he thought, almost gagging. He opened the nearest window and then bolted back out the room, shutting the door as quickly as possible. Heading for the kitchen to get himself a drink, he could tell Yorkie was a shambles. Sitting hunched over the coffee table he was building yet another spliff. This didn't bode well for Housty. If someone of Yorkie's legendary drinking abilities was feeling rough, then Housty was in for a very tough day.

'No idea how you can think of smoking more of that shit. No danger am I having any of it.'

'All the more for me then, eh? Lightweight. How's John Rambo? Bet he's doing push up's and star jumps and reciting his battalion's Latin motto.'

'He's fast asleep and by the stench coming from the room he's had an awful night. We better leave him to kip. Looks like it's up to you an me to alter The Anchor's plumbing the night.'

'Oh fuck man, no danger. What time we at?'

'It's the back oh twelve. Am going to need some fresh air before we do that.'

'Aye, me an all,' Yorkie replied whilst heading outside smiling, with his newly built spliff in hand.

As Housty sat nursing his glass of water, his mind wandered to yesterday's antics. He pieced the day together like a child's wooden jigsaw. Images of the chaos flashing through his mind like an old projector, beaming photos onto a wall. That was the most smashed he had been in ages. Great laugh though. It was hard not to start giggling again when he thought of the state of Matt and Tam in the front seat of the Vauxhall. Housty's daydream was interrupted by a spangled Yorkie coming into the van announcing he was now officially starving.

'Am so hungry I'd eat a Tynecastle pie. Cannae even mind when I last ate. While you two saps got stuck in yesterday, I had a rather enjoyable liquid lunch. Feeling it now but, man.' He was standing rubbing his groaning stomach.

'Let's go down to the other boozer for some scran. Then we can come back and get the plumbing gear. I'm just taking it easy though. No more powder,' Housty warned, then continued. 'It makes me feel rough as fuck.'

'Sounds like a plan. Am goin tae need a couple of swift ones before we do any plumbing. We tanned all the coke you'll be pleased to know.'

'You do surprise me.'

They both got cleaned up and wandered down into the village. On the way, they sneaked into the park where Tam lived for a laugh. Poking their heads round the corner, they could make out an obviously confused and distressed Tam trying to come to terms with the state of his vehicle of employment. He was standing next to the car, with all the doors opened, holding a bucket. The gargantuan Lonsdale Tracksuit he was sporting, was stretched to breaking point, as he bent down to clean.

Housty tugged at Yorkie's jacket, indicating that it was time to bolt before they were clocked but, to his dismay, Yorkie jumped out in full view shouting and waving to Tam. He then began striding up the road towards him. Housty followed awkwardly behind him.

'Some state you were in last night, Tambo my pal. Like the threads bud. Been down the gym have ye, pal?' Coming to an abrupt stop in front of Tam, he pretended to be surprised by the state of the car. 'Oh no man, whits happened to the motor?'

Tam stood up, sweating and wheezing. 'I dinnae ken. A woke up in the front seat, fucking covered in spew. Am never sick, never.'

'Aye, some state you were in. Matt had to drive us back. We tried to wake you bud but you were out for the old count. Sparko as they say.'

'Ah just dinnae get it. Ma ma says even as a kid I wisnae sick. Always loved ma scran too much.'

'Aye, it's a mystery pal, a real mystery.' Yorkie slapped his back in a consoling way whilst winking at Housty who was trying his best not to start creasing.

'The motor is in a bad way. Dinnae think you're customers will be lapping that stench up.' There was a solidified string of bile hanging from the rear view mirror. It would take a professional cleaning team a few days to sort this shit show out.

Tam had stopped listening, he just mumbled away to himself and shook his head repeating, 'I just dinnae get it.'

The two of them said their goodbyes, leaving the big man with the not insignificant task of returning the car to a state that would allow human habitation. Both of them almost jogging down the road, only starting laughing when they were well out of earshot.

'Funny, I was feeling brutal before I saw the state of Tam but now I'm almost fighting fit. That happens a lot with me. When you see someone in a worse state, it fair cheers you up, gives you a wee biscuit boost.'

Laughing again, Yorkie agreed. 'Aye, that was just the medicine. An intravenous hit eh wellbeing seeing that big lad in that state. Mind I think we're due him a bevvy....or should I say, Matt Rambo is.'

Both enjoyed a slap up feed in the pub. Yorkie went for the old favourite of fish and chips, Housty opted for one of the specials, beef curry. Both had the special rhubarb crumble with local ice cream. With the meal finished they sat back, relaxing and drinking their pints which had hardly been touched whilst they devoured the food.

'A could sit here aw day, man, an just chill out.' Yorkie was almost horizontal in his seat.

'A fucking wish, Yorkie. We're going to need to head over the road and do some plumbing soon. That lot are so hammered, they only pish a few drops each time. Mind you it's fucking dynamite.'

'Aye, credit where credit's due. They are proper pub soldiers that lot. Professionals. Three Michelin star jake balls.'

Enjoying sipping their pints, they chatted for another half hour, only getting one refill which was very un-Yorkie like. After paying the bill, they headed up the road to the van. The van seemed empty, no sign of Matt. Then they heard the toilet flush and Matt walked through with a glass in his hand, dressed only in his boxers and a t shirt.

'Hoollleeeee fuck, you look rough as a badgers arse, brother.'

'Dinnae, Yorkie, I feel brutal. Spewing an shittin all night and morning. Whenever I drink, I cannae keep it down. Goin do us a favour, get some bog roll at the shops when you're out. Oh and none of that tracing paper rubbish, I need some luxury soft stuff.'

'Aye, no bother. We're going to head down to the boozer to get our supply of you know what for the cooking. I'll need to take the lanny.'

'No bother, keys are there,' Matt pointed to the keys on the work top and then poured himself a large glass of water. 'Fuck man am……. oh no again. Cccccuuuuuuuunnnnnntttttt.' He spilled some water as he waddled quickly back through to his not so inviting, exclusive toilet.

Housty looked at a very amused Yorkie and just rolled his eyes. Picking up the keys to the lanny, they headed out, leaving Matt and the toilet to a rather predictable and uncomfortable afternoon. Parking the lanny at the park behind the pub, Housty got the pipe and container out whilst Yorkie went in the pub to open the back gate which led into the beer garden and then through to the toilet. They stashed the stuff out the back and entered the bar receiving the usual cheers and back slaps from the ever more smashed clientele. Pint poured, they grabbed a seat and enjoyed sitting back watching the perpetually pickled locals going about their daily ritual.

'It's a fucking mystery tae me how these cunts can do this,' Yorkie said.

'Look at C-o-l-i-n though, man. He's always smashed an god only knows how he's no deed.'

'Aye, but I need tae feed the slavering jake and get him cans. He cannae even get up and down the stairs without that fucking chairlift. These boys are so energetic with it, it's like a workout. Look at that pair there.' Yorkie pointed towards the old dudes playing darts. 'They two are in their eighties, they've just ordered triple cheapo whiskies wi halves of cider an they look like a couple oh lads in their twenties pissing aboot. Nuts man. These arnae pub soldiers, these boys are special fucking forces.'

'Must be all that sea air, bud.' As much as Housty enjoyed Yorkie's company, he wasn't in the mood to chat. Yesterday had taken a heavy toll on him.

'Ken what, there might be something in that. We've been having a ball down here an none of us, apart fae Rambo, but thats coz he's a greedy cunt, have been rough. A love it here, bud. Here's tae many more laughs.'

Clinking glasses, they sat back enjoying the show. Neither feeling particularly rough from yesterday's session, but both lethargic. It felt strange for them not having Matt there. The three boys had become close again during the last couple of months. A closeness they hadn't experienced since their late teens. Housty turned to Yorkie without speaking, all he did was wink at him and smile. Housty was a bit freaked out as he was certain Yorkie knew exactly what he was thinking. For all Yorkie's problems and nonsense he was an ultra marathon from stupid. The wink was just to say, 'aye mate, a ken, its barry eh?'

They kept a watch on who had been to the toilet, deciding after about half an hour that they had a window to install the container. Housty had seen Matt do it often enough, so Yorkie kept watch whilst he unscrewed the waste pipe and attached the container. It took no more than two minutes. The fixings for the ancient urinal were now so loose that it was an easy switch. Easy physically, but this was the first time Housty had done it and it was a shock to his fragile senses. This close, the stench was overpowering and he was almost sick. It wasn't one of the self-rinsing, not so modern numbers. It was a decrepit, porcelain museum piece. For some reason, it reminded Housty of swimming lessons in Primary school at Glenogle Baths in Stockbridge. When the school had first taken the class there, they had all been shocked to see actual baths on the mezzanine floor above the pool. None of the children could believe that people didn't have their own bathtub in the house. Housty managed to control his body's urge to empty his stomach and they returned to the bar. It was late afternoon at this point, a couple of pints later they decided a walk to the beach would be more beneficial than sitting in here watching the Coldingham drunken circus. Yorkie skinned up in the toilet and they headed off for a bit of fresh air. Not before they had promised to come back for a few more later. The weather had changed in the weeks they had been at the caravan. Autumn was in full swing and there was a constant cool breeze now blowing from the North Sea. The short walk to the beach cleared their heads for a moment, before Yorkie sparked the enormous cone shaped reefer. Finding a sheltered spot on the veranda of one of the brightly coloured beach huts, they sat back and chilled, watching the waves rolling relentlessly in and sweeping up the almost deserted beach. The only other humans they could see were the two surfers, braving the cold, unforgiving, dark and turbulent waters of the North Sea.

'Check out they cunts. Av no seen them catch a fucking wave yet, man. Reminds me of us try tae skateboard. When a say us, a really mean more like you. A wis a graceful cunt at whatever a did.' Yorkie was never found wanting for self-confidence, even in his lowest moments.

Raising his eyebrows, Housty's face broke into a mischievous smile. 'Graceful, aye? No mind that time you tried to skateboard fae the bus terminus on the hill down Blercrae Drive?' Housty had started creasing. 'You crashed into the old dear on the mobility scooter. A found her glasses in the hedge an her false teeth on the road. Your mum had to pay for new ones. They were scattered all over the shop like tic tacs.' Housty began laughing at the childhood memory of his friend's first road traffic accident.

A not so cocky Yorkie couldn't help but laugh. 'Not my finest hour, I will admit. It's funny looking back, eh? We had some barry laughs.'

'This place when it's so quiet makes me think of Martha and the Muffins, you know what I mean?' Housty looked at Yorkie raising his eyebrows, challenging him to think.

'Of course I know what you mean, ya radge.' He started singing......badly. '*Echo beach far away in time, Echo beach far away in time.*' Putting his arm round Housty, he said, 'You'll never catch yer pal out in a music quiz. Fuckin classic tune.'

'Sure is, man.'

Lost in their own thoughts, they smoked while watching the two surfers floundering in the waves. After enjoying the views for a while, taking bets on how shite the surfers would be on the next wave, they headed back into the village, stopping at the other caravan site for fish and chips. Both devouring them in their munchied up state, barely taking time to breathe. They heard The Anchor before they saw it. Some terrible singing was blasting out. Someone had got hold of a karaoke machine and the locals were not holding back. As they entered the bar, one of the old boys who had been playing darts earlier was giving Steppenwolf a run for his money, screaming the magnificent tune, 'Born to be Wild,' into the mic. The veins on his neck looked in serious danger of springing a leak. '*Fire all of your guns at once and explode into space,*' he wailed. This was not the vibe the still very stoned Housty had wished for, but Yorkie's asbestos like resistance was loving it. Pints were poured and he soon had his name up to sing 'My Generation'. The Who's classic teen anthem. The locals loved it, they really had taken to the boys. Housty had looked on as a couple of the pensioners jumped about threatening to break their fragile ankles.

The star of the night was the barman, singing a spectacularly honest and pleading rendition of Engelbert Humperdinck's, 'Please Release Me'. His gaunt, grey face and googly eyeballs, straining to convey his internal struggle with drink to the now quiet crowd of caked senior citizens. A few were even swaying from side to side, whether intentionally or not, with their lighters held above their heads burning. It was during this sobering moment that Housty nudged Yorkie and they rescued the container from the toilet, stashing it in the back of the motor before trudging up the road. Tomorrow was cooking day.

Chapter 18

A View from the Lodge

William Longridge had been spending as much time at his country lodge as his wife would allow. She had stupidly agreed to look after their two terribly spoiled grandchildren, three days a week, while their ungrateful parents were working. This was all the encouragement that he had needed to spend those days at his luxury holiday lodge in Coldingham. An arrangement that his long suffering wife was more than happy to accept. A man prone to embellishing everything about himself to others, he described his thirty two foot static caravan, as a lodge, to those in his golf club and the small circle of acquaintances, who were unlucky enough to be cornered by him. He believed that the small quiet section of the caravan site, his lodge was situated on, was the most exclusive section of the sprawling park. In fact, it was the same site fees wherever the caravan was, but that didn't stop him from telling those that would listen a small lie. Furthermore, he liked to tell people it was called little Morningside but it was him that had created the myth and encouraged the owners of neighbouring caravan to use it. Morningside was the type of area in Edinburgh where he had always aspired to live, but his small pension from the Scottish Office, meant that that would forever remain a dream. His caravan was his pride and joy, purchased with the lump sum he had received on retirement, five years previous. With the little money he had left and some savings, a massive decking had been built around the lodge, but his favourite purchase had been the reflective glass he had had installed in the caravan's front window. This allowed him to indulge in his favourite pastime of watching and ensuring that his neighbours behaved, without them being aware or so he thought. It was obvious to everyone that he

164

was watching all the comings and goings, but if he was hiding behind the glass, at least it meant they were not being bored by his relentless, dull, caravan site gossip. His wife would join him at weekends and they would enjoy bingo and some dancing in the site club. He did enjoy the weekends to an extent, although, his favourite time was the quiet weekdays when all the workers had returned to their jobs and he could survey his coastal domain in peace. At least that had been the case until five weeks ago, when the mysterious caravan that had lain empty for a long while, had suddenly began getting used by three undesirable men. To William's huge annoyance, these men, all obviously hooligans of some sort and no doubt up to no good, had been breaking his peace and relaxation time with their brutish behaviour. They had been constantly flouting the site rules like they meant nothing to them. He had tried to stand up to them regarding dogs being on leads and their total disregard for the 'No Ball Games' rule, but he had been met with pure cheek and what he regarded as thinly veiled, dangerous aggression. As a result, he had begun watching them closely whilst documenting their loutish antics. He was planning to produce an all-encompassing dossier, which he would present to the site owner, with the aim of having them removed. He had attempted to get the other residents of little Morningside behind him, but shockingly, none had shown the slightest bit of interest. In fact, most had never set eyes on the lads and if they had, they would undoubtedly have preferred them to the bitter, nosey William.

Monday 20th August 2018: *The three men arrived and immediately cause myself and Marjory distress. Their dog is not on its lead approx. 11am. Midday I once again reminded them dogs must be on leads and that ball games were strictly prohibited. Thankfully Marjory was now returning to Edinburgh so did not witness their insolence in this instance. The two stocky men appear to be in control of themselves at least but the thinner man is quite obviously drunk as he walks in the oddest way. Thankfully they left on the Wednesday having spent the whole three days drunk. The thinner man is not only drunk but is constantly polluting the air smoking. He is the one to watch! A bad egg if I ever I saw it.*

Monday 27th August 2018: *They have returned. I have now given up engaging them in conversation regarding site rules. The two heavier men are at least up and about at a reasonable hour. The thinner man seems to surface last and continually smoke before the three of them spend the days in the village bars. Need to find out what they are doing in the van. On certain days the curtains are drawn and they appear to be busy. It will not be them cleaning the van that's for sure, that thin one needs a good wash! It's strange I have a nagging feeling I have seen his face somewhere before but I just cannot place it. Probably on crime watch!*

Monday 3rd September 2018: *These brutes are indeed creatures of habit. Drunk again and then spend the day in the van before disappearing to the bars again. Need to find out what they are up to that will be the key to having them ejected. Where there is a will there is a way. Spotted one of the heavy set ones carrying a large bottle containing liquid when coming back from the village. What are they up to? It could well have been fuel of some description. Note to ones self to check site rules regarding the storage of flammable liquids.*

Monday 10th September 2018: *No change in their behaviour. The thin one will not see retirement if he continues smoking like that. Doubt he has worked a day in his life. Drunk again, how can they afford to finance such debauchery? The large bottle was again brought back to the van. They leave with it empty and bring it back full. Think man, think what could they be up to???*

Sunday 16th September 2018: *The men arrived a day early unfortunately. I hope they do not make a habit of this as Marjory again had to suffer the criminal's presence. She is putting on a brave face but I can tell they make her nervous. One of the heavier ones has not left the van after them being away all day Sunday. Spotted him running for the lodge long before the other two arrived back singing. Something must be done, this can not go on! The other brute returned on Tuesday morning with their ridiculous 4x4 car and I saw him again carrying the container. I must find out what they are doing. If only the thin one would refrain from smoking I could take a peek through the window.*

Chapter 19

Gin Head and the Castle to the Rescue

Yorkie and Housty slept in the living area again. Matt was still struggling when they got in and neither wanted to hear him on the toilet all night making noises like a stuttering tommy gun. All of them were up early. Housty still felt drained due to the recent excesses and Matt looked like he had acquired an overly aggressive, short term, heroin habit. Yorkie was the only one showing no signs of over indulgence, probably because for him, this had been a standard couple of days. Housty had collected the lanny and the cooking process had begun. Everyone was keen to get the order completed and to get home. Although Matt hadn't managed food, he had been drinking water again. He was determined to get through the day and drive home, no matter what the time. His own bed and home comforts were calling, big time. He had another trip to see Thomas lined up this weekend, he had bought tickets for the two of them to watch Ipswich Town. Recovery was paramount now.

The plan was to get the first batch complete, then get some of the daily fresh mutton pies from the local butcher. There had been serious debate about these being better than the Stenhouse ones. The Stenhouse pie had long held the crown in Edinburgh, so this was a discussion no one thought possible, before they came to Coldingham.

The first round of cooking went well. Housty had volunteered to get the pies as he fancied a walk and fresh air. The caravan was horribly hot and stuffy, despite the windows being open. He loaded the first crate of bottles into the lanny and headed down to the shops, leaving the others to start the next round. Housty noticed the nosey

168

man, watching him closely whilst holding what looked like a note pad and pen. He just knew the guy was conducting some sort of amateur surveillance on them. Back at their caravan, Yorkie was getting annoyed as he had wanted a break and a smoke, but Matt was insistent they kept going.

'You can have a smoke once we've got the next lot cooking. A need tae get the fuck out of here tonight, Yorkie. Am dyin, man.'

'Fuck sake man, right, right. Mon then geez a hand. Luckily you weren't around in World War II, you'd have been a fucking cert to join the SS. A can just imagine you goose stepping about torching books.'

They continued whinging at each other as they worked. If Yorkie was honest, he was also keen to get home. It was hard to comprehend, but he missed C-o-l-i-n and Smokey, big time. The caravan had been great fun at the start, but now the weather was changing, it didn't have the same appeal. Spending time down here in deepest Scottish winter was not Yorkie's idea of fun. Still, he'd had worse jobs but he'd never been one for sticking with a shite job. He was a free spirit, a modern day hippy. Obviously, without all the long hair and fucking incense or any of the decent morals.

Housty strolled down the road glad to be temporarily free from the incessant steam and heat in the caravan. After some small talk with the butcher, he headed towards the small grocers that served the village, for a paper. Whilst walking, he enjoyed eating one of the freshly baked mutton pies. The pie was finished in the short time it took him to get there. He grabbed a Ribena off the shelf and then turned to choose which crappy, lying, red top rag to buy. His choice was usually based on the paper that contained the least articles on Celtic or Rangers, therefore requiring him to pick them up first and check the back pages. He didn't get that far. Before his arm had extended far enough to pick a paper up, he was stopped in his tracks, unable to move. Oh fuck, oh fuck, oh fuckity fuck. Struggling to think rationally, he could feel himself begin to panic. Emblazoned over the front pages of the three papers he could see, was to lesser and greater extents, Yorkie's freakish photo fit. One headline read; '*Break Through in Broomhouse Breaking Bad Case.*' Panicking further, Housty picked the paper up, dropped five pounds on the counter and ran out the shop without a word.

Meanwhile, back at the van, Yorkie could feel his mobile vibrating in his pocket constantly. The pots were now on the stove, boiling away and he was contentedly rolling a big fat joint. He was in no hurry for his break to be interrupted by a phone call. Matt sat slumped on the sofa, sipping water. Finishing the spliff, Yorkie walked out the van warning a very lethargic Matt to keep an eye on things. Lighting up, he looked at his phone. It was his mother Lynne that had been calling. There was also three texts from her. Puffing away he opened it up wondering what the fuck C-o-l-i-n had done this time. Better not have fallen down the stairs again, that was a nightmare trekking back and forward to the hospital, sneaking full cans in and empty ones out. Yorkie read the first message three times, each time feeling his heart rate and stress levels increase. The other was just as worrying.

'*What the fuck have you been up to? The police have been at the door looking for you. Do not come home I think they are watching the house. Phone me!!!!*'

'*They are in the street. Do not come back. Where are you?*'

'*Phone me now son!*'

Shit, this was not good. Stuck between phoning her straight away and first working out his story, he sucked desperately on the joint. The strong skunk reefer burning down in ridiculously short time. Looking round, he went to knock on the window to signal Matt but noticed him getting up quickly.

Matt had a sudden, all too familiar, ferocious urge to get to the toilet. He knew he shouldn't leave the cooking pots, but he was desperate. I'll be quick, was the plan. Neither pot was at the unstable stage, so it was a matter of weighing up the risk and return. The main risk being that he shat himself and that was not going to happen. He bolted for the toilet, delighted to detect the cool reassuring feeling of the plastic seat on his tender arse.

As Matt was sitting down, Yorkie was finishing the joint knowing that he had to get in the van pronto as Matt was obviously, otherwise engaged. That's when he heard his name being called. It startled him due to the tone of Housty's voice. What the fuck is Housty doing he thought? He watched him sprinting across the site, waving a newspaper with what looked like the pies in his other hand. To his horror, the paper bag ripped, allowing its contents; those beautiful pies which Yorkie was now really wanting to eat, fall out onto the damp grass. Yorkie began to worry when Housty failed to notice the calamity and continued to sprint towards him with an ever more alarmed expression.

Gasping for breath, Housty launched himself up onto the decking that Yorkie was standing on. Housty had Yorkie's full attention now. He had that sense of impending doom, the same one he got when he knew the chairman of York City was about to rip up that beautiful, life changing contract.

'Oh fuck man, we are fucked, mate. Look at this.' Housty handed Yorkie the paper. This was one of the rare moments in his life where he was speechless. The photofit of himself stared back, expressionless. It felt like he could see into his own caricature's eyes and it was taunting him. Those eyes said, you are fucked me old matey. It's the end of the road for you pal. The party is over.

'Your coupon is all over the papers, mate. It's fucking linking you to the explosion at the allotment and the new drug the police are concerned about,' a still breathless Housty declared.

'Shit man, that explains why my ma's been on the blower. The bizzies have been round my gaff. Some cunt has dropped me right in it.' Yorkie began wracking his brain for who the culprit could be.

'That's not all. The police are keen tae trace a Land Rover seen at the scene and two other men that had been seen in the area. That fucking beechgrove cunt would have been on the blower. Nosey prick. Seems we are surrounded by them. I caught the cunt over there earlier watching me. Looked like he was taking notes. Hope he's no taken the car reg plate down, then we are really fucked.'

As Yorkie hurriedly read the article, Matt was still oblivious to the disastrous news. Every time he tried to get off the toilet, he would get another sharp, incapacitating pain in his lower bowels which would force him to sit down again. This would ensure that their current desperate situation was going to get exponentially worse.

Matt felt the vibrations first, followed very quickly by Housty and Yorkie. Matt only had time to put his body in the aeroplane crash position, while the others looked straight at each other, both understanding they were helpless to act.

One pot exploded, igniting the other and ensuring this was by far the most calamitous blast yet. The front side of the van opened up like it had been savaged by an enormous, blunt tin opener. Housty and Yorkie were thrown from the decking, luckily landing on the relatively soft grass, that surrounded the van. Matt was not so fortunate. Although unhurt, he was now completely exposed to the elements while perched on the toilet. In normal circumstances, he would have jumped up, but he was just not finished. Hurrying, he got himself sorted and jumped straight out the smoking van onto the grass. The three of them gathered themselves in front of the caravan to survey the damage. The van was a mess. Stevie Wonder would be able to tell its days of hosting fun family summer holidays were over and the lads' days of using it as a cooking shop, had definitely come to an abrupt and crippling end.

All three were in shock. They began checking each other for injuries that their adrenaline filled bodies had not yet conveyed to their brains. Miraculously, they were all fine. They may have been fine physically, but the explosion had not gone unnoticed on the thankfully, quiet site. A couple of dog walkers were looking on from a distance and the caravan owner who they had a mutual dislike for was on his balcony on the phone. At least he had ditched the pad and paper Housty had spotted him with.

Matt spoke first. 'We need to get out of here fucking pronto, that cunt is on the phone to the police, I guarantee you.'

No one spoke but they all sprang into action. All three rushed back into the van to gather any undamaged personal belongings, along with anything that could link them to this latest debacle. They were all conscious that the van's gas supply was now vulnerable. Yorkie was last out, the other two were already in the Land Rover and Matt had the engine running. Yorkie thought he could hear distant sirens in the wind. This scenario was becoming all too familiar.

Matt slammed the lanny into gear, driving straight across the grass and flower bed through the middle of two neighbours' vans and up onto the site road. Their pal on his decking was leaping about, apoplectic with rage, at what he was witnessing. Housty was first to break into nervous hysterics as the lanny got onto the main road and gunned it out of Coldingham, north towards Edinburgh.

'Did ye see the cunt's face, man?'

'That was some driving Matt, pure army escape shit.'

Matt had not initially seen the funny side but was soon creasing as well. 'Aye, I hope he has a coronary, fucking twat,' he said, in-between waves of laughter.

They sped away from the ruined van and the imminent arrival of the emergency services, desperately putting distance between them and the crime scene. Once things had quietened down, they were all concentrating on escape plans and trying to calm down as the miles between them and Coldingham increased. All three simultaneously panicked as a speeding police car hurtled towards them, but to their eternal relief went flying by, unaware that the perpetrators were so close.

They were on the A1, heading north, in less than fifteen minutes. This had to be an all time record for a Land Rover on that windy stretch of moorland road. The A1 was quiet and they made good time, until up ahead, they saw two serious looking police vans shadowed by a large military vehicle. Sirens were on, no doubt heading straight for the caravan. As the first police van passed, Matt caught the driver's eye and noticed his passenger was pointing at them forcefully.

'Fuck, boys, they spotted us. There must be an alert out for a Land Rover. They were definitely looking at us.'

'Aye, I think your right. The boys in the next van were staring right at me.' Yorkie sounded panicked, mainly because he was. He'd been in trouble before but this was getting way too fucking heavy. He knew he'd not survive in jail, long sentences were for people like Ray. He was a shark. In comparison, Yorkie was a wee rainbow trout. This knowledge had kept him away from incarceration up until now.

'That military vehicle was bomb disposal. They mean fucking business, boys.' Matt had recognised it straight away and it worried him. If the authorities suspected explosives were involved, they would be very quick to act and all resources would be available to their hunters. That meant helicopters would possibly be added to the chase.

Housty took the opportunity to fill Matt in on what he had seen in the papers, making sure to include the bit about the Land Rover. They all agreed that they needed to get off the main road. The first opportunity to do this was just past Dunbar where they took a back road to North Berwick. From there, they could head back to Edinburgh on the coastal road, hopefully giving them enough time to get back into the city and to hide the Land Rover. There were plenty of lockups and dead ends in the Blercrae jungle to hide a motor. The road was again quiet, with the odd tractor or delivery vehicle passing. They followed the coast roughly, winding round tight corners, until the mighty Bass Rock came into view and perched close by, the formidable fortification of Tantallon Castle. The huge castle once fought over by vast armies, lay in majestic ruins. Unfortunately, they were not able to enjoy the sight of these famous landmarks. At least a mile behind them, Matt caught sight in his mirror of flashing blue lights, coming in and out of view between buildings, trees and dips in the road. Slamming his foot to the floor, the Land Rover leapt forward, as if it too was aware of the severity of the situation.

'We need to get off this road. They are not far behind. Look for somewhere,' Matt desperately urged. He was having to work hard to supress his rising panic. He could feel the pressure in his chest increasing. Up ahead, there was a right turning which he almost took but stopped at the last minute, realising it was the Historic Scotland car park for castle visitors. Thankfully, between a group of houses ahead, there was another turning that he gratefully took. It was in the direction of the sea, on the headland, directly opposite the Bass Rock. After about two hundred meters, they came to a halt in front of some large gates that stood ominously, across the road. It looked like a compound of some sort. Eight foot high fencing surrounded it on both sides, with what appeared to be a guard house, on the far side of the gates. The Land Rover was now far enough from the main road that they would not be spotted so all three got out and watched for the police car. It shot past the entrance, not even slowing down.

'Nice one, that was close.' Housty glanced at his pals. Both were sweating, looking every bit as concerned as he felt.

Matt was looking intently on his phone. 'This is an old RAF listening station, it's called Gin Head, believe it or not.'

'Gin Head, a fucking wish, mate.' Yorkie didn't even bother smiling at his rather obvious joke.

'We better get away before we get spotted,' Housty said.

'Na man, it's not owned by the MOD now, it's up for sale. I think we're ok here for a bit. The houses are far enough away that we shouldn't get any company.' Matt headed for the back of the van taking out a pair of industrial bolt cutters.

'What are you doing now, man? We're in enough shit without breaking in here.' The circumstances Housty found himself in were a million miles from his previous life. Working in an office did little to help prepare him for this. Like the others, he had been in trouble with the law when he was younger, but until recently, he had thought those days were far behind him. His mortgage arrears were also a thing of the past but some time in jail would soon reverse that.

'I reckon there will be a helicopter out soon, looking for us. We need somewhere to stash the motor, I bet we can in here. Look at the place, no one's been here for donkeys, man. If it's up for sale, you can be guaranteed the RAF have stripped the place bare.'

Yorkie shrugged, 'We're fucked already, why not add breaking and entering into government property to the list?'

Right enough, it was overgrown. Even the warning, keep out signs, looked ancient. Matt strode forward and cut the chain easily, giving the cutters a loving pat before getting back in the lanny and driving forward while the other pair held the gates open.

They then closed the gates and Housty wrapped the chain back around to make them appear locked. In front, Matt drove the Land Rover slowly down what had once been a proper tarmacked road, but was now a single track, decorated with more pot holes than Edinburgh's George Street. A neglected piece of prime real-estate in the centre of the city. Both sides of the track were hugged by thick gorse bushes and bracken, providing great cover from any nosey tourist who had a clear view into the compound from Tantallon's mighty walls. Yorkie had taken a quick look in the guard house but as Matt had guessed, it was stripped back to its plaster walls. They followed the motor, admiring the views that appeared through breaks in the bushes. The early afternoon sun was shining down on them, providing a calming influence on what had been a rather stressful day.

Housty was first to speak. 'Fuck man, this place is creepy and beautiful. So peaceful.'

'No fucking kidding, bud. A keep expecting some fucking, special forces cunts to jump out the bushes an give us all a right shoe in but aye, the views would make C-o-l-i-n put his can down...... for a second at least.'

The track opened into a large tarmacked clearing surrounded by buildings of various sizes. Some dilapidated, with broken windows and doors, but others remained in a good state of repair and appeared secure. Matt had got out the lanny and headed over to what resembled a garage but with a door that was at least double the height of a normal suburban house garage. The others followed him over while he checked the lock.

'We need to get this open and hide the lanny. I reckon the chopper will be out fucking sharpish.'

'You really think so, man?' Housty wasn't convinced. From the relative safety of this compound, his earlier panic had receded.

'Housty, that was a bomb disposal truck accompanied by two major incident police vans. They are not messing about. As soon as these cunts think explosives these days, it gets handed to anti-terror units and those cunts are serious as fuck.'

'It's no going to take them long to put two and two the gither and realise it's the same cunts that blew up the allotment.' Housty looked at Yorkie. 'And you bud, are their number one lead.'

'Fuck, fuck, fuck,' was all their worried looking friend could reply.

'Ssshhhh, listen,' Housty raised his finger to his mouth.

They could all hear the distant sound of helicopter blades, slicing up the air, methodically making their way towards the coast. Matt bolted back to the lanny getting the cutters. He attacked the garage's lock ferociously.

'Housty get the lanny started, as soon as the door opens drive it in,' Matt shouted, without taking his eyes off the cutters and lock.

Housty didn't need a second telling. Yorkie had grabbed the bottom of the massive roller doors and was trying to force them up as

Matt was working on prizing the substantial lock open. It eventually snapped under Matt's vicious assault and the roller gave slightly. Matt dropped the cutters and joined Yorkie, both intent on forcing the door up. Housty had the lanny right behind them, as soon as the roller was high enough, he drove into the empty garage. They were just in time. The helicopter flew directly over the compound, out past the castle, before circling and following the road they had last been seen on, towards North Berwick.

'Ya fucking belter, you'll no get us that easy, ya cunts.' A jubilant Yorkie was looking out the doors, towards the helicopter, giving it the V sign.

'What the fuck have we got ourselves into, boys?' Housty questioned. Unlike Yorkie, he knew this small victory was only the beginning. The speed of the mobilisation of the authorities was a huge concern.

The same negative thoughts were running through Matt's head. How could he visit Thomas if he was locked up in jail and where would the money come from to pay for his treatment? He had to try and clean up this mess and he knew exactly who to get in touch with. Go back to what you know. He called his pals at the barracks and arranged for them to come down and get the lanny for him. Soldiers had a strong bond and Matt and his friends trusted each other implicitly. He didn't need to explain exactly what had happened, just told them where it was going to be. His plan was; if a convoy of army Land Rovers were on the road, they were very unlikely to be suspected or stopped. If his one was in the middle of a couple of real army vehicles, with any luck, no one would notice. It wasn't quite standard army issue, but it would pass a casual glance when amongst the real thing, especially if real soldiers were driving it. They agreed to take his lanny back to the safety of the barracks, where he could pick it up when the heat was off or more likely, given recent events, when he was eventually released from prison.

'I owe you big time, soldier. I'll leave the keys under the front seat. Oh and whatever you do, don't fucking touch any of the bottles in the back. Just trust me on that, it might look like whisky but it's not. Not even close. I'll be in touch.'

Hanging up, Matt realised Housty and Yorkie were looking at him in a none too happy manner.

'How in the name of suffering fuck are we going to get out of here, if we are leaving the fucking motor?'

'Aye, am no fucking swimming back tae Leith, ya bam.' Housty and Yorkie were not happy being left without transport so far from civilisation. Neither was sure where exactly they were.

'Calm the fuck down, you pair. We cannae drive this anywhere today. We'll need to walk into North Berwick and get a bus or a train. It's not far.' The army had trained Matt to accept situations and identify solutions.

Despite moaning about it, they had to agree that it was the only option open to them. Driving about in the lanny was the monopoly version of go directly to jail.

The helicopter had come back and was sweeping up and down, from the coast back to the A1. The boys took the opportunity to take a closer look round the place. Most of the buildings were accessible, with only a few doors needing gentle persuasion from Matt's shoulder.

'This is the type of place we should have cooked in from the start, man,' Housty pointed out. 'No one's going to break into a military compound.'

'Apart from us like?'

'Aye,' laughed Housty. 'Apart from us. Na, but think about it. I mean we could have blown this place up once a day and it would have made fuck all difference.'

Yorkie had suddenly stopped in his tracks. Sensing this, Housty turned back to look at him. 'You seen a ghost, pal?' Yorkie had a strange, unreadable expression on his face.

'Av goat it, ya cunt.' Yorkie was slapping his forehead in frustration. 'How the fuck did a genius like ma self, no think oh it before? You are spot on Housty. We need a place like this. Even more secure. A place close to home that we could blow the fuck out of and no one would even ken.'

'Sounds fucking perfect, mate,' Matt acknowledged. 'But where exactly are you on about, Yorkie?'

'The fucking bomb shelter, mind the place on Blercrae Hill? We used tae play in at lunch time at the school.'

'The cold war nuclear shelter you mean?' Housty was listening now.

'Aye, how many other bomb shelters on the hill do you ken about?' Yorkie was getting exasperated now. For a bright laddie, Housty could be a tad slow on the uptake at times. All brains but no common sense as his granny used to say.

'It was built to withstand anything but a direct hit from the ruskies.' Matt was warming to the idea.

'Fucking exactly, man.'

'Only thing is, how the fuck are we going to get in there? We spent hours trying and got nowhere when we were kids.' The boys and many others from their high school had spent their lunch hours running around the site of the shelter which was only ten minutes walk from the back entrance of the school.

'I'll work it out, boys. No amount of solid steel doors can stop this bam.' Yorkie was pointing at his chest proudly, exuding absolute confidence.

'Right lads, let's get back to the lanny, get our gear and head into Berwick. We'll need to stay off the road, so lucky for us, the tides out. By the look of things on google maps, we can walk along the shore. The polis will not be looking for us down there.' Matt was keen to get moving and had been checking his phone for possible safe routes into the town.

They trooped back to the lanny, each grabbing their own gear. Closing the garage door tightly, they made their way to the main gate, happy to see the helicopter appeared to have given up its search of the area. Again, the gate was closed with the chain wrapped around it. Skirting the compound, Matt found a path that led down to a sandy beach that gave great views of the Bass Rock and high up behind them was Gin Head. The walk into North Berwick took around an hour and involved a number of sandy bays and numerous slips and stumbles on seaweed smothered rocks. The boys all agreed that food was a must. No one had eaten anything all day, apart from the pie Housty had had, but he opted to keep that wee snack quiet. Matt was feeling faint but delighted that he had regained his appetite. The chippy at the south end of the high street was their first port of call. Once the food was demolished, they made their way to a small pub at the back of the main street called The Auld Hoose. It was an old school boozer. Three pints of Stella sat on the table, the three of them were stretched out next to the real log fire, that burned underneath a huge TV. For the first time that day, it was safe to chill for a bit.

'There's trains every half hour so no need to hurry, boys.' Housty had been studying transport options. There were buses as well, but they took forever, stopping at all the coastal towns on the way back to the capital.

'Am in nae hurry tae get hame, Housty man. My ma is still pestering me, she says the polis have been back at the door again. Some cunt is right out eh order. Who the fuck would grass me up?'

'Am hoping that nosey cunt from the campsite hasnae taken a note of the lanny's number plate. If he has, they'll be at my door in all.'

'Aye, I said that to Yorkie earlier and that's not our only problem. Ravanelli is not going to be overly chuffed we have now blown up the caravan and managed to get more publicity than a footballers' wives night out.' The numerous obstacles in their path were becoming apparent to Housty.

Yorkie's old confidence was returning with every sip of lager. 'Dinnae worry aboot the silver fox. When we get up and running in the bomb shelter, he'll be as sweet as a sherbet dib dab.'

'I think we need to knock this caper on the head, boys.' Matt was still having his doubts about continuing. Today had been a close one, too close. Unlike the other two, he had a son to consider. He would miss the cash though. 'Anyway, how are we going to get in a 1950s underground nuclear bunker without anyone noticing?'

'Stop being a big pansie, Matt. You were in the army, who dares wins Del Boy style.' Yorkie was now in full flow, the first pint hardly touching the sides.

'That is the SAS motto, ya tube, not the Royal Scots.'

'He's got a point but, mate. The bomb shelter will be a hard nut to crack.' Housty had also been giving this some thought.

'Am no sayin it's going to be easy but I ken who could get in there quicker than Rocco Siffredi wi a anally desperate nun,' was how he so delicately informed the other two of his plan. His idea was to get in touch with his old pals, the infamous Toto and Baggio. They too had been brought up in Blercrae, although they had had different circles of friends. Yorkie knew them both well though, from their days in the all-conquering Salvesen youth football team. Their real names were now a mystery, but they had earned the names Toto and Baggio from the legendary Italian forward line of Toto Schillaci and Roberto Baggio. They had even pretended to have real Italian roots, but as Yorkie had pointed out, the closest they had ever been to Italy was a sausage supper from Tony's Tower on a Saturday night. The three of them had made a fearsome forward line, sweeping all teams in that age group aside and only losing to a Welsh side in the youth UK cup final because the three of them had been arrested for robbery the night before the big match in Cardiff. While Yorkie had had a career of sorts in football, Toto and Baggio had obviously got a taste for pilfering as they went on to excel at stealing. Highland post offices were a favourite as the security was poor and the unsuspecting locals were just not prepared for two armed maniacs. There were numerous post offices, jewellery shops and smaller local banks up and down the country that had a visit from them. They seldom left empty handed.

'Surely, that pair are inside now. Nowhere was safe from them.' Housty had not even thought about them in years.

'Na man, you mean no safe was safe from them. A seen Toto a few months ago, up the town, trying tae get a couple of dirties back to his gaff in Stockbridge. Some boy. They live in a huge town house. Own a shit load of flats and houses across the toon.'

Matt had been quiet up until now. 'Mental eh. That pair looked like they had a one way ticket to jail and now they're living the high life, prospering off rents and robberies. There's no danger they are going to risk all that to bust into the bomb shelter. I mean we have plenty of cash the now but I dinnae want to just hand it over to them. Sounds like they are flush enough anyway.'

'Dinnae worry about payment. I ken how those boys' minds work. Al put it tae them as a sort oh challenge. They just cannae refuse. Mind you, a bit oh ching from Ravanelli would help convince them.' For all Yorkie's nonsense, he was a master at manipulating people to get his way. Few people could resist his charm when he put his mind to it.

The lads had a few pints, chilling out enjoying the pub. It was somewhat less hectic than The Anchor. There were the usual pub soldiers but none in the JK premier division like Coldingham. Darkness provided some cover for them when they eventually left. All three were aware that the police would still be on the lookout. During their time in the pub, Yorkie's mother had phoned again. He had managed to semi pacify her but had failed to convince her that everything was all right. She had seen the news and had endured several visits from the police. Anyway, he was taking her advice, no danger was he going home tonight. One of the others would have the pleasure of his company. Matt insisted on going back to the chippy for seconds. He had some catching up to do. Walking along the high street towards the station, they were quietly enjoying their food and reflecting on what had been a rather stressful, eventful day. Yorkie recognised the signs that the other two were considering calling it a day so he was desperately plotting his next step. He knew if he left things for a few days, giving them time to think, it may be curtains for the cooking business. He planned to get in contact with Toto and Baggio that night. He needn't have worried, Ravanelli had seen the Scottish news. There was no way he was going to let them just quit. He had immediately got in contact with Big Andy who had called Yorkie during the short train journey back to Edinburgh. As the boys walked out of the entrance to Waverley, Big Andy spotted them straight away. He pulled up beside them in his faithful white van.

'Jump in, cuntos,' came the shout.

'Fucking hell, Andy, I just about shat ma self.' Housty had understandably panicked when he saw the white van pull up, assuming for once the police had been efficient.

'Matt probably did shit himself,' Yorkie laughed. 'And not for the first time today.'

Matt was not amused, he sussed something wasn't right. 'How did you know we'd be here, Andy?'

'Cunto told me,' Big Andy moved his head in Yorkie's direction.

Now Matt and Housty were not happy. 'And you didn't want to tell us about your plans?' Housty said accusingly. The day's events meant Housty's fuse was shorter than a midges cock.

'A would have telt ye baith if yous hadnae insisted we sit apart in case the fuzz were on the train.' Looking at Big Andy he continued. 'Couple of panic merchants, man.'

It was Matt who restrained Housty, Yorkie was close to getting a dull one. 'No here, Housty. The last thing we need is the bizzies taking an interest in you battering your mate.'

Yorkie had jumped in the front, Matt followed him, deciding it was safer to keep Housty away from him. For Housty's part, he was quite happy to get in the back. He was knackered and wanted to get home and get his head down. Whatever Big Andy and Yorkie had been plotting was of no interest to him.

'Right, just get me home Andy, there's a good man. I am knackered. It has been a cunt of a day,' Housty said, fully expecting just that to happen.

'I'll get you straight hame Housty as soon as you and the boss have had a wee blether.' Andy replied matter of factly, no threat or malice in his voice.

'What the fuck?' Housty said, in a raised voice. He didn't like the sound of this.

'Aye cuntos. I told Yorkie he wanted a word. Yooz did blow up his caravan.' Big Andy started laughing. Lighting a fag he carried on. 'Some bunch you lot. Av seen smoother operations right enough. Honestly, yooz are no exactly staying under the radar.' Obviously the days disastrous events tickled Andy as he continued to smile, laugh and shake his head.

'Just drop me on the main road man, am no going all the way to Fife.' Housty was just not up for this.

'Nae bother cunto, the boss is in the town. We've to meet him on the way hame anyway. An yooz better get yer stories straight, he did not seem too chuffed about the news story. He loved that caravan.' Big Andy winked at them through the clouds of smoke. It was hard to read Andy when he was in this mood.

It was only Yorkie that was nervous. Housty was too pissed off to care. The caravan trips had been great but the three days a week they were down there had been taking its toll. Yorkie was not a healthy man to be around. Matt was neither pissed off or nervous, he was happy to have a quick chat with Ravanelli. If he wanted to be a wanker about it, Matt would just call it a day. He knew that caravan meant nothing to him, he had acquired it in a drug deal that had most probably spelled the end for the real owner.

Big Andy pointed the van towards Leith and from there, they headed along the front to Newhaven. Newhaven had been a small fishing village, but like so many others that surrounded the capital, it had been swallowed up, its relative innocence stolen by the city. He took them into an underground car park that lay below the last block of newly built flats, on reclaimed ground, adjacent to Newhaven Harbour. Getting out the van, the boys looked around expecting to see Ravanelli waiting for them in the shadows of the secure car park. It felt a bit like a scene from an old movie, where a hit man appeared from the shadows with a silencer on the end of a pistol.

Yorkie was not enjoying this. 'Where the fuck is he, Andy?' he said, while glancing nervously from side to side.

'You look like you're shiting yourself, cunto,' Big Andy said laughing. 'He's up the stairs in his flat, waiting on us. This isnae some American gangster film fae the 80s, cunto.' Andy was clearly enjoying himself now, he couldn't wipe the friendly smirk from his face.

Big Andy headed for the lifts with the others following behind. Once in the lift, Big Andy thought it wise to point something out. 'Dinnae call his gaff a flat, he got all annoyed when I did. Thinks it's a fucking penthouse. Another cunto living in the US of cunting A. This is fucking Newhaven, no Beverly Hills, cuntos.'

'A thoat these big dealers were meant tae be hard fuckers, right bunch eh drama queens.' Big Andy lifted his finger to his lips in a shoosh sign signalling Yorkie to keep quiet. They were on the top floor, the corridor had magnificent panoramic views of the River Forth, extending all the way to the bridges and the Ochil hills beyond. Big Andy had rung the bell and as they waited, all four of them took in the view.

'Tell you what, this is a fucking penthouse man, some view.'

'Indeed it is, Housty. Do come in gents. I think it's better for all of us that Britain's most wanted are not seen loitering outside my front door.'

Housty almost shat himself for the second time that evening. None of them had heard the door opening. Ravanelli was standing at the door with it opened wide, indicating they were all to get inside. Big Andy ushered them all past him into the flat. Housty was first in and was pleasantly surprised to shake Ravanelli's hand and see he was smiling warmly. He did the same with all three of them. They followed him through to a lounge that had equally impressive views over to Fife and down the Forth to Leith docks, the Isle of May and in the distance, the cold, unforgiving, open expanse that was the North Sea. Two large sofas and a massive TV was all that was in the sparsely furnished room. They all took a seat apart from the silver fox who remained standing with the impressive vista behind him. He surveyed the three friends, his manner and face now unreadable.

Matt was first to speak, being careful to use his correct name 'Bill………. you dinnae seem nearly as pissed off as I expected.'

Shrugging, his face remaining neutral, he said calmly, 'What's the point in crying over spilt milk……or should I say burnt out caravans? However, there is a point of crying if our lucrative business is affected.' He now looked back and forward at them all. 'So what do you propose to do to ensure its longevity?'

Before Housty could say, fuck all, we've had enough of this, Yorkie piped up. 'Dinnae worry raaaa, Bill. Av come up wae a plan.'

Raising his eye brow with a mischievous smile, 'Feel free to enlighten me and for your sake I hope it includes staying underground for a bit. Off the radar. That picture of you is scarily accurate.'

'A tell ye what mate, I'll be further underground than you can imagine. I want tae start cooking in the old nuclear bomb shelter underneath Blercrae Hill. Av goat a plan tae get in and once we're in, we can cook to our hearts' content under there. Nae cunt will ken we're there.' Yorkie spoke confidently, surprising the other two in the firmness of his voice. It wasn't often he spoke with such authority. His eyes never leaving Ravanelli's.

He had his full attention now. 'I remember hearing about that place when I was in the RAF. It was part of the WW2 radar system I think. I vaguely remember talk of the nuclear bunker being added. It would definitely be quiet down there. How do you propose to gain entry without raising suspicion?'

'Av goat a couple of pals, who are, let's just say professional in gaining entry.' Yorkie tapped the side of his nose and winked at Ravanelli.

'Of that, I have no doubt,' he replied smiling. Matt and Housty had kept silent throughout the exchange. Ravanelli was now looking at Matt. 'What are your thoughts on this? You are very quiet. Do you think this a realistic plan?'

How the fuck would I know thought Matt, he hadn't had a look at the place in years. He had only been near it recently when up the hill walking Roxy, but even then the high fence along with trees and bushes meant he hadn't been able to see the place. Trying to give the impression that he was interested Matt replied. 'It's certainly very private, the place doesn't look like anyone has been near it in years. As long as we can get in without raising the alarm, it's possible.' Wanting to give them a bit of time he added, 'Although until we get in its impossible to be sure.' Matt realised as he spoke that he actually hoped it was possible, not just for the cash although that had been a life saver in terms of his son, but also because he was enjoying himself in a way he hadn't in a long time. They had been on a proper adventure together in recent months. The dangers and excitement they had faced had taken him back to his early days in the forces. The good times.

'What about you?' Ravanelli turned to Housty, giving him one of his strange inquisitive looks, like it was some sort of test.

Housty was also coming round to the idea. He was getting used to the cash and if they were cooking in the bunker he could stay at home and keep up the gym visits his body and mind were crying out for. 'I agree with the lads, if, and it's a big if, we can get in, it could be the perfect cover.'

'Well, until you do, I've got supply issues. How much of this week's order did you manage to rescue? Before you answer, the right answer is all of it and the wrong one, is none. Somewhere in between is acceptable.'

Housty could sense Yorkie was about to speak so jumped in quickly. 'We have half of it, well kind of have half of it.'

Matt elaborated. 'Half the order is safe in the back of my motor. The only issue is it wasn't advisable to drive it home.'

Ravanelli interrupted, finishing off Matt's answer for him. 'With you all being hunted men you mean?'

Matt nodded, 'Aye, it's safe where it is and I have a couple of friends picking it up tomorrow. We'll be able to get the order to Big Andy in the next couple of days.'

'Right Andrew, let me know as soon as you have organised to get it. I don't want any more fuck ups. We have a good thing going here, gents. A bit of concentration is required. Yorkie, I may have misjudged you, I think the underground bunker is an excellent idea. Make it into reality, right.'

'No sure you have misjudged him,' Big Andy said, laughing and nudging Yorkie. Andy was beginning to enjoy watching the boys and Ravanelli circling each other. He usually just followed orders, take this here, pick this up, meet this boy etc etc but now he was getting some entertainment and getting a wage for it.

'Aye, comedy gold, Big Andy, right enough, yae need a fag, its well out ae character for you tae be this amusing.'

Smiling, Ravanelli said 'I think I am even beginning to like him, Andrew.' Turning serious and business like in a disconcerting flash he barked. 'Right boys. Get into that shelter ASAP. One week of having half rations is not ideal, any longer is going to cause us all problems. In this business it pays to keep ahead of the game.'

With that pep talk over, they were all pretty much dismissed. Yorkie was the only one talking on the way back. Big Andy had some fags to catch up on and the other two were keen to get to bed and catch up on some much needed sleep.

'He's just a pussy cat, I had him eating out ma hand. Glad he's finally noticed am the brains behind this operation. Toto got back to me straight away, he says there is not a building in the toon they couldnae get into. That cunt loves a challenge. Oh Andy, tell yer silvery haired pal we're on but he'll need to provide a wee incentive for Butch Cassidy and the Sundance Kid. An incentive of the white powdery variety. Oh an mind Housty, am staying at yours for a wee bit.'

'Oh fuck, no danger man.' Housty's heart sank at the prospect of having Yorkie as a lodger.

'Fuck you, man. I cannae exactly head hame, can ah? The polis are havin a fucking tea party ootside ma hoose, ya moanin faced auld woman.'

'Right bud, whatever, just dinnae make a mess an stink the place out. Joints on the balcony. I fuckin mean it, man.'

'Aye, good yin, ah ken the drill. What's your favourite rock band, OCDC, ya radge?' Yorkie was pleased to see his attempt at a joke got a snigger out of both Andy and Matt.

Matt was delighted to get out the van in Davidsons Mains. Not so delighted to hear Yorkie tell him he'd be in touch first thing. Housty was equally happy to be back home, it had been a long day. Within in about ten minutes of being in the flat he was ready to crash.

'Yorkie, am hitting my scratcher,' he said, popping his head out onto the balcony. His face instantly engulfed in a pungent cloud of skunk smoke.

'Right brother, sleep tight, dinnae let they wee jambo, bed bugs bite.' Yorkie blew him a kiss before turning to look out over Blercrae and plan his next move.

Chapter 20

Scrabble with the red head

This day had been on the horizon for ages, scrambling through the darkness to get to him, but at last it had come. C-o-l-i-n had drank sparingly that morning. He hated Jennifer seeing him blootered. Drinking had ruined one of her visits and he vowed it wouldn't happen again. Moving tiny scrabble pieces around a board, when you were highly intoxicated, was just not possible. He had rationed the cans that morning to only four which was a fifty percent reduction in his usual early morning consumption. Four was just enough to quash the demons, whilst allowing him to speak without slurring his words and stay alert enough to play his beloved Scrabble. It was not advisable for alcoholics with his pedigree to stop drinking suddenly. He had been warned by the doctor that it could send his battered body into shock. On the few occasions that he had made genuine attempts to stop drinking, with the help of his wife and daughter, he had sought the doctor's advice. The doctor had prescribed diazepam tablets to take the edge off the horrors his body and mind would undoubtedly experience with a dearth of alcohol. Within hours, he had been sneaking down to the local shops for more cans. The pills, even when taken in large quantities, were no match for the monkey on C-o-l-i-n's back. He was a hopeless case which his family and himself had reluctantly accepted long ago.

It was a clean, relatively well turned out C-o-l-i-n that walked carefully down the stairs upon hearing the doorbell, clutching the banister to stabilise himself. He had made an effort to tidy himself up and was determined not to let her see him descend in the chair.

Instantly, he knew it was her, he could make out the distinctive red hair through the frosted front door glass. Soon they were both seated in the living room on opposite couches, with the Scrabble board Jennifer had brought, set up. She had a cup of tea which she had made herself and C-o-l-i-n had one of the four cans of weak lager she had brought as a gift. Not his usual tipple but it would keep the demons in their dark unwelcoming holes for the length of the visit. He had pretended when he opened the can that it was the first of the day and she had gladly gone along with the charade. Both determined not to go over old ground or rekindle arguments of the past. Although they would play games during her visits, they tended to concentrate more on discussing tournaments long finished and often won by C-o-l-i-n. Jennifer generally encouraged this as she hoped it would stimulate his brain to be reminded of his past triumphs. It did and her efforts were greatly appreciated. If only they were able to last longer than a few short hours every month.

She loved to remind him of some of his wildest words and moments. Qabalistic, the adjective form of Kabbalist, describing an ancient Jewish follower was a particular favourite. He had loved using words beginning with Q that were not followed by a U. Many opponents were not familiar with these words and his use of Qabalistic had caused heated scenes in a tournament in a miners' club in Bonnyrigg. As always, back then C-o-l-i-n had just sat back and enjoyed the show, knowing full well he was correct. His vocabulary was legendary, but sadly, was steadily and systematically being destroyed by his other legendary hobby.

Unlike in the tournaments, the two would always go over the twenty five minutes allocated time. They were friends after all and had long since given up timing their games. Often, it was the conversation and laughter's fault. Jennifer occasionally got close to C-o-l-i-n's score but even now he still frustrated her with the variety of words he would use. Never a meeting went past that didn't involve a heated discussion before the dictionary proved C-o-l-i-n to be correct. It was after one of these jousts that Jennifer showed C-o-l-i-n the paper she had brought along.

'C-o-l-i-n, is that not a picture of your grandson? It looks very like him. Is he okay?'

They very rarely discussed Yorkie, or Steven as she knew him, but Jennifer had been worried when she recognised his caricature staring at her from the morning newspaper. Yorkie and Jennifer got on well but he always tried to make himself scarce during her visits. Mainly, to give them peace, but also because unlike any other house guest, he just did not feel comfortable smoking skunk around her. It seemed disrespectful, she just belonged in another world or so he thought.

C-o-l-i-n sighed, 'Aye, I ken Jennifer. I'm certain it's him, he's no been around much and the laddie has cash on the hip fir a change. Not a good sign where that boy's concerned.' C-ol-i-n's mind wandered back to his York City days and how he had spunked that particular excellent wage.

C-o-l-i-n dropped one of his word bombs as they chatted placing 'COOEES' on the board and winking at Jennifer.

'Oh come on, what is that? You are at it this time.'

'Check if you like hen but you should know by now a dinnae joke wi Scrabble. Cooee is when you say hello, an cooees is the plural,' he answered, with his usual smugness where Scrabble was involved.

Jennifer began to check then put the book back down giving C-o-l-i-n an annoyed accepting look. She knew the dictionary would prove him right, it always did. She took her shot whilst they returned to talking about Yorkie.

'Maybe he's finally getting his act together though, C-o-l-i-n.' Jennifer said this and immediately thought to herself; no chance, nice boy but a troubled, lost soul.

C-o-l-i-n had a similar thought; no fucking danger, he's a chip aff the auld block that laddie. 'No, I've seen it oan the news, it's

194

definitely him. The dates back that up but al tell yae, the real reason a ken its him is because the polis are parked outside the hoose aw the time. Lynne and him think am too pished tae ken……..' His face went redder than its permanent tomato shade as he realised he had made a slip in her company. She pretended not to notice the fact he had just confirmed that he was still an absolute and permanent drunkard. He continued, '……but av seen thame when am up checkin the fish. An a ken he was up tae something in the kitchen, cooking something lethal that exploded. A heard him that day, an a ken every time ah see that photae on the news its linked tae an explosion. Must be making hooch and strong stuff at that.' C-o-l-i-n couldn't have been closer to the truth.

Chapter 21

Toto and Baggio

Housty woke with a jolt. Usually he dreamt, but not last night. He couldn't recall any thoughts or dreams, just darkness. A long, warm, trouble free, comforting darkness. It sounded like he had left the telly on, there was voices, actually one voice, coming from the other room. No, he hadn't left the TV on, it was Yorkie. For a blissful, calming moment, he had forgotten about yesterday's troubling events but they poured back into his consciousness. He lay back and closed his eyes. He was bound to be on the phone to Toto or Baggio, either that or it was Lynne giving him more grief. He swung his legs out of bed. Sitting up, he moved his head around, trying to loosen off his neck. He had to get back to the gym and stretch before he seized up entirely. Slipping his feet into his baffies, he walked through to the toilet, passing the living room where he saw an animated Yorkie was marching up and down, deep in conversation. Yorkie gave him a big smile and the thumbs up before he carried on. Housty tried not to listen to the conversation, happy to wait until his friend felt the need to unburden himself with his next wacky idea.

Housty washed his hands and then splashed his face with cold water in an attempt to wake himself up. How was that spangled nuisance so lively at this time of day? It just wasn't fair. Heading straight for the kitchen, he got the kettle on and poured himself some cereal. Opening the fridge, he took the milk out, pleased to see it was still in date. Housty jumped when he heard Yorkie's voice right behind him.

'Morning, ya radge. Some kip you had, it's almost lunch time. Must have needed it, eh pal?'

'It's no almost lunch time, ya bam, it's ten am.'

'Aye, well, it's C-o-l-i-n's lunchtime. Usually has his lunchtime can about now.'

Exasperated, Housty just had to put him right. 'You cannot set the time of day by C-o-l-i-n. He's not a fucking sundial, he is an alcky and a locally renowned JK. He's a greedy bastard, so he tans his cans as early as he can. Drinking his lunchtime can at ten does not mean its fucking lunchtime.' Housty was beginning to rant, he could do with some Yorkie free time.

'You make a good point, my man, but it does feel late to me. My ma was on the blower the back of seven. Says the polis have fucked off now. Obviously realised I'm hardly going tae march in the front door while they are oan a t bone steak out. Wankers. Then a buzzed Toto. He was strolling round the Inverleith Park trying tae look poash. If only they Stockbridge toffs knew about his entrepreneurial past.'

It was hard to understand the mindset of Yorkie and his pals. They lived by different life rules than most. This used to make Housty jealous. As he attempted to make his way in life, Yorkie and his pals appeared to do exactly the opposite. To Housty's eternal annoyance, he could never quite break free and here he was back in the midst of the Blercrae madness. He just kept getting dragged back in.

'I take it he told you to bolt?' Housty replied, more in hope than expectation.

'Told a man of my standing to, as you so beautifully put…..bolt???? I think not young man. He's meeting us at the car park with Baggio at one pm sharp. I have already informed our friend and colleague Matthew to be there. No excuses from you sonny Jim. The wheels of industry have ground to a halt and a will not stand for it.' Yorkie slammed his fist down on the kitchen work top to emphasise the point.

'Oh bloody hell, he now thinks he's Winston fucking Churchill.' An exasperated Housty left the room and slumped down onto the couch already fearing what the day may bring. He needed a holiday, being around Yorkie was fucking exhausting.

Yorkie followed him through. 'We will fight them in the bookies, we will fight them in the boozer, we will fight them in the Co Op.' To Housty's relief he then went out onto the balcony to smoke yet another pre rolled reefer.

Matt's putting him up the night Housty thought. It was like babysitting a large Rastafarian child on speed. Total fucking nightmare.

Housty and Yorkie walked up through Blercrae, to the car park used by the local dog walkers, that was closest to the bunker entrance. Yorkie had a black sun hat on he had borrowed from Housty. Housty didn't have the heart to tell him he stood out a mile wearing it in what was now almost winter. They could see Matt was already there, standing straight like he was on the parade ground, with Roxy sitting next to him.

'Fuck sake man, he's brought that fucking fluff ball with him. We're meant tae be gangstas, not friends of the frigging earth. Fucking rainbow warrior twats.'

'Shut it you, I love that wee hairy nosed mutt. At least I can play with him while you act the fucking goat with your old football chums.'

As they arrived Yorkie was still moaning about Matt bringing the dog. 'How can you expect they cunts to take us seriously when you are standing there wi a fucking designer, rabies ridden dug, man?'

'How can Housty and my good self, expect to be taken seriously, when we are standing with a boy stuffed full of designer drugs, ya loony?' Pointing at his dog, Matt continued. 'An that is as far from a designer dug as you will get. The wee cutie is that ugly, his dad was probably a capybara.'

'Dinnae even start, I am sober as a vegan, lentil munchin, pansy boy.'

Housty cut in, 'Aye, a really stoned vegan lentil munchin, pansy boy, who is named after a dog. Never thought of that, did ye?'

'Good point Housty, my man,' Matt acknowledged before turning to Yorkie. 'Where's Bonnie and Clyde anyway? Am no hangin about all day.'

'Chill out GI Joe, they'll be here.'

At that moment, they heard car tires crunching over the rough gravel that was scattered over the small car park. A souped up white Fiat 500 had pulled into the car park. Toto was driving it. Pulling in, he jumped out the car and headed straight over to Yorkie with an enormous smile on his face. He gave Yorkie a massive cuddle, holding the embrace for what may have been uncomfortable for some men. When he eventually let go, he warmly shook Matt and Housty's hands.

'Great to see you, muckers.' Toto was around five foot eight and very stocky. Not in a body building way, just naturally chunky. His low centre of gravity and physique had been an asset during his early playing years, but it was his stubborn persistence that would wear his opponents down. His head was shaved clean, in complete contrast to his face, which was sporting a thick brown beard. Baggio was there behind him, also hugging Yorkie and giving the others a very friendly, welcoming handshake. He was taller than Toto, almost six foot, with very short curly hair and stubble. Baggio even had an Italian look with dark skin and eyes. It was easy to imagine him strolling through Rome with some model girlfriend. Like Toto, he was also what men would bluntly describe as a shagger. Toto went back to the car, opening the door and pulling the seat back, to allow a light brown and white squat French bulldog to waddle out. He had to then reach in to get a miniature black and brown sausage dog.

Yorkie was looking on bewildered. 'Aw no man, no yooz in all.' He looked crestfallen now. 'What the fuck has happened to you all? Daft wee dugs all over the place. We are meant tae be breaking into government property but we look like five poofs goin tae pump each other in the woods.'

'Glad tae see your vocabulary has improved since we last met, Yorkie. What you dinnae understand and therefore cannot see, is that these wee pooches almost guarantee you a ride. See, taking one of these wee bams round Inverleith Park gives you a reason tae chat to all those rich, lonely, bored housewives wi loads of spare time. I have never shagged so many women as I have wi this wee diamond.' Toto tickled the ridiculously small sausage dog under the chin.

'That thing is so wee it looks like you had it lowered on pimp ma ride. It must be scraping its boaby along the ground, man.'

Matt was laughing. 'Now I know where to walk this wee radge,' he said, whilst tickling Roxy under the chin.

Baggio had bent down to say hello to Roxy whilst Housty and Matt were stroking the French Bulldog. Only Yorkie had remained standing and was surveying the scene with a look of disgust.

'How are we going tae get anywhere wi they dugs in tow? Ah jist dinnae ken whit the fuck has become of ma old pals. You've all gone soft in the fucking heed.'

Baggio stood up laughing, 'Check you out, Yorkie, yer awfy up tight. These wee creatures are our cover. It would look dodgy if the five of us were wandering about the bomb shelter without the dugs. At least now we have a reason for being here.'

'Aye, chill out, man. These wee furry bastards are our cover. An let's face it, you need all the cover you can get. Your puss has been plastered across the national news.' The picture had not escaped the attention of Toto and Baggio it seemed.

'Aye, I suppose,' Yorkie conceded.

The lads carried on, catching up whilst they walked into the woods, following the muddy track towards the main entrance of their target. The buildings were located in an old quarry protected on two sides by its towering sandstone walls. There was fencing running all the way around the compound, even along the high cliffs. The gates were securely closed, so with Toto leading the way, they walked around the fencing looking for a weak point. It would have been easy to get through, but any new holes would create suspicion amongst the local dog walkers, who would be passing here almost daily. Dog walkers, like most people, were creatures of habit. On the far side of the compound, the path left the fence and headed down towards Queensferry Road. The boys ignored the path and followed the fence into the overgrown woodland. About twenty metres in, Toto found a small hole big enough for them to sneak through one by one. Once they were all through they walked towards the buildings, coming out into the quarry in only a couple of minutes. Once in the quarry, they were well covered by the trees and bushes that had sprung up around the fence in the years since the shelter had been abandoned. This enabled them to give the single storeyed brick structure a proper look over in peace. The building was flat roofed and built from old red bricks. The few doors or windows there had either been bricked up or had enormous blast proof steel doors or shutters blocking them.

Matt, Housty and Yorkie had assumed that these would be the weak points worth targeting but the other two had given them the once over and carried on around the building to the two sides that were adjacent to the cliffs.

The three pals were confused by this and stood watching the two of them checking out the brick work deep in conversation.

'What are they up to?' Housty asked. 'Surely we could prize one of the windows or doors open?'

'No sure about that, man.' Matt had been looking at them. 'These things are solid. Even the double steel door looks like it would take some serious industrial cutting gear. That would be noisy as fuck.' The double door Matt had been examining looked big enough to drive a small vehicle into. 'Must be some size of bunker,' he said, almost to himself.

Toto was waving the boys forward. He was up near the corner of the right angled cliffs.

'Right lads, we reckon this is the best way in. We'll probably need tae take ten tae fifteen bricks out.'

'Wit, you mean go straight through the fucking waw?' Yorkie was not impressed.

'Aye, chill out, stressed Eric. We robbed a post office in the highlands by removing bricks at night from the back wall. Took the two of us a couple of nights but it was well worth it.' He gave Baggio a big smile that was returned. 'We kent it was giro day and half the population up there is on the take. We went down the road happy and those lazy cunts just had to wait another couple of days. Would have done their livers the world of good. Should have been fucking thankin us.'

'Aye, everyone was happy,' Baggio confirmed.

'How long will it take?' an unconvinced Matt asked.

'No as long as you think. This is old mortar obviously, it's a wee bit crumbly now.' Toto ran his finger along it to demonstrate. A fair amount of sandy mortar crumbled under his touch. 'Baggio, away and get the tools from the back of the car. You three, geez a hand clearing all this shit out the way.' It was obvious that Toto had been the brains behind their partnership.

Baggio headed off whilst the others beat back the brambles that had taken over the gap between the cliffs and the shelter walls. By the time Baggio reappeared with a small holdall, they had made a big enough impression on the brambles to give them ample space to work.

Toto took a heavy looking hammer and chisel from the bag. He started smashing his way through the mortar. It came away relatively easily. Realising a nosey dog walker or jogger may hear them, he placed an old bit of cloth over the hammer end of the chisel.

'Learn from your mistakes,' he winked at Baggio. 'We almost got busted coz of the noise we were making last time we did this.'

The first brick came away after about twenty minutes, they had all taken turns at assaulting the aging cement work.

'Geez a look, man,' Yorkie almost shoved Housty out the way to peer through the small gap. 'Fuck sake man, there's more bricks.'

Laughing, Toto explained. 'Aye man, of course there is. A building like this will have three layers, each with a few inch gap in between.'

'Oh no, man, that will take fucking ages.' Yorkie thought they would be in the place in a matter of minutes. He was not a person famed for patience.

'No as long as you think, watch.' Toto took the hammer from Housty and hit the brick above the hole with some force. The brick popped out effortlessly. 'Once you make a hole the others come out much easier.'

'Much easier,' Baggio confirmed, nodding his head with his most serious expression. The lads couldn't decide whether he was taking the pish or was indeed that slow minded. He had at one time had a fast football brain and immense thieving skills, along with legendary shagging powers, all of which may have hidden his other grey matter limitations. Although, on the other hand, he was a wind up merchant so it was anyone's guess.

Using the same technique, they cleared a hole around three foot squared. The next layer of brick was harder to break through, the mortar had not been exposed to the elements, therefore had aged considerably better. After forty minutes the first brick was out and they began smashing out those surrounding it. The afternoon light was fading but they were all desperate to see what awaited them inside.

'Boys, its going tae be too dark tae see soon. Let's chisel oot one oh the bricks in the last layer. We can take the dugs hame and get some torches.' Toto was calling the shots now, he was focused. Yorkie had called it correctly, he was seeing this as a challenge and was now as keen as the others to gain access.

'You sure there will only be three layers, man,' Matt queried.

'Aye, cannae imagine there are four. The main bunker is below ground, this is just going to be for stores and access. Would have been overkill tae build the waws any thicker. Especially with the extra protection of the quarry.'

'Tidy, lets ditch the mutts and rendezvous here at ten the night, when there's no dog walkers daft enough tae be wandering aboot. If we are panning fuck out this wall in the dark when it's meant tae be quiet, a do gooder dug walker or late night jogger is going tae raise the alarm. These cunts cannae help themselves. Love a bit a drama in their boring lives.'

'Very sensible for once in your life, Yorkie,' Toto pointed out, smiling widely.

'Very sensible,' Baggio predictably confirmed, winking and therefore only adding to the intrigue regarding whether he was on the wind up.

They were all in agreement. Sure enough, as Toto had envisaged, the next brick fell inwards, landing with a dull thump onto what sounded like a solid concrete floor. A damp, stale, unpleasant smell came through the gap. Like the air in a long abandoned cellar. Air that's not been disturbed for a while. They took turns at looking through the gap using the torches on their phones. It appeared to be a corridor with closed doorways running along the opposite side. It took a monumental amount of self control for them not to just keep going but it would have been stupid. The only way of illuminating the bunker was the crappy lights on their phones and a small torch Toto had in his kit bag. The batteries having long run out of power. They did however, knock more bricks out the way ensuring that all they had to do that night was climb through the gap. Using branches broken off trees, they covered up the substantial hole they had made. There was little chance anyone would happen to wander by, but they weren't prepared to take any chances. The scattered bricks were stashed in the under growth to conceal their afternoons exertions. All five of them had grown up in the area, fully aware of the existence of the legendary nuclear shelter. They had all explored its surroundings and attempted breaking in as kids. Now, as adults and despite their age, they were all still desperate to see what the government had so secretly built below their hill. Toto and Baggio headed off in the small Fiat while the other three walked into Davidsons Mains village to drop Roxy off at Matt's place. Yorkie was pleased to be heading away from Blercrae, he had been experiencing paranoia, surprisingly for the first time in his life. He was certain that people were talking about him and that every second parked car held some of Edinburgh's finest detectives, trying to capture him. He was probably half right, most people he knew would have recognised him from the photo fit but he was a well known radge, so no one would have been in the slightest bit surprised. There may have been some gossip and obviously someone had alerted the police, but the vast majority would have had a ten minute laugh about it in the pub, bookies or takeaway before forgetting all about it. This was Blercrae after all, there was always another bam just around the corner intent on stealing the limelight. Unfortunately, the attention of police was not so easily turned. They may have stopped staring at Yorkie's front door but they were still working in the background trying to identify the new drug and he remained their best lead.

Chapter 22

Polis

Bryan Carver was in work early, very early. The Chief Super, Gordon Swinton Hughes, had phoned him the previous night while he was at the Hearts game. His apoplectic rage had been a welcome break from another Levein horror show. It turned out that it was Bryan's fault that next to no progress had been made in the new street drug case. The mysterious orange liquid capsules, which had been nicknamed 'The Damage', had turned up in the Chief's son's posh private school. Not quite turned up. From what he could gather, the Chief's son was lucky to still be a pupil, as the enterprising little shit had been selling them to his fellow students. If it wasn't for the Chief's special relationship with the school, he would be looking for a new one. The Chief had been kind enough in the past to assist in keeping the school out of the news. A good deed which had been a huge benefit to both. Reputationally for the school and financially for the Chief. A private education was not cheap after all.

So Bryan found himself sitting at seven am in front of the Chief, who was a pompous wanker at the best of times, but this morning he really despised him. And his privileged drug dealing son.

'Carver, have you made any progress at all?' the Chief barked.

'Well, Sir, as you know it is a complex case.'

'Complex case? That's all I fucking hear from you lot now. Life is complex. In my day, we just got on and got our hands dirty. No namby pamby shite. Real policing.'

'That may be true Sir but times have changed, I can hardly drive about like the Sweeney.'

'More's the bloody pity, Carver. That's what these criminals need.'

As does your son by the sounds of things, Bryan thought; but that particular dig would come later in the discussion. Bryan didn't necessarily disagree with the Chief's point but if he had mistakenly assaulted an innocent member of the public, he knew the Chief would be the first to throw him to the mercy of the papers and courts.

'Agreed, Sir. We have still had no luck with the Malone boy. The one known locally as Yorkie.'

'Bloody stupid being named after a chocolate bar. If these people are that thick, we should have caught them by now.' The Chief's mood did not appear to be improving.

'It's nothing to do with the chocolate bar, Sir. He had a failed stint as the star of York City Football Club many years ago. His mother told me that much, but nothing else. She's not daft. The brains of the family, I suspect.'

'Only these types of low lives would celebrate failure like this, Carver. Are there no other family members we can lean on?' The Chief was now doing his deep in thought face, pleased to be coming up with suggestions even a special constable would have thought of.

'I did attempt conversation with the grandfather, Sir, but it was a waste of time. He is an incoherent drunk.' Bryan shuddered at the state he had found C-o-l-i-n in. 'Harmless enough though, Sir.'

'How do these people afford it? I wish I could spend my days drinking but there's work to be done.' The Chief rested back in his chair as if waiting for Bryan to confirm that he was the hardest working man that he had met and who made unimaginable sacrifices in the line of duty. He looked disappointed when the compliment failed to arrive.

We all thought you did in the masonic club was what Bryan would have liked to have said. 'I know, Sir, it's a mystery. I do know from my sources, Sir that Malone is an associate of Andrew Forest, the delivery man we have discussed on a number of occasions. Do you think we could get the go ahead for surveillance?' Bryan had tried in the past to get funding for this but without success. He thought it worth a try now in these special circumstances.

'Now, there's a thing. He is known to have worked, I use the term loosely of course, with a certain infamous Edinburgh man, Ray Dean, who is in the very near future going to be walking the streets of my city again. Yes Carver, I think we could arrange that. Wouldn't it be nice if we could capture them all in the same tangled web? Yes Carver, I will get you a warrant and funding. Do not let it be said that I don't give my officers the backing and tools to do their job.'

'A tracking device would be advantageous, Sir.' Bryan again thought it was worth try.

'Yes, yes, whatever you need. Now if you don't mind Carver I have calls to make.' The Chief's sweeping hand gesture signalling the conversation was over.

'Of course, Sir.' It was you that called me up here, you cretin, Bryan thought before asking. 'And Sir, do you want me to press charges?'

'Press charges? Yes, when you catch them, of course!' The Chief looked at him like he was simple.

'No Sir, I mean your son, he was caught dealing drugs was he not?' There goes the pension thought Bryan.

The Chiefs face turned beetroot, he looked like he was struggling to breath. His rasping voice was quiet. 'Get the fuck out my office, Carver. If anyone in this station hears about this, I will know it's come from you. Your career will be over. Now fuck off and nail these scum bags before I nail you.'

Bryan closed the door behind him, suddenly feeling better about the day. Not only had he almost killed the Chief, he now had the tools to go after Big Andy and Yorkie and maybe, just maybe, it would lead him to that English ponse, Bill Middleton in Aberdour and then to Ray. Not a bad mornings work after all.

Chapter 23

Stepping into the darkness

It was pitch black when the lads walked back up to the bomb shelter that evening. They had been forced to travel on foot due to Matt's Land Rover now being housed in Penicuik Army Barracks. His friends had called him to confirm the rescue mission had been a success. Big Andy and Matt had organised to meet them the following day, to pick up the bottles of The Damage.

Matt had provided head torches from his huge personal supply of pilfered army kit.

'These torches are fucking barry, man. Bright as fuck. It lights up whatever I am looking at,' Yorkie said. He was very impressed by the hardware he had been provided with.

'Funny that, Yorkie, with it being stuck to your heed.' Housty couldn't help but laugh at that wee golden nugget of information.

'Shut your hole, Housty, am just pointing out that they are the business. Showing my gratitude to Matt for chaffing them from the British Army.'

'Aye, it's no wonder the army are struggling, you had half a battalion's kit in your spare room.'

Matt had a huge dislike for the armed forces now. 'Cunts deserved it, man. Just take the pish out of you. It's a great life when you're younger mind. See the world and all that shite. That's how they sell it anyway. What they don't mention is you see all the totally fucked up parts of the world.'

'Aye, it was good for you when you left school. Mind you had a job in the council, you hated that.' Housty remembered them getting the bus into town together for a very brief period in their youth.

'Must have been really shite, if he preferred to be shot at in Ireland, than work in the Housing Department,' Yorkie was laughing.

'Working, stuck at a desk, was shite right enough,' Matt confirmed. 'Dunno how you managed it for so long, Housty.'

'Fuck all else to do, should have been a joiner when I had the chance of an apprenticeship.' Housty had been offered an apprenticeship when he was sixteen with his grandfather but for whatever reason, he hadn't taken it. A decision that still rankled with him over twenty years later.

'All in the past now, boys. We are about to start the biggest drugs factory in the country. Narco mutha fukas.' Yorkie made childish gun noise, pretending to fire automatic weapons into the trees.

'I just cannae wait to explore this place, could hardly finish ma chippy I was that excited.' For once in his life, Housty had left some chips on his plate.

'A cannae wait either, Housty, but dinnae lose sight of the goal. We'll have a scout about and then get our new super duper cooking shop planned. Ray will be out soon, we can start supplying him in all.'

Housty was incredulous at Yorkie's suggestion. 'Dinnae be so fucking stupid, Yorkie. If Ravanelli found that out, he would go absolutely radge. You might think you are freelancing but he's got us where he wants us. We blew up his caravan and he kens how to get liquid into the capsules. Anyway, if Ray ever found out we had been helping Ravanelli, while he was inside, he'd give us a right kicking in all. We'd have tae lock ourselves in the bunker to hide from our own, very personal, cold war.' The thought of their betrayal to Ray made Housty shiver.

Yorkie considered this for a moment. 'Aye, you might be spot on, Housty man, no like you, pal. These gangster dudes can be right precious aboot things. Right fucking dramas, man.' Housty and Matt just looked at each other, rolling their eyes. This was prime time Yorkie, understating the obvious.

Arriving at the point where they left the path earlier that day, they then found the hole in the fence. Up ahead, they could see slithers of torch light dancing through the leaves and branches. They followed the light into the woods, through the gap in the fence and caught up with Toto and Baggio in the quarry.

'Now then, now then, no red ribbons or shiny badges, just a 1950s bomb shelter to explore.' Housty was doing a brutal impression of disgraced and thankfully dead, celebrity monster, Jimmy Saville.

'Now is no the time tae remind us of that paedo cunt. This is a happy time, boys. I am fucking buzzing,' Toto replied.

Baggio turned to face them, a huge smile on his handsome, permanently suntanned face. 'Fucking buzzing,' he confirmed.

'Right, let's get to work.' Toto clapped his hands together, disappearing around the side of the building. The others followed and they began quietly removing the branches. Instead of hammering the last layer of bricks out, Toto put the head of the hammer on them and leant on it, forcing the bricks out one by one. The remaining ones were now loose enough just to remove by hand. He did this, throwing them into the undergrowth, where they landed silently.

Turning to the expectant faces, 'That's us in, boys,' he announced triumphantly. There then followed a fair bit of handshaking and back slapping as the five hyped up friends celebrated their success.

Matt had brought two larger camping torches that he now took out his rucksack. He leaned in the access hole, lighting up the corridor. 'This place looks the fucking business. The airs still pretty rank though.'

212

'Aye, I noticed that,' Toto agreed. 'Give it a couple of minutes, this hole's big enough to ventilate the place quickly.'

'Big enough,' a very happy and clearly elated Baggio confirmed.

'That'll be shining bright, there's no danger I am waiting. We're pioneers, boys. Tally ho.' Yorkie nudged himself past Toto and Matt and peered in. He lifted his leg through the gap and climbed in singing Kylie. 'All you can do is step back in time.'

'Fuck it,' Housty said. Taking the big torch from Matt and handing it to Yorkie. He too climbed in, followed not so reluctantly, by the rest of them.

The corridor led in one direction to the huge steel blast doors that they had seen and inspected that afternoon in the quarry. The other way took you on a gradual slope down to another set of thick steel, double doors. The corridor was painted in grey standard MOD battleship paint on the lower wall and white above. It was dotted with substantial wooden internal doors that were painted in the same neutral colours. Above them, the ceiling of the corridor was lined with so many pipes of varying thickness that at some crowded points it looked like huge matted bits of spaghetti. Now they were inside, any background noise from the city had vanished. The bunker had consumed them. It was deathly quiet, absolutely silent. None of them had gone far, they just milled around, taking their new surroundings in. The corridor was more like a tunnel, big enough for a small van to drive in. Moving towards the lower steel doors, Matt and Toto forced them open using the naval style door handles. Everything from switches, to door handles, to the doors themselves was on a grand scale. Matt shined one of the powerful torch beams through the gap in the doors.

'It looks like the London underground, man. Creepy as fuck, gadgies.'

A circular tunnel descended into the darkness, the air smelt seriously damp. Each took turns staring into the gloom before they decided to explore the upper section, giving time for some fresh air to circulate below. No one had spoken much, all of them were mesmerised by their new surroundings. Toto took the lead opening the door nearest to them. It took them into a small dorm with six metal bunk beds. Each had a thin mattress with a pillow and a rolled up grey, itchy looking blanket. The next door took them into a similar room, everything was untouched and sterile. The following door opened into a standard sized corridor, again with more doorways. They spent about an hour trawling through the upper floor, finding food stores, offices, toilets and some bigger plant rooms. These contained what looked like generators, water and air purifiers and general large industrial units that no one could fathom. Matt and Housty were looking for fuse boxes and anything that resembled a power source. The other three were raking around in the cupboards, filing cabinets and desks for anything of value. It appeared the saying, 'old habits die hard,' was appropriate in this instance.

Having exhausted the whole floor, Matt shepherded them towards the main tunnel again. On arrival at the colossal steel doors, he was pleased to note that the air smelled considerably fresher, although it was much colder here. The others must have also felt it to as they were zipping up their jackets. Housty helped Matt wrench one of the doors wide open. They high fived each other before they began their descent into what looked like the abyss. Masses of cabling, wiring and piping were held in metal cages above their heads. Further blast doors were at the far end of the tunnel. These opened into a staircase that appeared to be three or four stories deep.

'We really need to find the power in here,' Matt said, leaning over the banisters looking down. 'This place is fucking massive.'

'Aye, you've still never said what you want the place for,' Toto mentioned.

'It's a long story, bud. You'll no believe it when we tell you,' Matt replied. He had no problem letting them know, as he trusted them implicitly, but before going into what would no doubt be a long conversation, he wanted to get the power going and recce the place properly.

'Aye right, if this daft cunt is involved, al believe anything.' Toto had his arm round Yorkie laughing.

'Cheeky cunt,' a chuffed looking Yorkie responded.

Deciding to split up, Housty, Toto and Baggio chose to head down the stairs in search of a power supply, whilst Matt and Yorkie ventured through a doorway into another similar corridor to the ones above. They were now in the heart of the bunker. Large, green, boxy ventilation pipes were overhead. These would have ensured, the chosen lucky few residents, survived long enough once the big red Soviet button had been pushed. Going on recent conflicts, the British would be in as much danger from their so called allies, the Yanks, hitting their own button. The Americans loved a bit of so called friendly fire.

'This place is a fucking labyrinth, man,' Matt whispered to Yorkie.

'What the fuck are you whispering for? We're one hundred metres under the ground, ya radge.'

'Aye, I ken, but this place gives me the serious heebie jeebies.'

'I know what you mean.' As if to illustrate this, Yorkie moved closer to Matt. The constant shadows from the moving torches were jumping out at them, adding to their frayed nerves.

They had found toilets, dorms, a large kitchen and dining area and were now in what resembled an office. It had ridiculously thick glass windows that looked down into the impenetrable darkness. Their torches weren't powerful enough to illuminate what appeared to be an impressive room below. At the same time Housty had found a room full of very dated electrical equipment. Oversized fuse boxes covered the walls, all intricately detailing the purpose of each switch. Eventually Housty found what looked like the master switch, a two pronged metal lever. Toto and Baggio recoiled as he forced it into the on position.

Lights in the room flickered on instantly, at the same time a humming sound slowly began to build from an adjacent room. All three panicked, close to doing a runner, until realising it was the bunkers creaking ventilation system gurgling into life. Matt and Yorkie heard the noise where they stood but neither were tempted to run as the room they were peering into simultaneously burst into view as numerous bright light bulbs were supplied with long awaited power.

'Fuck.... In..... hell, man,' Matt muttered to himself.

'Ho lee fuck,' was Yorkie's response.

The room was hexagonal, they were on the top floor. Below were two other levels, with similar glass fronted offices, encircling the ground floor which contained two large map tables of the British Isles. All the offices contained desks and phones. This was to be the central control for Britain if nuclear war hit. The vision in front of them was staggering and one not enjoyed by human eyes for decades.

'Wow, man, just fucking wow. I've heard of places like this when I was in the army but never seen one so untouched. This should be a fucking museum.'

'Smart as fuck, man.' Yorkie was looking down but also surveying his surroundings. 'What's a piano doing in that room over there?' He pointed to one of the other offices they had a view into. A wooden object the same size as an upright piano was against one of the walls

'That's no a piano, ya radge, it's an ancient phone exchange. You can see the wires and receivers.'

'Aye, right enough,' Yorkie was laughing. 'I thought they could play the death march to everyone if things got really bad. Da da dada da da dada.' Yorkie danced about pretending to play the piano.

Matt turned sharply when he spotted movement below. Housty and the boys had entered the room, all looking equally as impressed as

Matt and Yorkie had moments before. With all the excitement, Baggio looked to have escaped Toto's shadow. He was moon walking back and forward in delight. This place was immense, every time they looked in a different direction, they spotted something they hadn't noticed. Clocks showed the time in different parts of the world, all had long since stopped. Signs littered the walls and small models were on the tables that indicated targets and defensive positions on the solid, three dimensional table maps.

Matt and Yorkie made their way down to join the others on the lowest floor.

'Check it out, lads,' Yorkie said, pointing at the clocks on the wall. 'We are going international ya cunts, in fact, fucking continental with a gang hut like this.'

'What a fucking place, boys,' Housty said, giving both of them a big hug. 'This is where we will cook. Smart as fuck.'

'Cook?' Toto enquired. He was a sharp boy. 'I'm intrigued what are you three up tae? I think you can tell us now.'

Between the three of them an explanation was provided that left out some detail. Mainly Ravanelli's involvement and the possible cash rewards. They needn't have worried.

'I like it lads, I reckon this place is perfect for your needs. Glad tae have been of service. It was nice tae feel the auld excitement of breaking and entering. Cannae beat it, the natural high oaf adrenalin from illegal activities.' Toto performed a sweeping bow to them.

'Glad to have been of service,' Baggio repeated, smiling and also bowing theatrically.

'Look lads, we'll sort yous out. You've been barry like, an it's been great tae catch up. Like the old Salvy days. We were thinkin of rewardin you with a nice bag eh ching?' Yorkie could tell by Toto's expression he wasn't interested so tied again, 'Or some cash, boys?'

Toto smiled warmly at Yorkie, like a father or older brother would. 'Na man, we dinnae get high oan drugs anymore. No need. Just no need. Take thae new raves at the show ground at Ingliston for example. We went along tae one to check out what the kids were up tae. They are not raves, no fucking way. They are packaged nights out for wee birds dressed in nowt, wi daft luminous make up oan and young blokes that just look out oh their fucking depth. No one dares let loose now coz theres always some cunt wi a phone recordin you tae take the piss oan Instagram, I mean, what even is that? When we were leavin there were some birds headin tae McDonalds for a scran. I mean, for fucks sakes, when we went raving you didnae eat for a day afterwards. Oor stomachs were more shrivelled up than Jimmy Saville's boz after a night in the kids' loony bin. The cunt.' Toto spat the last few words out in revulsion. 'These folk are rave tourists. They want tae be us. Fucking us!' He points at his chest, in full flow now. 'They cannae be, coz we are a one off generation. My ma always asked wit happened tae us aw. We won that's whit a tell her. She thinks we're aw bonkers. Folk take drugs tae feel good. We already feel good coz we fucking cracked it. We dinnae need drugs now an defo dinnae need money. We are sorted.' Toto smiling, put his arm around the much taller Baggio's shoulder.

'Aye, sorted,' a beaming Baggio repeated.

'So na, man, keep the ching, but do yourself a favour and chuck it down the bog. We made it, pal. The ravers an headcases of our generation are this generation's idols. We were happy tae help youz, we would have chummed you into hell if you had asked. We were always there for each other, oan the pitch wi Salvy or up to no good, like in Cardiff that time. We stuck the gither. Not one of us said a word to the bizzies. Mind when we played, the three of us just knew where the others were? You would hear Scott, the coach.' He looked at Matt and Housty so they would know who Scott was. 'He would be shouting, look up, look up, but we didnae need tae. We just knew where each other would be. Instinctive man. We're tuned tae the same frequency. It was beautiful, man, telepathic. No one could touch us.'

Yorkie had a tear in his eye, he had forgotten just how close the three of them had been. It was a long time ago now, but Toto's emotional speech had brought it back, great memories of a time when life was simpler. The football they played together had been mesmerizing. He was afraid to answer back in case his voice cracked.

Baggio must have sensed this as he stepped forward and hugged him, whispering in his ear, so only Yorkie would hear. 'We love you brother, always have, always will.'

Toto was next with a massive grin on his face. 'Come here ya big sap.' He also grabbed him. 'We love you brother.' Maybe, they really did know what each other was thinking and saying.

After Matt and Housty had given the lads a hug to thank them, the group wandered round the bunker checking out every corner. They reminisced about old times and old friends, some no longer around and others that should have been gone but were still ripping it up. Parties and fights. Tears and raucous laughter. Who said youth was wasted on the young? They hadn't wasted a minute.

During the wander they found impressive concrete ventilation shafts rising high above their heads, in another large tube shaped tunnel, at the bunkers lowest level. It eventually took them to a set of double blast doors that exited into yet another quarry, this one at the bottom of the hill next to Queensferry Road. A possible escape route if ever required. The bomb shelter was unreal and perfect for their requirements. Above all, for the moment at least, this cold war relic was theirs.

Chapter 24

Renovations

After thanking Toto and Baggio again, they said goodbye as the pair of them walked through the upper blast doors. It was now almost daylight. Their time underneath the ground had flown by. The boys locked the blast doors. In front of them was the building's only weakness. One they had engineered themselves.

'What kind of idiot would spend time building this monstrosity and leave a hole in the wall like that?' Housty asked, laughing and beginning to pick up the few scattered bricks that had fallen into the corridor.

'Typical British workmanship,' Matt answered, smiling.

'It's this slap dash approach that gives the decent British tradesman a bad name,' Yorkie agreed.

They spent the following hour planning their next moves. Just the sight of the place had reinvigorated Housty and Matt. Both were well on board now with Yorkie's plans. By the time the three of them got their heads down in one of the bunk rooms, a plan of action had been agreed. It wasn't worth them heading home as Matt was meeting with Big Andy in a couple of hours to retrieve the bottles of The Damage from the barracks. All of them were reluctant to leave their new found premises unsecured. Yorkie was going to tag along with Matt and Big Andy. Therefore, in their absence, Housty had been set the task of bricking up the outer wall. In the long distant past, when Housty had left college, he had laid patios so was the closest to a brickie they had. Yorkie's task was to acquire what was required to cook on an outrageously bigger scale. He was to be dropped off at an industrial kitchen supplier on the outskirts of the city. He planned on buying the biggest pressure cookers they stocked and would then wait for the lads to pick him up on their way back into Edinburgh. All three had been nervous about Big Andy finding out about the bunker, but it was a case of needs must. He had the van that could accommodate the equipment required. Going on past events, Ravanelli would have him spying on them anyway, so at least this way they saved their friend that task.

Big Andy picked the two of them up in the car park, a couple of hours later, as agreed. As always, he was bang on time. This meant it was down to Housty to guard the bunker. They would pick up some sand and cement on their travels. Housty had been uneasy about staying in the bunker alone but was so fascinated with the place that the initial nerves soon faded. It was an immense structure and in the hours that followed, he methodically explored its workings. Housty had been enthralled with military history from a young age. This probably stemmed from childhood visits to various historic battle sites and castles. Both his male grandparents had served in World War II which had fuelled an interest in more recent conflicts, the cold war being one of them. For him, this was like having the best, most accurate, personal museum to explore.

Big Andy was not his usual self, although prompt as always. The well polished cunto greeting was non existent. He just nodded at the lads and aggressively smoked as they jumped in. His mood seemed to rub off on the others as they all settled in quietly to their own thoughts. Matt and Yorkie were now feeling the exertions of the previous twenty four hours, coupled with little sleep. As if god himself had realised this, Yorkie felt something drop onto his lap. Looking down, he saw a large bag of white powder. He picked it up and examined it, looking at Matt who was also looking at it. Both were confused and turned towards Big Andy looking for an explanation.

'That's the ching ye asked for. Mind, fae Ravanelli?' Big Andy hadn't even turned round. 'He says it's oan the house, just dinnae fuck things up again was the general message.'

A large smile spread across Yorkie's face and, as if he also had control of Matt's features, a huge grin emerged from his too. This was meant to be payment to Toto and Baggio and the soldiers. It turned out that Toto and Baggio's share was now going spare. Yorkie already had his phone out, passing it to Matt to hold.

'Am tired so time tae get wired,' he said, beaming at Matt.

'Aye, count me in, I'm shattered. Would be rude not to.' This was just the tonic Matt needed. He was not that kid who had once stayed up all night digging trenches anymore, the previous night had been fun but exhausting.

'Me in all, cunto,' Big Andy demanded, rather than asked.

Matt and Yorkie glanced at each other and then turned to Big Andy. 'What the fuck man? Av only seen ye smoke some turf wi me. What ye oan aboot?' Yorkie asked. He was taken aback by this request, his big pal had never shown any interest in anything stronger than a joint and a pint.

'Long story, cunto. Let's just say am under some pressure the now, right,' he snapped.

Raising his eyebrows to Matt, who shrugged, Yorkie chopped out three chunky lines on the phone screen Matt held out. Rolling a note, he hoovered his share up like the professional he was. Holding the phone for Matt, he did the same. They both settled back to enjoy the excellent gear seeping into their veins.

'Fuck me, the silver fox gets some barry gear, man' a wired Yorkie acknowledged.

'Geez some, fucking now!' barked Big Andy.

'Steady on man, easy tiger. A wiz waitin til we fucking stopped. You're doing eighty along the fucking bypass, heed the baw.' Yorkie was beginning to worry, this was totally out of character.

222

Soon, they had Yorkie and some enormous cooking pots in the van. Some more east coast main lines were consumed which appeared to improve Big Andy's fragile mood, to an extent. Matt and Yorkie were melted by the time they strolled into B&Q for sand and cement. Yorkie's Iggy pop knee replacement walk, was exaggerated by his cocaine intake, as he robotically wandered around the massive DIY store looking lost.

'Check the state of your walk, man. You look like you are being electrocuted.' Matt was pointing, laughing now.

'Shut it you, it's ma dodgy hips fae too much football.'

'Aye right, too much bad living more like. Your brain's wiring has gone wrong.'

'Stoap talkin pish and help me with the cement. You're the one wi the fucking muscles.'

Loading the stuff back into the van they could hear, Big Andy on the phone.

'Dinnae threaten me, cunto. Your no Ray, you are his fucking performing monkey. Fuck off.' He then ended the call with a further string of expletives.

'Am going to batter that CCCCUUUUUNNNNNTTTTTT.' Big Andy screamed as he thumped the steering wheel and door. 'Thinks he's the fucking man coz he works wi Ray but he's fuck all.' A couple of women walking past the van with their rolls of new wallpaper looked so frightened they started breaking into a run.

Matt raised his eyebrows at Yorkie whispering, 'He's losing it big time. Dinnae give him anymore ching.'

They both knew Harvey was a cunt but he was a big, dangerous, conniving cunt. Neither of them would have fancied a square go, but that went for Big Andy too. If the truth be told, it was a fight, they would pay money to watch. A definite heavyweight contest. Unfortunately, the new no ching for Big Andy agreement did not last long. He was still muttering about Harvey when he pretty much demanded more of the drug before he would leave the B&Q car park. So in full view of the passing public, Big Andy had his nose in it again. Obviously Yorkie felt duty bound to join him. Soon, they were driving back towards Blercrae Hill and their very own bomb shelter. The drugs removed any awareness of risk from Big Andy as despite repeated warnings, he drove the van right up to the main entrance gates of the perimeter fence, in full view of a group of well to do joggers. Thankfully, they appeared to be too busy discussing something dull, like a school PTA meeting or the dire goings on in Downton Abbey, to take any notice of three bams in a white van.

During the morning, Housty had found a neatly labelled key box in one of the store rooms. He was there to meet them at the gates as agreed during a warning call from Matt. Opening them quickly, Big Andy drove in, right up to the open bunker door. Housty had also discovered a key for one of the single steel doors which meant they could now leave the bunker secure when it wasn't time to cook.

It was obvious to Housty immediately, that Big Andy was not his usual, matter of fact, jovial self. He did help empty the van and showed some interest in the bomb shelter but his clear objective was to sniff and smoke his way through the day. When he did disappear into the depths of the bunker, his path was easily followed by the smell of smoke. He would emerge from one of the many doorways looking for a hit. On most occasions, Yorkie would have joined him, not today though, there was work to do. Housty began rebuilding the outer wall as Matt and Yorkie transferred the equipment into the kitchen area situated centrally in the bunker. Amazingly, the antique heating elements still worked.

'Things were built to last years ago. Not like now, where they are designed to break.'

'Aye, nae fucking expense spared on these dignitaries while the likes of you an me were toasted by Ivan. Cunts.' Yorkie certainly had a way with words.

'Nothing changes, mate. We are still their cannon fodder. I know that only too well.'

'A kin just imagine aw they big wigs hanging aboot here, havin a brandy an a cigar an a big posh line, laughing heartily about how they survived the nuclear holocaust but wee Daz, Maz and Baz fae the cooncil scheme were obliterated. Wankers, man.'

'You ever thought of becoming a politician, Yorkie. The people's poet. The voice of the underground.' Matt was enjoying himself now.

'Aye, that'll be shining bright. Every one of they cunts is a prize, lying arsehole.' Matt couldn't have put it better himself.

With the 1950s kitchen now set up to cook the world's newest and arguably best designer drug, the two of them set out to find Big Andy and then check on Housty's progress. Big Andy was puffing away furiously on a cigarette, looking over the map table in the hexagonal glass room.

'Av done deliveries all over the shop. Here, here, here, even fucking here cunto. Ah always deliver.'

If Big Andy's rantings were correct, and there was no reason to doubt them, Ravanelli or Ray's influence spread further than the boys thought. It wasn't a good idea to question him too much in his rubber man state. At least he had stopped asking repeatedly for more cocaine. He must have been getting close to an overdose, especially considering he didn't normally indulge. They managed to coax him up through the bunker to the corridor where they had first entered early that morning. It was strange to think that not even a day had passed. The place was like a time capsule. Housty was squeezing the last brick in from the outside when he spotted them.

'Just about done, boys. Just this last brick and a bit of pointing to sort. Am starving, lets get a scran after this.'

Matt and Yorkie were not going to argue, it was ages since they had eaten. The look of revulsion on Big Andy's face, suggested that he may not be joining them, which was understandable after his class A consumption that day. Housty completed the wall and after some final rough, external cement work, it was passable.

'It'll no survive a frontal assault by a ned's size ten but no a bad job, Housty,' Yorkie said, whilst running his hands along the repaired wall.

It wasn't like Yorkie to issue compliments so Housty was pleased to hear his verging on kind words. 'Pretty fucking pleased with that. Scran time,' he said, clapping his hands together.

It seemed strange locking the bunker and leaving it unguarded. It was their pad now. Big Andy agreed to drop them at a local curry house that doubled up as a boozer. The Spice Lounge was formerly the legendary pub, 'The Rainbow'. Situated in the west of Edinburgh around ten minutes walk from Blercrae. At its height, it was fondly known as the Rambo due to the locals' love of a fight. Saturday was fight night. In the old days Housty would sometimes head down at closing time just to witness the almost guaranteed brawl. The pub's days were threatened as police became aware that it was doing a roaring trade in not only beer and spirits, but also Peruvian marching powder and other mind altering drugs. As trouble heightened and its reputation spread, the pub began to lose customers and its owners, like Selkirk FC, lost goals. It was left empty for years as rumours circled it would be demolished for the predictable construction of more cheap flats. Cheaply built anyway. An unlikely local man bought and opened the Scottish drinker's utopia. A boozer that sold curries. The Spice Lounge was born and is now firmly settled as a great restaurant and even greater pub, run by the best bunch of Indians you could meet. The lads ordered after exchanging some chat with the drinkers and owners. Choosing to sit far enough away from earshot they enjoyed their food and a couple of drinks. All three were struggling to keep their eyes open. It had been a while since any of them had had proper sleep. It wasn't long before they left, jumping in a cab straight home. It was Housty who once again got the pleasure of Yorkie's company. By this time, he was too tired to argue or care, the lager and spicy food combining to create an effect like a powerful sleeping pill.

The following day they met at the bunker to sort out the last obstacles standing in the way of them starting to cook. With the loss of The Anchor's reliable urine supply, the boys were forced once again to find a new source. This was more straightforward than they could have imagined. Yorkie had remained at the bomb shelter while Housty and Matt called in on Jacks the plumber, their former source and good friend. He was now spending his days drinking warm cans of lager in what he called, the gang hut. It turned out his gang hut was in fact a drinking den, used by the numerous drunks in Blercrae to escape the wrath of their families, during what should have been the working day. The gang hut was an abandoned house in the centre of Blercrae that the council appeared to have forgotten about temporarily. The lads managed to negotiate an acceptable deal for both sides without any difficulty. Jacks would encourage his friends to fill the large containers provided with their grade one urine, while in return the lads would supply the gang hut with a huge carry out. Where one problem was solved another potential issue arose. They would have to be purchasing huge amounts of booze weekly which would theoretically raise suspicions. Along with numerous bottles of vodka required for the planned boost in The Damage production, they had now agreed to supply Jacks and his pals with vast quantities of warm lager. This resulted in a tour of the supermarkets in the west of Edinburgh once a week. Buying a relatively small amount in each appeared to be the solution. During one of these tedious shopping trips, the lads noticed a couple ahead of them in the queue with two shopping trolleys full of various types of alcohol. The checkout assistant did not even blink as bottle after bottle of spirit went through the till. From then on the number of shops visited was reduced and the amount bought in each increased. Drinking was Scotland's national sport after all, what had they been worrying about?

All arrangements were now in place. All they needed to do was wait a couple of days for Jacks and his pickled pals to produce enough potent urine and it was all systems go. He was as good as his guaranteed word. The bunker proved to be the perfect cooking shop. It became like a second home over the next few weeks or in Yorkie's case a first home. He loved the place. One of the bunk rooms was now unofficially his. Clothes, trainers and various other personal possessions were scattered across the spare bunks. He had been making late night visits back to the house to shower and change and of course enjoy the energetic straight laced company of C-o-l-i-n. He was pleased to see skag hag had been looking after old red barnacle nose. In fact, although C-o-l-i-n showed glimpses of being glad to see him, he also made it clear he preferred skag hag's bed side manner. His new carer had fitted in very well.

'Dinnae think you're sneaking back here, ya Hibs pleb. Am in love an am no wantin you ruining it. Hertz rule this hoose.' C-o-l-i-n usually began one of his grandson's clandestine visits by making it clear he preferred a Yorkie free house. In a jovial way, of course.

'Ye cannae be in love wi skag hag, ya bam, she's spoken for.'

'No she's no, she's a free spirit just like C-o-l-i-n,' his grandfather replied, pointing at his chest which sported a clean Slazenger polo shirt. Yorkie wasn't sure if this was her doing or C-o-l-i-n finally making an effort to tidy himself up.

'Free, free?' Yorkie started creasing at this and continued. 'She's no free, ya old plum. It'll be twenty smackers a blow job and thirty if you want her tae take oot her teeth.' C-o-l-i-n was not amused at this slur on his new loves character.

As much as Yorkie enjoyed the abusive friendly jousting with the old man, he was always glad to get back to the solitude and safety of the bunker. It almost felt like home. He had brought Smokey to the bunker for company, but the cat kept appearing out of ventilation pipes scaring the shit out of Yorkie. He just couldn't settle, so he was returned to enjoy sleeping on top of C-o-l-i-n once again.

Some mornings in the half light, Yorkie would emerge and walk over Blercrae Hill through the woods to the benches at the Rest and Be Thankful. A place made famous by its mention in Robert Louis Stevenson's epic novel, Kidnapped. It was here that David Balfour and Alan Breck had parted company. In fact, a few streets in Blercrae were named after the rascal of a Highlander, Alan Breck. Yorkie would sit and smoke in the peace and quiet of the woods, the only noise being the nearby animals of the zoo awakening. The shadow of the city spread out in front of him. The prominent seven hills of Edinburgh, formed by cooling volcanic discharge 400 million years ago, were partially visible in the early morning light. Yorkie knew from chats with C-o-l-i-n many years ago, that there were other hills in the city that were now hidden by the towering old town tenements. These hills' names had been lost to most but not C-o-l-i-n who had passed on their ancient names to him many years ago and thankfully, for once, Yorkie must have been concentrating. Even now he can remember their names; Multrees, Bunkers, St Johns, St Leonards and Heriot Hills. The city's earliest tenements surrounded them whilst bridges connected them. These bridges' arches could now only be seen in a few places, like in the lower streets of the old Cowgate. The damp dark vaults of the bridges once providing homes for the city's poorest residents. Further away in Leith, the green steel struts of Easter Road stadium came into his sight and beyond, Berwick Law, Traprain Law and the Bass Rock. A sight that made him shiver given his recent proximity to the white looming rock. It was in this spot that a long lost uncles's ashes had been scattered. Yorkie would look back on his childhood memories with his uncle who had been only a few years older than him. It was kind of because of his him that Yorkie, Matt and Housty had become close friends. His uncle had taken him to a church hall in nearby Corstorphine one Friday night to his first and still his best rave. The church had rented the hall being convinced by a local DJ it was for an innocent teenage disco. This couldn't have been further from the truth. The rave had been an eye opener for all who attended, including Matt and Housty. They had been present when another local lad had grabbed Yorkie around the neck, dragging him outside at an opportune moment when his uncle wasn't there to protect him. Yorkie was due the lad money for hash but his finances back then had been as chaotic as they were in his adult life so he had been unable to meet his obligations. Luckily for Yorkie, Matt and Housty had witnessed his forced exit and followed them out. They weren't close pals back then but knew each other well enough from Blercrae. Everyone knew everyone back then. Yorkie had got them into trouble as kids many years previously by encouraging them to play the trick with mentos and coke in their local shop. Matt had grabbed the lad's right fist and held it tight just before it started its assault on Yorkie's chalk white panicked face. The lad was a known wannabe hard man and hadn't taken the intervention well. 'What the fuck are you sticking up for this fucking waster for? He's a fucking bam.' Matt's response had been along the lines of, 'Aye he's a bam but he's our fucking bam.' This had made Housty start laughing at the same time Matt had planted his wide forehead on the bridge of Yorkie's attacker's nose. Yorkie's uncle had emerged from the heat of the church hall to finish the job Matt had started, sending the wannabe hard man home to think again. The rave was ending so the four had headed back to Yorkie's house to smoke their come down into oblivion and cement a friendship that would last forever.

The boys were now cooking as much as their supplies would allow. Ravanelli was more than delighted to buy whatever quantities of The Damage that was available. Big Andy for his part had calmed down in the following weeks and appeared to have got over his earlier episode. For the first time in a while, everything was going swimmingly but in this caper it just couldn't last.

Chapter 25

Out

Edinburgh's Saughton prison dominates a large site to the west of the city centre, not far from Ray's spiritual home of Blercrae. He could see the hill from his small foot square window in solitary confinement. In fact, he had spent more time being moved around her majesty's dwellings than he had spent in Blercrae, although his shadow had remained during his incarceration. Not that he had ever been a bully to the residents, in fact his presence had helped the area by warning off others who may have ordinarily fancied taking over.

Anyway, it was time to put it all behind him because today was the day he was getting out. As the long process of actually being physically released stumbled on, Ray's thoughts wandered to his youth and the misdemeanours that had paved the way to all the wasted years. To be fair, he mused, he had been a bit of a rascal but in a more serious moment he decided never to return to prison. He would take a step back, let his cohorts run things. They had done a decent job for him while he'd been away. Although, he was under no illusions that they would have been taking bigger cuts than he would have liked but it was only natural. He had done the same to his predecessor after all.

Ray faced a new challenge on his release, one he hadn't seen coming. During his reign, supplying Edinburgh and the Lothians as well as the Kingdom of Fife with narcotics, he had only had to deal with great pretenders going up against his authority. Never had he planned for, or expected, that the dynamics of his trade would change so hugely that the bottom would fall out of all the markets that he ruled. No longer were people wanting his relatively uncut party bags or in some cases, suitcases. There was a new hit in town. What perplexed

Ray was no one that had been leaned on, or in one case chucked of a relatively high quarry cliff in the Pentland Hills, had any idea who was supplying this orange liquid that was so sought after by the locals and increasingly, not so local, consumers.

Most of the screws were class A dick heads so Ray was chuffed to see it was a local lad standing in front of him. Chris, who was going to process the final stages of his release, knew Ray relatively well. They both nodded at each other. Neither up for conversation and both keen for differing reasons to get things finalised. All paper work signed and personal belongs returned, Chris extended his right arm towards Ray and wished him good luck. Unlike most of the others, he meant it. Ray considered leaving him hanging but only for a second. Gripping his hand tightly, 'Same to you, pal. Next time I see you I might even buy you a beer.' They both lived in the same area of the city, a fact they had established during one of their infrequent conversations.

'You never know, all the best. Oh and Ray, dinnae come back.' Chris winked at him and turned to get on with another day in the violent unpredictable bams' Butlins.

A thick cover of thin, wispy rain and cloud comforted him as he left the prison compound. He could see the old black sovereign jaguar waiting. It was as far from the prison door as possible without being parked illegally on the dual carriageway. Harvey, his driver, just didn't want to go near the place. He had also wasted time in prison and just being close to the entrance gave him the fear. Ray knew this and enjoyed the walk down towards the car, the fresh rain washing the smell of prison from his nostrils. As he opened the car door, he glanced back towards his former lodgings pleased to see the mist surrounding and suffocating that horrible monument of despair.

'Alright, gaffer?' Harvey said as he turned his huge head towards Ray. Smiling, showing a not so fine set of damaged and rotting nashers.

'Harvey, take me home, bud. I want to wash and get out of these fucking clothes, pronto.'

Harvey, a more dangerous version of Pluto from Popeye was a bit hurt by the lack of emotion Ray showed him. They had been together since childhood and Harvey had always been loyal, not through fear as was the way with some but because they were pals.

'Oh and Harvey,' Ray said, turning towards him and switching off the shite radio channel. 'It's fucking great to see you, brother.' He grabbed the big man's head and cuddled him while ruffling his thinning hair. They both laughed, settling into each other's company again.

'Let's get you away from here, pal' Harvey said, as he floored the big cars 3.2 litre engine, all four wheels gripping the road sending gravel from the prisons crumbling car park flying towards its walls in a final fuck you.

Harvey could tell Ray was impatient to get home so broke as many rules of the highway code he could, to speed up his return. Something he would never usually do as he hated drawing unnecessary attention to himself. As they neared Blercrae, Ray became calmer until he asked his friend to go slower so he could enjoy the moment he had dreamed of for so long. Eventually arriving at his home after causing an almighty tailback as Harvey had slowed to a snail's pace as instructed. Harvey opened the door letting Ray step through first and handing him back his keys now that his stint as caretaker had finished. He was delighted to be able return to his family home and ensure his fucking head case of a wife was not spending his ill-gotten gains as quickly as he could earn them. There was delivery drivers turning up at the house throughout the day, like formula one cars going into the pits. They were delivering all manner of designer, ill-fitting shite for her and his vast squad of kids. In fact, maybe he'd ask Ray if he could have one of the spare rooms as he had begun to enjoy the peace that the bachelor life had afforded him.

Thrilled to be back in Blercrae and even more so in his own house, Ray took a long shower, savouring every moment of the prison being washed down the plug hole. A plug hole full of Harvey's mangrove like pubes. In fact, looking around he decided to get professional cleaners in, the place was a frigging tip. He wasn't used to all this clutter and mess. Once dry he headed through to his room, pleased to note unlike the rest of the house it looked untouched by Harvey. Choosing a pair of jeans and a smart shirt, Ray was chuffed to see they still fitted. He had a big frame but had never had issues with his weight. It had remained constant throughout his turbulent life. God knows how his hair hadn't fallen out either. It had greyed at the sides and apart from a bit of receding, was in good nick. Adidas Sambas and Barbour jacket finished off his look. He hadn't realised that in his time away, Barbour jackets had dropped out of fashion but had become trendy again. Without putting the Sambas on, he headed back down the stairs and looked around. Aye, the place was honking, Harvey may like living in a pig sty, but no danger was he going to. A few calls later to announce his return to some associates, he headed out for a stroll with the intention of passing one of his old drinking haunts. Apparently, it now doubled up as a restaurant which was handy, he was starving. In the excitement of the day, his breakfast had remained untouched but now his appetite was back. His empty stomach making itself known to him by growling away.

There are few downsides to a boozer that sells curry but there was one for this particular establishment. It attracted some old faces, some visited out of curiosity and others because their options were limited due to their behaviour after a few light refreshments. This meant that there was an eclectic mix of clientele, most of whom would be completely oblivious to one particular drinker sitting by himself at the bar. Although he had his back to the door, his eyes were heavily focused on it using the mirror behind the bar. In Ray's position, it paid to stay focused. He still had enemies, some employed by the government, who would love to see him locked up again and some others who were intimately more dangerous. The type that didn't bother waiting on a jury to settle a man's fate. Ray sipped at his pint while noticing some familiar faces entered through the double doors of the curry bar. He hadn't seen Housty, Yorkie and Matt in a long time but he recognised them instantly. He smiled to himself, Yorkie's weird robotic movements were hard to miss, even after fourteen years.

The lads grabbed the table in front of the TV no doubt wanting to watch whatever dross, unatmospheric English football Sky television had paid an obscene amount of money for that day.

Yorkie and Matt stayed at the table while Housty headed for the bar, finding a place between a well dressed gentleman, who was a bit worse for wear and Ray. Housty obviously knew the guy as they exchanged some small talk about the weather and how hungover they had been after they last met. As Housty signalled the bar man, he turned catching Ray's penetrating gaze, like a guided missile right into the centre of his brain. He immediately recognised Ray and went to shake his hand. Ray hadn't spent so long in jail without learning about mens' body language and he knew that although on the outside Housty was pleased to see him, he sensed a sniff of worry in Housty's handshake. Ray was sharp, intelligent and a fucking bam which made for a dangerous combination.

'Fuck me, man. How's it going, Ray? Great to fucking see you out, mate. You look well.' Housty was torn inside. He really liked Ray but he knew his emergence from jail was going to have complications for their booming business.

'Good to be out Housty and great to see you an the boys. Mind if I join you for a bit?'

'Aye of course, man. That would be brand new, good to catch up, mate.'

Again Ray sensed hesitancy from Housty but chose to ignore it......for now.

Housty got Ray another pint and the two headed over to hear Yorkie laughing at Matt about something to do with an explosion. Both shut up immediately on seeing they had company and looked visibly worried when they realised it was Ray. It was too late, he had made a connection between his current lack of sales and stories he had heard about some kind of local operation being behind this new substance and the explosions he had read about in the papers. As he turned to face Yorkie, he had a flashback to the photo fit he had seen on the news while cooked up in his cell thinking. Always thinking, always planning. Another connection.

Matt and Yorkie stood almost simultaneously and in turn gave Ray a hug saying how good it was to see him. Both meant it but were also aware that they were encroaching on a dangerous man's livelihood. Ray had asked Yorkie instinctively how C-o-l-i-n was. Ray was another young lad that C-o-l-i-n had tried to steer along the correct path. Although his efforts had obviously failed, Ray wasn't going to allocate any blame to C-o-l-i-n, his situation was entirely down to his decisions.

As he took his seat, Ray's brain was flying. Pieces were falling into place like big wooden chunks from a child's jigsaw. Harvey had told him that Big Andy had been seen with the three friends on a number of occasions. In Blercrae, even the houses have eyes, or so it seemed. No one got away with anything unless they were extremely careful. He had always known about Big Andy's dealings with Bill and didn't mind. A man had to work after all and it hadn't got in the way. Harvey had told him about Big Andy's reaction when he had suggested he should just be working with them. A picture was forming in his brain. Had Big Andy been the connection between these three and Bill? If this was the case, these boys must be making a lot of money for his rival. That could not be allowed to continue. Ray decided to put these thoughts to the back of his head and see what he could learn. Business could wait, he had already ignored lots of calls that day. He just wanted a laugh. The four of them had just that, combined with numerous drinks and food. When Ray had, almost innocently, asked what they had been up to, Yorkie's panicked expression had been the last piece in that child's jigsaw. He saw it clearly now. Their hurried explanations of how busy they were, didn't add up. As far as he could evaluate, they were the busiest unemployed people he knew. Of course, Ray kept quiet, he had no intention of violence. As always, he just wanted in on the action, his cut.

The boys had discussed things the following day while cooking and simultaneously trying to cope with huge hangovers. Deciding that the only solution was to keep low profiles. They continued in the safety of their very own nuclear bunker. It was hard to feel threatened deep underground, cocooned in metres of reinforced concrete. Big Andy didn't have such a shield. His only cover was the three millimetre thick steel of his transit van. Unfortunately for Big Andy, it was proving to be inadequate. Ray's release had meant a step up in work but it was time he could not afford. The Damage was now taking up most of his driving hours and the stress was beginning to tell. He had been coping using some powder he had syphoned off from a few deals. To his knowledge, there had yet to be any complaints and there were unlikely to be any. Not his most professional moment, but needs must. He had an almost constant feeling of being watched which he blamed on tiredness and paranoia from the drugs. This may have been partly to blame but unbeknown to him he was now under heavy surveillance. The Chief had been as good as his word for once, the comment about charging his son no doubt still ringing in his ears. Bryan had arranged for a tracker to be hidden in the van and whilst the overtime budget would allow, a team was now watching Big Andy's every move. Not an easy task, it soon became apparent that Big Andy was a busy boy and took his own precautions to avoid being followed. Blercrae's intertwining streets meant before he set off anywhere important he would have a quick drive around the scheme to determine whether he was being followed. Using this method, he unknowingly lost the police relatively frequently. It was during one of those moments that the surveillance team wasn't on the ground that disaster struck. The van was parked outside Big Andy's house when some opportunistic thieves were driving around searching for tradesmens' vans, to steal tools and equipment from. These lads were not local as no one from Blercrae would have the bottle to steal from Big Andy. He had only left the van for half an hour while getting his tea but this was ample time for the thieves. Although the van was locked, the back doors were forced easily enough. The pilferers were disappointed to find no expensive power tools but the sixty or so bottles of what looked like whisky would do for now. They quickly carried the crates to their van and drove off looking for further possibilities.

Billy and Chaz were not the brightest of human beings. The brothers had had very little help or encouragement of the right kind during their early years. As teenagers, their parents had sent them out every evening to burgle houses. They would take gold and cash and anything that was untraceable. The gold would be melted down to feed their parents vicious drugs habits. Their mode of transport would be the first car they stole that night during a burglary, it was easy taking the keys from the house and driving off into the darkness. Sometimes, they managed this without the inhabitants waking, giving the boys all night to enjoy the luxury motor. If the next Corstorphine suburban villa had a better car in the drive, they would just do a swap. Why not? They needed some enjoyment in their lives, what did they have to lose? Their education was non existent, attending school at eight am was difficult when you weren't home until five am. Their parents had lived out with the normal social system for so long that the boys had been forgotten by school and social services. Both parents succumbed to the inevitable, slow, wasting death. Their demise had begun an upturn of sorts in the boys' lives. Everything is relative after all! No longer were they having to pass all ill gotten gains to their parents. They could now use them as they so wished. The family home had resembled a concentration camp, it was so full of disease and lack of food. The boys had turned the place around so it was now habitable. They had also invested in an ancient semi roadworthy van instead of having to steal transport every evening. The bottom had fallen out of the house breaking business. All the local youths were in on the act and the police were all over it now as it was seriously pissing the middle classes off. Power tools were the new targets. No longer were they required to break into closely guarded houses. Most tradesmen were doing long hours, using very expensive tools and were too exhausted to empty their vans every evening, despite invalidating their insurance. This meant that the boys could drive around after dark emptying hard working peoples' vans. There were so many tradesmen on the look out for tools as they kept getting robbed, that the lads never took long to move them on. Often joking that they were stealing the same tools every second week. There was a high probability that this was the case. Both liked a drink, so although no expensive tools had been wrestled from their owners they did have an old decrepit van stuffed with whisky. On the way home, Billy, the older brother had reached into the back of the van, taking one of the bottles he went to take a drink but sniffed it first.

'Ya cunt, ya fucking cunt. That is honkin. No danger am I drinking that, Chaz. Worst whisky ever, cunty baws.'

'Dinnae talk pish, geez it here, ya wee lassie.'

Billy held it out so Chaz could smell it while driving. 'Fuck me, that geez ais the boak, get it as far as possible tae fuck.'

It was settled quickly that neither were going to drink this particular brand of whisky with the strange childlike writing on the labels. Therefore, there was only one other option open, sell it. The lads had a rule; never go hame without earning so they headed down Ferry Road towards Speirs Bar. It was a distant second uncle that ran the place, he was bound to be interested in some knock off whisky he could poison his fumbling arthritic clientele with. Having phoned ahead, he had agreed to stay behind after closing time to meet them. Luckily, Degs, their uncle twenty times removed, was not bothered about the quality of the product. He took the lot, planning to sell some of it the following day at the Giant Jenga Championships he was hosting and off load the rest to a pal in the trade who ran the masonic club in North Berwick. It wasn't good business to have bootleg grog on the premises for too long. The brewery could take the hump big time and with his previous indiscretions he was on his final, final warning.

Billy and Chaz headed home happy with the measly amount Degs had given them, completely ignorant to the fact that a man in a posh corner of Fife would have paid them thousands.

Chapter 26

The Fall Out – Three things then happened in what is a great example of the ripple effect

1. Fettes

Before Big Andy's stomach could begin digesting the mince and tatties he had shovelled into his thick set face, he had sniffed a not unsubstantial amount of marching powder. This would provide the energy needed for his night's work. He had moved seamlessly from a chain smoker to a chain sniffer. This just couldn't go on he was thinking to himself as he headed down his path to the van. His head was swimming and heart banging away powerfully in his chest as he unlocked the front door and jumped into the driver's seat. Immediately something felt wrong. There was a cold breeze blowing through the van. Panicking, he looked round seeing one of the back doors was lying slightly open. His eyes then fell to the empty van floor. He yanked his door open and charged around the side of the van pulling both doors wide open.

'Yyyyoooouuu ccchhheeeekkkkkyyyy cccccuuuuuuttttttttsssss,' he yelled into the transit, his cries echoing around the empty vehicle. Seething with rage he kicked out at the back of the vehicle, dislodging something from the van that clattered onto the road. Confused, he looked down at the tarmac to see a smallish black metal object that looked like some kind of transmitter. His heart rate reached a dangerous level as it dawned on him what it was. Surely to fuck its no!!! No, dinnae fucking tell me, dinnae, FUCKING DINNAE!!!!! His thoughts were racing through his head. This was his ultimate nightmare. Cunt, cunt, cunt, he thought to himself as he picked it up and examined it thoroughly. His worst fear was realised. He was absolutely certain it was a tracking device. Turning, he slumped into the van, sitting and juggling the metal device from hand to hand. Those blue nosed cunts tracking me, he thought. What had they seen? Where had they followed him to? As more and more possibilities raced into his head, he got more and more worried. The worry soon turned to anger and rage. He knew there was a good chance that him being followed would mean a lot of his customers and suppliers were in danger. The main ones concerning him, being Ravanelli, Ray and the boys. He had been to the bunker so often recently. Calming down slightly, he realised the tracker wasn't that dirty so could only have been on the van a short time. Not all bad news. He heard a car coming into the street and looked up, a standard non descript Ford Mondeo came into view moving slowly. The two men in the front spotted him straight away, making eye contact and then immediately tried to pretend they hadn't.

'Fffffkkkkkkkiiiinnnnggggg bizzies, al show they cunts.' The car had accelerated away as soon as it had passed the van. By the time Big Andy had jumped in the driver seat it had disappeared out of sight.

'Bbbbaaaaasssstttaarrrdddds,' he screamed, whilst fumbling about in his pocket. Taking the wrap of remaining coke out he shoved his nose in it, sniffing as much as possible, before licking what remained. Now tuned to the moon, with a numb mouth and nasal passages, he slammed the van into first gear, spinning the wheels saying to himself determinedly, 'I'll show those cuntos.' His face wearing a demonic smile.

He drove like a competitor in the whacky races towards Edinburgh's Stockbridge. Fettes Police Headquarters were situated just outside the posh Edinburgh district. On Queensferry Road, he hammered it past a patrol car on the wrong side of the carriage way and around a traffic island. Doing close to seventy miles an hour meant the driver of the police car had to floor it to keep Big Andy's transit in sight.

'Catch me if you can, you filthy, nosey, spying cunts,' an ever increasingly manic Big Andy screeched as he slammed his massive fists into his steering wheel. The van's engine was screaming with him as it piled down the road into the outskirts of Stockbridge. The well-built stone tenements rising up on either side looking down sternly as the transit went through a red light and turned left to face the dominating Fettes College. An absolute masterpiece of a building. Its architecture resembled something out of Harry Potter. The school for politicians loomed above the police headquarters. Sirens were now blaring behind Big Andy as he homed in on the entrance to the police station. He drove directly towards the front door reception, only coming to his senses quickly enough to pump the breaks when he saw a woman at the front desk. The van destroyed the reinforced glass as it pulverised the reception area. Thankfully, the PC and member of the public had heard the commotion, along with the van's engine screaming for mercy, so had been able to dive for cover. The force of the impact had slammed Big Andy's body onto the steering wheel while his chunky forehead had cracked the windscreen. As the blood flooded over his face, he wiped his eyes clean and exited the van.

'Fucking track me? You've been tracking me. YA NOSY FILTHY CUUUNNNTTTTTSSSSSS,' he bellowed.

The first policeman to reach him was met with a head-butt that began in Big Andy's feet. The officer's body lifted off the floor and fell limply next to his colleague who ran past him only to be met with a fist that crushed his right cheek bone. He too hit the deck, joining his colleague in the land of nod. By now, there was a number of officers running to meet Big Andy's challenge. He knocked another three to the ground before eventually being overpowered. It took around half an hour to get him in cuffs and safely in a cell. In a further half hour, they had established who he was and were amazed to find out he was meant to be under surveillance. Someone had fucked up.

Bryan Carver was at his desk high up in Fettes headquarters. He was completely oblivious to the carnage that had taken place below him. Of course, he had heard sirens and some noise, but that was common here, there was always a drama taking place. It was Scotland after all, a country full of bams.

'Inspector Carver, Sir?' Hearing his name broke his concentration. Looking up, a dishevelled officer he barely recognised with a stonker of a black eye and a tear in his uniform was standing before him.

Intrigued, Bryan answered. 'What can I do for you, are you all right? That is a cracker you've got there, mate.'

'I believe you have had an Andrew Forest under surveillance, Sir?'

'Yes, aka Big Andy. I have indeed. What have you got for me?'

'We have him downstairs in a cell, Sir. I think he wants a word with you.' Before the PC could continue, Bryan punched the air. He was so pleased he shouted across the office. 'Ya beauty, a breakthrough at last.'

'Aye Sir, it was a break through, alright. He just drove his van through the reception front doors. The place is absolutely fucked. He's sent half the nightshift to A&E.'

Bryan's jaw dropped and remained hanging open as the mildly concussed officer returned to his duties.

2. Giant Jenga

Robert's day started as normal, a couple of well fired rolls with his cup of tea. They didn't taste the same when he made them. His wife Betty had passed away a few years earlier and since then life had seemed pointless. Like he was waiting in line on the platform for a train to take him to meet his maker. Still, you have to take the positives when they come along and today was the Giant Jenga Championships at his local pub, Spiers Bar. The best day in the social calendar. Robert would get down there early to get a front row seat, one as close to the bar as possible, obviously. He always had a few nips in the evening to help him sleep but today would be a good session. Not like the old days when him and his pals would go on all day fishing trips from Dunbar that would end in the last bus back into Edinburgh. Honking of old fish as they hid as many of the decomposing sea creatures, caught that day, as possible under the back seat. The seat was right above the engine bay so the heat would speed up decomposition. On some occasions, one of the lads would get caught short and his pish could be seen winding its way down the bus, mixing with the other passengers' feet and rubbish. Embarrassing to look back on, but a great crack at the time.

Once Robert had washed his breakfast dishes and freshened up, he got dressed, put on his jerkin and cap which balanced just perfectly above his thick black NHS glasses. Right, let's get ready to rumble, he thought to himself, grabbing his keys and what remained of his paltry state pension before heading out with what just about felt like enthusiasm in his stuttering steps.

It was a short walk to the pub from Robert's tenement and one he usually took with ease. Not today though, he attacked the five hundred yards with determination he had not felt in months. After negotiating a busy Ferry Road and passing the usually tempting bookies without a second glance, he pushed open the boozer's double swinging doors to find the party had already begun. One of his longtime friends, Gordon, clocked him straight away and signaled for Robert to join him at the bar.

'Alright, Rob. Big day the day, pal,' Gordon beamed. Gordon like Robert had been waiting for today for weeks.

'You better believe it,' Robert replied, eyeing the bar for his favourite tipple.

'Go easy on the whisky, word is that moanin faced twat, Degs, got his hands on a case for today. He's doing a deal wi his regular clientele i.e. you an me an the boys, tae sell it at a very favourable price to his best customers. In other words, my man, that's you and me getting blootered on the cheap.'

'Fucking dancer, pal,' Robert replied whilst giving him a friendly slap between his old pal's somewhat shrivelled shoulder blades. Aye, that wide unyielding bastard, time, was catching them both up right enough. Was it the Stones that said time waits for no one? Whoever it was, they were bang on he thought.

This cheap whisky talk was like angelic music to Robert's ears. Cash was a bit tight so some cut price, golden nectar was just the ticket. He ordered a half of cider for himself and a half of porters for Gordon.

They both stood relaxing at the bar, discussing the usual trauma Hibs put their fans through on a weekly basis whilst surveying the occupants of the boozer. They could see the Judge from their vantage point arguing with Table For Two about how he had set up the jenga for the first round. The Judge was a well to do gentleman and long time patron of Spiers Bar. With his long beige overcoat, shirt, brogues and white swept back hair, he had an air of pub royalty about him. This had meant he was quickly elevated to a position of trust in the pub's giant jenga community. He had earned himself the name, the Judge, as he had the final say on any disputes which would invariably become more frequent throughout the day as more and more ale was drunk. Table For Two was a man of Gordon and Robert's age, who had lost his wife around a similar time to Robert. He insisted on carrying an

A3 portrait of his Doreen everywhere he went to the extent that he required two seats in the local café or pub. Unbeknown to him, this had meant his pals and social acquaintances now referred to him as Table For Two. After some serious afternoon sessions, it hadn't gone unnoticed that he would buy his portrait of his late wife a sweet sherry. Once, when he was at the toilet, one of the boys had downed it after being encouraged by everyone. They wanted to see his reaction. He hadn't missed a step or appeared unnerved. He just gently patted the frame and said something like, 'You always loved a sherry, Doreen. Always loved it.'

As the day's entertainment moved into the more competitive and interesting phase, word had spread through the bar that there was a case of whisky, hidden from view, soon to be going cheap. Not the type of patrons to show the proprietor any undue respect, Degs was constantly having to field calls to crack open the whisky. 'For fucks sake,' Degs shouted over the ever increasing shouts from the bar. 'I've got to make some profit off you miserable, end of life cunts before I crack open the cheap stuff.'

As the boos and shouts of 'tight cunt' echoed round the boozer, Degs smiled coldly to himself, remembering that he paid a pittance for the entire case. He was going to make an absolute killing from these old retards today. Best to get it out soon though, everyone was already well oiled. He would need to sell the lot today before word got to the local police who already had their eyes on him for his cannabis operations in the convenient cellar below his very feet.

Half an hour later, Degs had finally had enough of the constant abuse and lined up around thirty small glasses on the bar. Pouring decent measures into all of them. 'Right boys, one fifty a nip. Fill your fucking auld boots.'

The bar was hit by a tsunami of pensioners, keen to get stuck into the cheap drinks.

'There's plenty to go round, ya old smelly leaches,' he yelled as skeletal hands were coming through the crowd snatching glasses. Within minutes, the first round of glasses had disappeared and Degs was happily lining up more, delighted at the tidy profit he was going to make. One that he wouldn't have to share with the increasingly profit orientated brewery.

Robert gave the amber liquid a sniff. Even his age ruined nostrils were telling his brain this stuff was rank. 'Degs, this stuff is honking, I hope it tastes better than it smells.' Still, it's cheap he thought as he threw it down his throat. Most of the others had done the same.

Boom, the mood in the bar changed instantly.

The potent elixir took immediate effect on Roberts's body and mind. His brain was experiencing utter joy wrapped tightly in total confusion. He rose from his bar stool just as a spare piece of jenga flew past his head, smashing one of the not so potent bottles of Ben Eagle, gut rot whisky on the optics behind the bar. Degs hollered in his thick Scottish accent, for the perpetrator to get the fuck out his bar. Unfortunately for Degs, his call was lost in a child like wave of excited noise as the locals began to feel the effects of what they all thought was bootleg whisky. One of the pensioners staggered towards the jukebox with the sole intent of putting Elvis, The King on. The palms of his hands are hotter than a stolen black limo in Dubai, making it impossible to extract any coins from his manky, shell suit bottoms. In what seemed like a moment of divine intervention, another patron staggered by, throwing coins in the air, shouting 'SCRAMBLE,' seconds before falling straight through a table, sending glasses, phones and false teeth flying. A coin now in the jukebox, Elvis pumped out the pub's creaking speakers as Robert bellows, 'BRING ON THE DANCE, MUTHAFUKAS.' The pub descended into a rock n roll, pensioners, late 80s, illegal, Chicago House party.

Robert's time abused body could not cope, so like others around him he slumps to the sticky floor. Lying in his heavenly, semi-conscious coma watching the chaos and now genuine public disorder unfold, he started giggling like he had not since childhood. For some reason, he remembered his grandchildrens' name for his wife Betty was Yoda or wrinkly old tortoise. This really tickled him so he lay back on the greasy pub's carpet and laughed his big bald head off. If he ever returned to planet earth and made it home he would have to call them. They would have a right laugh about this. He didn't know what was happening to him but he had to admit he liked it. In fact, he fucking loved it.

Looking at one of the untouched bottles, Degs decided he deserved a nip of this stuff after surveying the apocalyptic scene in front of him. He cracked it open and took a monstrous slug. His brain was almost immediately paralysed by a euphoric sense of well-being. He tried to take a few minutes to compose his flopping head but soon realised it was a lost cause. He looked up from behind his wrecked pub's bar bringing a smile to his usual dour demeanour. 'Drinks are on me, ya decrepit, reptilian, fucking beautiful smashers,' he shouted.

Luckily for Degs, it was the cheapest free bar he had ever offered and as it happened, the only one. Jenga had now been forgotten about, the pieces were scattered all over the boozer. Everyone was too busy trying to cope with the large dose of Yorkie's creation to care about a free drink. Not so luckily for Degs was the police involvement that was to follow. Ambulances were called by a passer-by who saw an old man fall out the front door of the pub onto Ferry Road and proceed to shit himself while laughing manically. The good Samaritan had glanced inside the pub only to panic and call 999. The pub looked like it had been hit by a KGB chemical attack.

3. The March

Charlie, Davie and Billy were preparing for the day's lodge meeting. North Berwick masonic hall was a small structure compared to the one that dominated Edinburgh's George Street but it was equally as ornately decorated and historical. The downstairs held the bar and toilets, important facilities in a masonic club. Upstairs was the small, comfortable hall that was intricately covered in the organisation's history. All the meetings were sombre affairs held in the upper hall. Afterwards the brothers would retire to the downstairs bar for a refreshment or ten. It was here that Charlie had left the case of whisky he had procured from his friend, Degs, the owner of a grotty bar on Ferry Road in Edinburgh. He had got it at a very reasonable price which would mean his fellow brothers could drink, even more cheaply than normal, that day. This should raise his standing among them. The whisky looked a bit dodgy but he hoped no one would notice after a couple of nips of the real stuff.

'Should be a quiet day, lads,' Charlie said, smiling as he unloaded the bottles to a shelf under the bar. Best to keep it out of sight for now.

'Aye, brother Charlie, your contribution will not go unnoticed,' replied Billy. He was the head mason in the North Berwick branch. He had been a serving officer in her majesty's army, in fact the majority of members had. They kept to the masonic codes but he tried to keep things light, unless of course they had initiation ceremonies with high ranking brothers present. Things had to be done by the book then.

'I'll get the sausage rolls in the oven, boys. Should be ready straight after the gathering. A few of them and some of that golden nectar will go down a treat.'

'Aye, they will that, Davie.'

They headed upstairs to the main hall to get the chairs in position. There had been a cinema night for the town the evening before so the hall needed sorting out. The lodge had been trying hard to integrate into the community, much to the annoyance of some of the inner city lodges. Unlike those places, it was mainly ex service men in North Berwick which meant not many rich patrons to assist with the ancient buildings upkeep.

Within half an hour, the place was packed. Obviously, word of the whisky had got round the sleepy town that was situated about forty minutes drive from the capital. A cheap piss up was guaranteed to swell the ever dwindling numbers at the club. Some had made the journey from other lodges. One particular honorary guest was Gordon Swinton Hughes, Chief of Police. He often popped in when he had been golfing on the renowned local course, North Berwick Links. He owned a second home in the town which he used frequently at weekends. The local brothers were glad of his association, even though it meant listening to the pompous prick. They welcomed him as he had assisted the ones on the periphery of the law on the occasions they had gotten in bother.

Billy started proceedings and was pleased to see they were flying through the day's agenda. Like him, the ageing members could obviously smell the sausage rolls. Within half an hour, he had wrapped things up with the usual Queen and country bollocks and was ushering everyone down to the bar.

Davie was getting the sausage rolls out on the tables whilst Charlie had the glasses lined up and was pouring large measures of what he thought was whisky into glasses.

'Going straight for the hard stuff, Charlie boy?' Billy shouted, struggling to be heard over the large crowd.

'Aye, the boys are keen to try it, Billy. Smells rough as fuck though, brother. I hope its okay.'

'Dinnae worry, brother, these animals will have drunk much worse.' Billy gave him a friendly reassuring slap on his withering back.

It was a lodge tradition that the first drink of the day was taken by all at the same time, enabling them to toast the Queen properly. Glasses were now in the forty or so brothers' hands. Billy raised his, momentarily disturbed by the vicious toxic whiff it emitted as it passed his nose.

'Tae the Queen, my brothers,' he shouted.

'The Queen,' came a chorus of voices.

Everyone tanned their glasses contents in one go. There was a stunned silence that followed. Then from the back of the bar came a lone, gurgling, slurred shout, 'Fstuck the pope, the tim cunt.' The less staunch among them couldn't believe that they were joining in with all that bigoted nonsense, but they were. For the first time ever, no one was asking for seconds, to Charlie's great relief, because he was absolutely trousered. Like many around him, he had no idea what the strange warmth was that was currently engulfing him, but he knew he fucking loved it. Some of the older, frailer members, were slumped on the floor drooling and a number had already soiled themselves.

To the astonishment of the two smokers, enjoying a cigarette outside The Auld Hoose bar, over the street from the hall, the masons began to spill out on to the road. Gordon Swinton Hughes was leading them singing at the top of their voices, 'We're up to our knees in fenian blood, surrender or you'll die.' This morphed into what looked like an impromptu orange march up North Berwick's café strewn High Street. With Swinton Hughes leading the charge, they blocked the road, stopping all traffic on the busy thoroughfare. The well to do, afternoon shoppers and tourists, escaping Edinburgh for the peaceful seaside, were stunned to see the relatively well turned out men behaving like a degenerate rabble. The local police were quickly on the scene. What confronted them was to be the stuff of legend within the force for many years to come. They immediately recognised the Chief Super at the head of the march clearly off his tits. Other well known faces of retired colleagues and a judge were spotted falling in behind him, singing offensive songs, all clearly off their heads. One of the less mobile brothers was being pushed up the street in a shopping trolley. Using an empty plastic shopping basket as a drum, he attempted to keep time with the procession. To try and save the chief embarrassment, one of the more experienced officers had tried to have a quiet word, only to be throttled and shoved out the way.

'Do you know who I am, you fucking pleb?' the chief had screamed in his face.

'I do indeed, Sir' was all the mortified sergeant could offer after brushing the pickled, staggering Swinton Hughes aside.

Help from stations as far away as Edinburgh was requested but by the time they were half way down the coast, the effects of The Damage had begun to wear off. A hugely indignant Gordon Swinton Hughes attempted to sweep his involvement under the carpet. This proved to be impossible as some of the younger officers present had in fact filmed his antics and of course shared it with their colleagues. The man who took the brunt of the chief's anger was Bryan Carver who was enjoying immensely the fact that the chief's son and now the chief himself, had been caught with the very drug that he was investigating. This revelation did mean that his case now took top billing at Fettes and that meant resources were not going to be an issue.

Chapter 27

The Dark Dark Wood

Housty had a familiar and unwelcome feeling of anxiety or nervousness, he was never sure how to describe it, when he entered his stairwell. The boys had been in the bunker cooking until the early hours of the morning. Matt and Housty had headed home for some kip, declining Yorkie's predictable invitation of a walk in the woods and a coma inducing puff on one of his massive reefers.

Since childhood, Housty had had what he would call premonitions or very random moments of future sight. These, combined with some visions of ghostly figures, had convinced him that life and death may not be as clear cut as most believed. Obviously, sharing these thoughts and incidents with his friends had only led to him being ridiculed. He had experienced one such incidence at Dalguise School camp in Perthshire when he was around ten or eleven. He had entered the toilet block situated in the converted attic of the ancient house to see a woman clothed in white standing in front of him. She had then proceeded to walk straight through one of the walls. A young Housty had been unsurprisingly upset by this ghostly incident but his pals had understandably ripped the piss out of him. He learned that day that he should keep these things to himself and as he grew into a man, these strange happenings had receded, only occurring very occasionally.

On his walk home from the bunker, he had felt exhausted but as he neared his flat and the feeling in the pit of his stomach intensified, he became more alert. Something was wrong, he was sure of it as he took the stairs to his flat two at a time, slowing up as he got to the last flight. On the final landing, half way up to his front door, the buckled hinges came into view, his relatively new door standing open, the frame smashed beyond repair. He had been sold this door on the pretence it was burglar proof. Burglar proof?? He thought to himself, aye fucking right, might stop your normal thief but not a Blercrae bam. The old dear that lived across the landing would have heard nothing, she was as deaf as a lump of wood. His pace slowed as he realised that whoever had broken in may still be there. On reaching the door, it was clear it's attacker had not gained access easily. The doors locking mechanism closed in four different places ensuring that it had been forced in more than one location. The flat was quiet. Housty always had a sense when someone was about but he wasn't getting that at all. For a guy who took pride in his house, he was seriously pissed off when he opened the living room door to see the place was wrecked. His stuff was scattered everywhere, the other rooms were in a similar state. Whoever had been in was searching for something which by the look of things they hadn't found. Surveying the mess, Housty couldn't actually see anything that had been taken. Yes the place was a fucking state but nothing appeared to have been stolen. His iPad sat on the floor in his bedroom not far from where he would have left it. Your average junkie would have had that traded for smack in less than an hour. This was no ordinary break in, that much was clear. Housty began picking up random objects as he wandered around the rooms, a worrying explanation for the intrusion was forming in his head. He was having visions of Ray and Ravanelli flashing through his brain. He knew the police were watching for them but this wasn't their style and the more he thought about it, why would Ravanelli do this? He was getting all of The Damage they could make. A crude warning like this just didn't fit with him but it did with someone in Ray's organisation. The callous face of Harvey entered and darkened his thoughts further.

While he mulled this over, he realised his phone had been vibrating in his jacket pocket. As he pulled it out to answer, he saw it was just past four am, there could only be one caller at this hour. As expected, it was Yorkie's name showing on the screen. Housty swiped answer not bothering to even speak, expecting his caked friend to burst into life at the other end of the line. This didn't happen, all he could hear was breathing and Yorkie's voice whispering something.

Housty had to concentrate just to make him out. 'Am being followed, cunts are defo following me, mate. Am shitting maself, this is dodgy as fuck, Housty. Can ye hear me, pal?'

Immediately, Housty snapped back to reality. Was it Harvey and the gang now targeting Yorkie? It was only a matter of time until Ray coaxed his crew into life. There is only so long you can step on a spider's web before it comes out to bite you. 'Where are you, pal?' Housty said quietly, aware that whoever was on to Yorkie may be very close by and would be listening intently for signs of his friend's position.

'Am at they steps just below the tower, man. Am hiding though in some bushes. A dinnae think they can see me but a kin see thaim.'

Blercrae Tower was constructed at the highest point in the woods, built in 1871 as a memorial to the famous Scottish author, Walter Scott. Housty knew exactly where he was and told him to sit tight which was advice, for once, Yorkie was glad to follow. After ending the call, Housty woke up a pissed off Matt and filled him in on developments. The two arranged to meet in the woods not far from where they knew Yorkie was. Housty grabbed a claw hammer from the cupboard and shutting the door as best he could he began jogging to meet Matt. What had started out as a laugh all those months ago had now reached the levels of seriousness that Housty now knew had been depressingly inevitable. Those regular gym visits paid off as he settled into a nice paced run, making the meeting point in fifteen minutes. Matt's army training was obviously still fresh in his mind as he emerged from the darkness without a sound, shortly after Housty's arrival.

'Alright, man, this is fucked up,' Matt said, stating the bloody obvious.

'Aye, I ken,' Housty replied. 'We should have seen this coming, bud. No fucking way were we going to get away with this without any come back. Cannae believe we let dafty talk us into this. What the fuck were we thinking?'

'I know,' Matt sighed, resigned to what would come next. 'We better get up to those steps, man. Stay behind me and no talking,' Matt instructed while removing a small cosh from his inside pocket. Housty showed him the hammer he had, Matt looked at it, nodded his approval and turned away focused on the job in hand.

Both kept low but moved quickly along the well trodden paths before moving into the undergrowth as they neared the steps. Matt turned sharply as with his heightened senses, he heard the noise of a twig snapping somewhere in the gloom directly ahead of him. In the dark, suffocating silence of the woods, it sounded like a sharp cracking sound booming from a huge set of speakers. There, in the shadow of some fir trees, close to the steps were two men having a smoke speaking in hushed tones. Neither Housty nor Matt recognised them but they could tell they were local from their aggressive, rough Edinburgh accents.

'The wee cunt has sneaked off but he'll have tae come back this way tae get tae the bomb shelter,' one said.

'Aye, the wee cunt is getting it, never liked him. Fucking jake ball. Always thought he was the big man coz he could play a bit oh fitba. Fucked that right up in all. Twat!'

Both men were stocky and dressed in dark clothes. One had a pony tail and was wearing army fatigues, he obviously fancied himself as some black ops commando. The other wore a dark shiny tracksuit and baseball cap. They mustn't have felt they were under any threat because although they spoke quietly, they were not making a huge effort to disguise their whereabouts.

'Want a wee livener, its fuckin dynamite?' The one with the ponytail asked as he reached into pocket. Matt or Housty never heard a response but it must have been a positive one as they could see the two men passing a small bag between them and making audible sniffing noises. In fact, to be more accurate, a number of sniffing noises. This was driving Yorkie mental, he hated missing a party, even when those attending were looking to do him damage.

Matt was thinking differently to Yorkie. He knew they must be amateurs if they couldn't keep their snouts out the trough when they were meant to be working. He would give the drugs a minute to kick in and then hit them with everything.

Housty could see in the gloom the clump of bushes Yorkie must be in, he must only be five metres away at the most, with him and Matt a further ten back the other way. Matt tapped him on the shoulder, indicating it was time to attack. This really wasn't Housty's speciality, he could handle himself well enough, in reality better than most, but attacking two obvious bams in the dark who were probably tooled up was way out his comfort zone. Matt, on the other hand, looked like he was enjoying himself. He had a manic look across his face and what appeared to be something between a sneer and a smile. Whatever it was, it instilled a bit of confidence in Housty. If his pal was this relaxed with the situation, he'd just have to follow his lead. He had no option after all, he would have chummed his pals to certain death if he had to.

Matt gave Housty a final nudge and sprung from their cover, charging straight toward his prey. He made up the ten metres in a matter of seconds giving the pair of them little time to react. Smashing the cosh hard over the pony tailed one's head, he sent him to the ground instantly whilst almost simultaneously head butting the other one. The smaller one staggered back under the blow, his cap had offered some protection and he was now trying to shake himself into action. He didn't stand a chance, Housty leapt on him, both men crashing to the ground taking the wind from them both. Before Housty could do anymore, a shadow appeared and with precision kicked the man in the side of the head. Housty scrambled to his feet to see Matt checking for a pulse on the bigger man and then turning as Yorkie landed a further powerful boot to the other man's ribs. Both men were lying on a combination of hard packed mud and leaves. By the look of them, they would be there for some time to come.

'That was fucking magic, boys. You pair were like ninjas. A didnae have a clue yooz were here. Fucking shat maself when yooz appeared like that.' Yorkie was delighted, buzzing with a mixture of relief and adrenaline. The same could be said for Housty, although Matt seemed calm. He had established that both men were unconscious but still alive so could come round any moment.

'Right boys, time to boost. This pair won't be out for long,' he said.

'Aye right, man. These cunts are sparko. Havin sweet dreams,' Yorkie replied, taking a closer look at the bigger man lying in front of him.

Housty was more than happy to make their escape. However, Yorkie was now busy trying to extract the powder from the bigger man's pocket. This annoyed Matt. 'Leave it, ya bam. You get enough of that shit as it is, mon time to go,' he encouraged, grabbing hold of Yorkie. When it came to drugs Yorkie was not a man to miss out though. He managed to wrestle free of Matt's grip and grab the bag from the man's jacket.

'Why should they have all the fun, dodgy cunts. This one's Davey Peace by the way. He's one eh Rays boys, av bought some ching off him from time tae time.' He nudged the bigger man with his foot.

'Are there any drug dealers in Edinburgh you've no bought gear from?' Housty asked, already knowing the answer.

'Very few, my man,' Yorkie replied proudly, as if this was some sort of achievement. Even after all these years of being friends, it was still hard to tell if he was on the wind up, his face gave nothing to indicate either way.

Neither Matt nor Housty cared about that at this moment, escape the only thing on their minds. Both began heading back the way they had come. Yorkie soon followed close behind, the adrenaline making him feel cold and shaky as it wore off, only accentuating his robotic manic movements.

They headed back towards the bunker without thinking, none of them considering that further trouble may await. Rounding a particularly dark corner not far from their destination, a large shadow emerged silently from the trees and proceeded to calmly thump Matt on the side of head with what looked like a baseball bat. Matt staggered to his side, close to hitting the floor and clearing the way for the new assailant to swing it at Housty. Without thinking, Housty reacted, ducking in time to feel the solid wood flash by the top of his head. In the same instant, he had raised himself up, feeling the comforting solid moulded black plastic handle of the hammer. He in turn swung it into the centre of the attacker's head. The blow landed perfectly with a dull thump rendering what was obviously a large man, unconscious. The next noise was his body hitting the ground followed by the bat. He had dropped like a stone, not uttering a sound in the whole incident. Although the attack had only lasted twenty seconds, it had all been in slow motion for Housty. Seeing Yorkie was helping Matt, Housty bent down to check their third victim of the night. His already high heart rate increased further when he recognised the ugly pale face of Harvey with a now additional lump in the centre of his oversized forehead. Having established Matt would live, Yorkie joined Housty, both now leaning over inspecting the egg that was growing out of Harvey's misshapen forehead. It was as your granny would describe, a beauty. Matt had taken quite a knock and was feeling groggy. He was pleased there was no sign of blood when he checked. It seemed he had been lucky and that they had probably surprised Harvey. He had no doubt presumed his two colleagues, from earlier, would have been more than enough to deal with Yorkie and had not foreseen the arrival of Matt and Housty.

Yet again, all three were aware that the big man would not be out for long so their second escape of the night began. This time, they took a different direction all agreeing that the bunker was out of bounds for tonight. Seeing as Housty's flat had already had a visit from one or all of the three men they had bumped into in the woods, they set a course for the safety of Dmains and Matt's pad.

Chapter 28

Re light ma coal fire, sexy high scorin words are my only desire

C-o-l-i-n sat across from Ruth, struggling to concentrate on the letters in front of him. The letters that had once been so valuable, so precious and powerful, like guns in a fist fight, were now obsolete. The can of lager next to him, brought to him by Ruth an hour earlier, sat expectantly on the carpet by his slipper clad feet, hardly touched. Ruth had bought him the faux sheep skin slippers a couple of weeks ago, along with other simple domestic things. She had immediately felt a need to help him, hating seeing him look so neglected. After all, he had once been the Caesar of the scheme. Nowadays, he might have been referred to as the top boy, a term that would never do him justice. On agreeing to look in on C-o-l-i-n, she had initially merely been interested in observing what had become of the once handsome, scheme heartthrob. His long deceased wife had been the envy of Blercrae at one time and although some of the local wives had tried to convince him to break his marriage vows, he had never even appeared tempted. Many of the women had later scoffed at his demise into alcohol oblivion, but not Ruth, even after all those years of him being a recluse, she hadn't forgotten him. So to be offered, out the blue, an opportunity to go and witness what his current life had become was an irresistible opportunity and a miracle like stroke of good fortune. The booze as payment was an added and very welcome bonus. Like all women, Ruth was a nosey, gossiping rascal and this was the type of gossip she could dine out on for months.

The first few days had not lived up to her expectations or those of her excited friends, who were all dying to hear her tales. Ruth had found herself feeling paternal towards C-o-l-i-n and had immediately begun making changes. A marathon clean up operation had begun. His clothes, bed sheets and body had all been given the Ruth treatment. She may have had a checkered past but her knocking shop had always been immaculate. When suggesting a bath, Ruth had expected some resistance but he was so inebriated he didn't care. During the bath, she had not failed to notice that the rumours had been true, he was a very big boy. No wonder she had heard the lucky few refer to it as Mons Meg back in the day. Mons Meg is a medieval cannon of huge proportions that to this day could be admired from within Edinburgh Castle. It was one of the biggest she had had the pleasure of encountering and there had been too many to count. This revelation was one in normal circumstances that she would have been unable to keep from her pals but strangely she had decided early on to say nothing to anyone. She was going to take pride in saving this man, not from anyone or anything that was dangerous, but simply from himself.

Ruth had popped through one afternoon, shortly after Jennifer had visited. To her surprise, she found an abandoned Scrabble board left on the coffee table. She had then discovered C-o-l-i-n in the kitchen with his head in the fridge downing a can of lager along with a half bottle of vodka. Ruth was by now, very fond of him and for her, enough was enough. She had snatched the vodka from him and given him the sharp end of her tongue. Surprisingly, he had been apologetic and actually looked like he meant it. With what remained of the can of beer, she had steered him into the living room and in an act of desperation had asked him to teach her how to play. Without her knowing it, this was a masterstroke which would have ramifications long after that first game had finished.

The first few games had been a challenge for both of them. It was a long time since Ruth had been at school and in her chosen profession, words and spelling were not usually required. Well, there had been some filthy talk but that didn't translate into a nice friendly game of Scrabble with the neighbour. Or so she thought. The games became more regular, until they were a daily obsession with both of them, to the extent she spent most of the day with C-o-l-i-n. He was now drinking noticeably less and even leaving the house with her for short walks in between games.

One particular afternoon, they had sat down for their post lunch game after enjoying a light meal of chickpea and onion salad on flat breads. The days of toasties with smoked sausage were long gone. Ruth had been met with resistance when she began introducing the healthy lunchtime menu. C-o-l-i-n had not been keen, rightly pointing out that this womens' food was never going to soak up the bevvy like a good cheese toastie could. A woman with a sharp wit and tongue, she suggested less drinking may be the solution rather than unhealthy food. Put firmly in his place, he could hardly argue against such an obvious and well rounded argument. As their time together continued, he had begun to drink less, especially in her company. Therefore, as that increased his windows of opportunity decreased.

That afternoon, the game started as normal with C-o-l-i-n talking her through her options, correcting her spelling and suggesting different tactics. Ruth was playing well and this pleased him so much. Today felt different for some reason, he sensed an electric charge between them. There was an atmosphere in the air. Ruth's limited vocabulary had led her to use the word "sexy", which they had both laughed nervously at, like teenagers would in a sex education class. In a strange twist, the letters in front of C-o-l-i-n called to him as they had done in big tournaments in the past. The word they called was "copulation". He placed the letters on the board. Ruth was well versed in every word that related to the art of sexual intercourse. She looked at the letters as they formed the word in front of her then her eyes raised up to focus on C-o-l-i-n's weathered face. The years fell away. She now saw the once proud, socialist man in front of her. The man she remembered, straight back and sturdy shoulders conveying a solid dependable strength. The same shoulders that had once lifted a massive undersea pipe, that they had no business to lift, from a young apprentice whose mistake had almost seen him killed. A deed he had been hailed as a hero for.

Just like the steady road into extreme alcoholism that he had walked had stripped away his self respect and physical appearance. The realisation that all was not lost filled him with hope. The reptile like red scales of torched skin on his face appeared to drop off, revealing the handsome man they had been hiding for all those years. Neither spoke but their eyes never wavered from each other's gaze. Locked together by some invisible power. C-o-l-i-n felt a movement down below he hadn't expected to ever have again. A woman of Ruth's expertise and experience had not missed it. Her hand reached over to his and without a word spoken they began to make their way up stairs. C-o-l-i-n felt young again, for the first time he saw a future away from bevvy.

Had Ruth achieved in a short time what family had attempted and his poor attitude had refused to let him do for decades? Had he finally crossed the alcohol infested Rubicon?

Chapter 29

Knock knock

Big Andy's incarceration and Harvey's failed attack in the woods was a turning point for the boys and everyone involved. The gloves were now off and their cover blown. As long as supplies were available from the drinking club, they would be cooking in the bunker knowing that their days were numbered. Make drugs while the pish flows, as Yorkie had so delicately described it. They were now extra vigilant when entering and leaving their underground realm. Housty had been using his mum's car to deliver to Ravanelli, a man who was now on the edge. His calm composed persona having slipped. The stress of losing Big Andy's services and Ray's reappearance meant Ravanelli was now having to get his hands dirty. This was not a situation he was overly enamoured with. So the three of them were now continually holed up in the bomb shelter, working as the cash was accumulating far faster than they could spend it. Although the bunker still felt secure, the outside negative forces were becoming more obvious. They had stopped their regular visits for curry and drinks as they didn't want to bump into Ray or Harvey and there always appeared to be a customer that just didn't fit in the surroundings. Initially, they had put it down to Ray being there regularly which seemed reasonable as a man with his past was bound to be kept an eye on by various authorities. More and more though, things were adding up to trouble. One day, when Yorkie had snuck home over the back fences, he had peered out the front bedroom window to see two men sitting in an inconspicuous family hatchback watching the house. It was hard to tell due to the distance and dwindling light but one of them resembled a man who had been at the table next to them the previous evening. All three had noticed him and had curtailed their chat from business to the mundane, leaving as soon as their food was finished. When they had left the bar, Housty had spotted him through the window, still at the table, but now on an animated call. Instead of heading straight home, they had taken a route through a nearby grave yard and park, only heading back to the bunker when they were sure no one was following them. Their general lives were becoming difficult and uncomfortable as the situation worsened. They didn't belong in the underworld.

On one side, the law was closing in, on the other, their friend Ray was now obviously on to them. Harvey had been following Big Andy before he had been locked up, when he had the chance and from a safe distance. For all his bravado, he had been taken aback by Big Andy's aggressive, threatening response. Harvey was not used to being spoken to like that. Although he had the comfort blanket of his association with Ray, a face to face with an increasingly psychotic Big Andy was to be avoided. On more than one occasion he had seen Big Andy driving into the Blercrae woods. Unlike the police, Harvey was local, as was Ray. They both knew what lay under the ground there. Not only that but all three of the lads had been seen with Big Andy at one time or another. This was the final piece of the puzzle for Ray. The photo fit, Ravanelli, the lads reaction to seeing him, Matt's missing Land Rover, Big Andy's behaviour and the police being all over Blercrae, especially Yorkie's street. It was Lynne, Yorkie's mother that had let that little rare gem slip when she had met Ray at the shops. A casual remark to Ray about having the police outside the house constantly, was basically an admission of guilt on Yorkie's behalf. He still was unsure what this drug was or how they were making it but if he knew them, it would be some story. He was genuinely looking forward to hearing it. Ray was annoyed but also seriously impressed. The three lads had knocked out two of his associates and managed to mould a huge egg to Harvey's now deformed paving slab of a forehead. The nuclear bunker had been sitting on his patch all these years and he hadn't utilised it. It had taken three amateurs to show him the error of his ways. Well, he would soon have it as his own and if he played his hand well, he could keep all those beautiful concrete underground square metres to himself. The finest, safest storage unit of any illicit supplier in the world.

Ray and Ravanelli were both missing Big Andy's valuable services and were both desperate to get word to him. Bryan Carver had foreseen this and ensured that Big Andy was kept away from the general prison population. Since his arrest, he had been kept in Fettes, his treatment not quite in line with the country's laws, although surprisingly, they hadn't had any complaints from Big Andy. There was only one person Big Andy blamed for his situation and that was Big Andy. He knew every rule in his very simple rule book had been broken, hence his current predicament rested firmly on his square shoulders. He had no intention of telling the police anything, despite their repeated crude attempts. His simple, very direct approach to his life and work had fooled the police into thinking they could at least get him to drop a few nuggets of information but much to their dismay, Big Andy was back to following his simple rules. Number one on that list was, say fuck all to the bizzies. From the direction of their questioning, Big Andy knew that his three pals were in real danger. Folk like Ravanelli and Ray were used to this world but he feared for the lads future if the police caught them red handed in the bunker. If he could have, he would have warned them but so far making contact had proved to be impossible.

The police knew they couldn't keep Big Andy here indefinitely so it was imperative they move quickly. High above Big Andy's cell a plan was being hatched to end the scourge of The Damage on Edinburgh's streets. It was inspector Carver himself that had discovered the bunker after analysing the data from the tracker. The tracker had been showing Big Andy's van going to the bunker for a number of weeks but the police assumed this was for a handover between vans. None of the detectives on the case were aware of the nuclear shelter, it was a well kept government secret after all. As the trackers that the police used were often faulty or inaccurate to certain distances, it was not immediately obvious where the van kept stopping. Inspector Carver decided to investigate for himself. After arriving at the identified point in the woods, he soon discovered the large fences surrounding the bunker's perimeter. Once he had established that this must be the place, it didn't take long to find out what the fence was hiding. The Ministry of Defence had been very accommodating to the extent of providing detailed maps of the moth balled facility.

Inspector Carver immediately paid a visit to the chief's palatial office to convey his findings and request further resources for surveillance. This was to be the final push.

'I am a man of my word, Carver. I promised you anything you needed to end this circus before people get hurt. This is one city that will win the drugs war and it will be on my watch.'

'Thank you, Sir. I knew I could rely on you,' Bryan Carver had replied with a massive hint of irony which was of course missed by the chief.

'Keep me posted, Carver. I would very much like to be there when you nail these devious bastards.'

'Yes, Sir,' Bryan Carver agreed as he left the office sniggering. He had to hand it to the old drunken, pompous slaver. He had almost managed to brass neck his way out of the North Berwick masonic lodge incident. Despite footage circling the internet and a number of public complaints, there had been very little in the papers. It helped to have contacts in the media and backed up most probably by a super injunction.

The next few weeks of increased surveillance produced results Bryan could only have dreamed of. Photos and video taken by the surveillance team were the best he had ever seen in his career. He now had Steven Malone, the lad known locally as Yorkie, who they were sure was the man in the photo fit. He had been photographed and filmed with two others leaving and entering the bunker. These two men

270

were of a similar age to Malone and Carver was fairly sure local as well. With a bit of digging, their names would soon be known. Bigger though, much bigger was the photos of Ray Dean and his sidekick the not so glamorous or infamous Harvey. The sighting of Ray Dean would give Carver all the ammunition he needed to get this case sealed up. That was the type of arrest that could see him on the promotion ladder. One other diamond was a grainy photo of one of Yorkie's associates with another man in a car park. The man's silvery grey beard and hair gave him a certain dignified air, Carver was very excited by this footage but kept it all to himself. He was ninety percent sure this was the ever illusive Bill Middleton. Ex RAF man long suspected of making a fortune in the drugs trade. There were few reliable photos of him and even fewer convictions. Carver wanted to keep this beautiful piece of evidence for himself. Always wary of people like Swinton Hughes trying to steal the limelight, he knew if he could put together a case against Middleton that promotion ladder would turn into a fucking skyscraper's super fast lift. Dean and Middleton would be bigger box office than those Hibs scum bags from Leith bringing in that womanising drunk George Best. Carver had to admit though, he was very jealous at the time. What a signing that had been.

Bryan put his case to the chief, making a big deal about the photos of Ray but making sure to keep the silver haired gentlemen out of the discussion. He had taken the photo to the chief's office but held it back in case of emergency. He needn't have worried, the chief would be more than happy to crack this case, which had been an obvious personal embarrassment to himself. The added incentive was the chance to again snare Ray Dean, a man that had been a constant pain throughout his long police career. Bryan got the green light from the chief to mount a joint armed targeted operation with the help of explosives experts from a nearby army base. The MOD were insistent that they were involved which seemed fair given it was one of their own facilities. Judging by the size of the steel doors Bryan had got a distant look at, the explosives would certainly come in handy.

Back in the depths of the bunker, Matt was surprised to feel his phone vibrating in his pocket. Thankfully, he had it on vibrate as there was no chance he could hear over the constant banging of Yorkie's feverish techno music. He rarely got a signal down here so was surprised and concerned when he saw it was one of his soldier pals. His first thought was, the police have found my Land Rover.

Answering it quickly, Matt couldn't make out a thing his friend was saying. 'Yorkie turn that crappy techno off, I cannae hear a fucking thing, man.'

'You're no putting any of the pet store bufties oan, ya radge. I need techno when am cooking. Keeps me oan ma toes. That's 808 state man. Classic tunes.' *The American system is failing to deal with the real threat to life, the bomb...In Your Face* blasted out at a dangerous volume. All three putting their long term hearing prospects in doubt.

'It's ma mate at the barracks, a cannae hear him. Sounds fucking serious, man,' Matty implored. Grudgingly Yorkie turned the music down. Both himself and Housty had their eyes on Matt as his face turned disturbingly serious. 'Fuck, fuck, fuck,' was all he kept saying, then he finished the call abruptly with 'Right, cheers, I owe you.' He hung up and looked at his two pals. He now had their focus, it was unusual for Matt to look so rattled. He had begun to rub the sides of his chunky head like he could feel a migraine coming on.

'We need to make ourselves very scarce,' he said slowly, 'NOW!' The way Matt emphasised the word now left the other two in no doubt that trouble was coming.

Yorkie and Housty still didn't move, they knew something monumental was in the offing but needed more detail.

Matt continued, 'Ma pals at the barracks have got wind of a big job in this area involving the explosives team from the army base and the police. Armed police. I reckon they are on their way here. It makes sense especially with Big Andy's arrest.' Matt's soldier friends knew he lived in the area and had joined the dots thinking it wise to alert him just in case he was involved. They had been bang on the money.

'Big Andy would tell them fuck all, you ken that,' Yorkie pointed aggressively at Matt keen to defend his pal.

'Aye, I ken that but it doesn't mean he wasn't followed here before he got lifted. If they were following you, they could easily have been doing the same with him. That fuckwit Harvey could be involved, who knows.'

It was Yorkie and Housty's turn to swear repeatedly.

'We better get the fuck out of here,' Housty said, stating the obvious.

'Aye, let's fucking scram boys. Fucking shame, real fucking shame.' Yorkie looked round the bomb shelter wistfully, sensing their time here was over. What a time it had been.

From far above, they heard an ominous racket that sounded like hammering on the steel doors. The noise added to their panic. In their haste to leave, they forgot to turn off the cooking pots. They did remember to grab the hold all that contained the cash accumulated over recent weeks. Things were serious, but not serious enough to leave that much cash for the police. Matt still had his son's health bills to consider, Housty had the mortgage and Yorkie, well he had his lifestyle to fund.

Meanwhile, in the woods above them, Ray was lowering a none too happy Harvey into one of the huge ventilation shafts. The pair were completely oblivious to the raid that was happening simultaneously at the quarry entrance, a good distance away.

'Of course I can take your weight, pal.' Ray assured Harvey, although he was unconvinced by his own statement. As was a very worried Harvey who was staring up at him aware he was now past the point of no return. He could no longer reach the top of the shaft and from his position it was clear that Ray wouldn't manage to haul him back up. The only thing that kept him from a gale force ten panic was the thought of surprising the three lads down there and getting revenge for their sheer cheek. He had been mortified, telling Ray about his poorly executed plan in the woods a week or so earlier. Even more embarrassed when whispers began swirling around Blercrae about him getting a doing. It was hard to deny with an alpine sized lump on his head.

Looking down at Harvey's expression, Ray had to fight the urge to start laughing. He looked so helpless and frankly the situation was ridiculous on two counts. One, he could have just confronted the boys, they would be in no position to deny it but that would have ruined the thrill of the chase. Catching them in the act would mean he had them exactly where he wanted them. Two, was how had he managed to talk Harvey into this, his recent fall from grace had made him susceptible to this crazy idea. He would have agreed to anything if it meant returning to Ray's good books. It was becoming clearer by the second that Ray couldn't take the big man's weight for much longer. Again, the urge to burst out laughing had to be controlled. Unfortunately for Harvey, he had put on a bit of timber in Ray's long absence. Ray on the other hand had slimmed up with the rubbish prison food and trips to the gym to relieve the hours of boredom. Ray, for his part in this fiasco was finding the fact he was not overly concerned about dropping Harvey, disturbing but explainable. He had heard, from a number of friends and associates that Harvey had been leaning on people too heavily and using Ray's name around the town. He had annoyed a lot of people, Big Andy being one of them, which still irked with Ray. Big Andy was the best in the business and was now locked up. Not only locked up but uncontactable as well, despite Ray's best efforts. Even on release, Big Andy's delivery business would now be under too much scrutiny to make it viable. Looking down into the abyss, Ray could just make out the look on Harvey's face, he really shouldn't have. This time he couldn't control the giggles, he looked away and started laughing. The waves of laughter engulfed him and he started shaking. Harvey could feel this in the rope, he mistakenly thought it was Ray struggling to hold his weight. Eventually Ray's grip gave and the rope shot through his hands disappearing into the gloom below. Harvey didn't make a sound as his large frame was lost to the deep, murky, stale darkness.

Meanwhile, under the ground the lads had initially taken their normal route out the bunker by heading up in the direction of the quarry entrance. It was crystal clear after they heard the charges breaking the powerful locks on the main blast doors that this escape route was blocked. Without speaking, they did a one hundred and eighty degree turn and bolted for the shelters lower exit. In their panic, their lack of focus would prove to be their salvation. An ominous sound was coming from the cooking area. All three friends realised how unstable the large vats must have become. After all, they had been here before. There was the kitchen, the allotment shed and then the static caravan. It looked like this concrete monstrosity was about to be added to the list. They were one hundred percent correct, the pots were now vibrating dangerously and due to their size would provide an infinitely more powerful explosion than the previous ones.

Housty who was out in front, leading the charge, was almost crushed by a falling object. Suddenly, directly in front of him, was the buckled figure of Harvey. He was alive but clearly in a bad way. The hammer damage to his head was still horribly clear, although in his current physical predicament it equated to a mere scratch. The noise and commotion in the upper part of the bunker, plus the rumble from the cooking pots, was enough to spur Housty straight past him followed closely by his two friends. There's no way Harvey was popping in for a cup of tea. If he'd had his way, the three of them would be getting a good old fashioned kicking or worse. Housty realised at some point in the distant, past he had seen this very scene unfold, he had that familiar spooky feeling of knowing this would happen. He also now knew that fire came next and the thought made him shiver. He now urged himself and the other two onwards.

'FUCKIN MOVE, LADS!' he screamed.

The escape route doors were now in sight. A final push from the boys straight down the lower tunnel brought them to the heavy steel double doors. All three grabbed the metal handles and pulled them down forcing the old doors open just in time. Above them the pots had ignited big time. The ensuing blast meant the lads had to dive to the floor as its power was funnelled down the long dome shaped corridor. A powerful burning force exploded out the tunnel. It missed the boys as they lay looking up at it disappearing into the atmosphere.

Now lying in amongst leaves and gorse bushes they looked at each other relieved to still be alive. All jumped to their feet laughing at the miracle of their escape. Without a word, they made for Queensferry Road where they could hopefully grab a taxi and make good their escape.

Chief Gordon Swinton Hughes had insisted on being the first through the upper doors into the bunker. Not a man to shy away from the limelight, he had been imagining the headlines in the local press and most probably national newspapers depicting him as the hero. Bryan Carver knew exactly what his intentions were, the chief had been a good thirty metres into the tunnel before Bryan had got through the doors. He had almost knocked one of the explosive guys off his feet, he was so keen. Unfortunately for him, the yellow liquid named The Damage, that was responsible for his son's school issues and had threatened the closure of North Berwick masonic hall, had one final message for Swinton Hughes. As the blast pulverised the lower part of the bunker, it sent a powerful back draft of vapour upwards which knocked the chief clean off his feet. The little hair he had left was singed and his face scorched. The Damage had finally given the chief a red face at the third time of asking. A bitter sweet moment for Bryan Carver. He knew by the size of the blast that it was likely any incriminating evidence would now be destroyed along with the three perpetrators. This in turn would mean getting any evidence on the Mr Bigs like Ray Dean and Bill Middleton was going to be somewhere between very hard and near impossible.

Bryan Carver proved to be correct in his estimations. The explosion and ensuing fire had ensured that any physical evidence linking the boys with the bunker was destroyed in what the fire brigade estimated to be temperatures of two thousand degrees. Photos of the destroyed shelter were eventually given to the papers. The inch thick glass, which once looked down onto the control map and the lad's preparation area, had actually melted in the extreme heat. It was days before the fire crews could get the blaze under control and allow Inspector Carver and the forensic team to get access. The damage was so extensive that any evidence of Harvey had evaporated in the ferocious heat which was perversely similar to that of a nuclear explosion.

Ray had felt the heat power its way up the ventilation shaft so much so that he had jumped back in surprise. It was obvious from the noise that something catastrophic had happened. A man with an instinctive danger warning system, he knew the authorities would be swarming all over this area soon, so he too headed for the anonymity of the city's busy Queensferry Road. As he emerged from the woods, high above the bunker's lower entrance, Ray could make out three figures he recognised instantly. None of them were aware of his presence as even at this distance he would have been unmistakable and they would have known retribution was guaranteed and would be swiftly sought. Yorkie's unusual walk was difficult to miss, he couldn't help but smile to himself. Fucking bams, he thought, as he began to laugh and leg it with the sound of sirens shrieking beginning to engulf the North West of the Capital.

On reaching the relative safety of the busy road, the three lads were also aware of the sirens beginning to stifle the usual constant traffic noises. They stopped running and tried to walk calmly to avoid attention. The emergency vehicles from all services were soon speeding past them, ignoring the three friends. No one had spoken a word until Yorkie started up a familiar football chant to the tune of Freed from Desire.

'The bunkers on fire, the Edinburgh police are terrified.' Matt and Housty soon joined in, the ridiculousness of their situation not lost on any of them. As they headed to the northern limits of the city, a taxi came into view which to their relief stopped and took them as far as

Queensferry where they planned to get a train to Dundee or Aberdeen to lie low for a while. Little did they know that the authorities would eventually list them as missing, presumed dead, therefore ensuring their freedom, for a while at least.........